The 55 Best Mountain Bike Trails in Ontario*

* til the next edition

© Copyright 2020 Dan Roitner
mediaMerge Ventures Inc.

ALL RIGHTS RESERVED

No part of this publication may be reproduced or transmitted in any form or by any means, electronic or mechanical, without written permission from the author. Exceptions are for reviewers or academics, who may use brief passages of the content for published reviews and critical study.

First Edition, 2020

paperback ISBN: 978-1-9991353-5-5

No government funding was provided for this project.

All photos taken by Dan Roitner, unless otherwise noted
Extra photos for reviews courtesy of Hardwood Ski & Bikes , Horseshoe Resort, Sir Sam's, Joyide 150 - cover photo of winter Fatbike & rider on rock - Paulo LaBerge

Cartography map styling by Dan Roitner
*Basemap data credited to © OpenStreetMap contributors licensed as CC BY-SA and information licensed under the Open Government Licence Ontario.

Terms of Use

We hope you enjoy using this guide and have a great bike ride.
By using this guidebook, you agree to take on all
risks and responsibilities.

This book is for informational purposes only. The author takes no responsibility for, nor guarantees the accuracy of, the content of this book. Efforts were made to be up-to-date, but trails and conditions do change frequently, so do not assume the information and maps to be accurate.

By using this published information, you agree we cannot be held liable for any injury, inconvenience, or financial loss that may occur while visiting any area mentioned or when dealing with any club, organization, or business listed in this book or on the website.

Ride safely, and within your own skill level. Always wear a helmet, be sure you can be seen, and have lights at night.
Bike riding can be dangerous,
so
RIDE AT YOUR OWN RISK
but have FUN, too!

Table of Contents

Location Map — 4
Introduction — 5
Using This Guide — 8

Central Ontario

Agreement Forest – MTB Trail — 12
Albion Hills – MTB Trail — 14
Centennial Park – MTB Trail — 16
Christie Lake – MTB Trail — 18
Copeland Forest – MTB Trail — 20
Coulson's Hill – MTB Trail — 22
Dagmar – MTB Trail — 24
Don Valley – MTB Trail — 26
Dufferin Forest – MTB Trail — 28
Durham Forest – MTB Trail — 30
Eldred King - MTB Trail — 32
Ganaraska Forest - MTB Trail — 34
Greenwood – MTB Trail — 36
Hardwood – MTB Trail — 38
Hilton Falls – MTB Trail — 40
Horseshoe Valley – DH MTB Trail — 42
Jefferson – MTB Trail — 44
Joyride 150 – MTB/BMX Park — 46
Kelso – MTB Trail — 48
Midhurst – MTB Trail — 50
Oro Network – MTB Trails — 52
Palgrave – MTB Trail — 54
Ravenshoe – MTB Trail — 56
Short Hills – MTB Trail — 58
Waterdown – MTB DH Trail — 60

Western Ontario

Blue Mountain – DH MTB Trails — 62
Brant Tract – MTB Trail — 64
Carrick Tract – MTB Trail — 66
Fanshawe – MTB Trails — 68
Guelph Lake - MTB Trail — 70
Hydro Cut – MTB Trail — 72
Kolapore Uplands – MTB Trail — 74
Puslinch – MTB Trail — 76
The Pines – MTB Trail — 78
Three Stage – MTB Trail — 80
Turkey Point – MTB Trail — 82
Wildwood – MTB Trail — 84

Eastern Ontario

Forest Lea - MTB Trail — 86
Harold Town – MTB Trail — 88
Larose Forest – MTB Trail — 90
Limerick Forest – MTB Trail — 92
Northumberland – MTB Trail — 94
South March – MTB Trail — 96

Northern Ontario

Bracebridge RMC - MTB Trail — 98
Buckwallow – MTB Trail — 100
Georgian – MTB Trail — 102
Haliburton Forest – MTB Trail — 104
Hiawatha – MTB Trail — 106
Laurentian – MTB Trail — 108
Minnesing – MTB Trail — 110
Porcupine Ridge – MTB Trail — 112
Seguin – Rail / MTB Trail — 114
Sir Sam's – MTB DH Trail — 116
Torrance Barrens – MTB Trail — 118
Walden – MTB Trail — 120

What Is Mountain Biking — 122
MTB Groups & Clubs — 127
Ontario Geography — 128
Trail Building Concepts — 130
Trail Hazards — 131
Loose Bike Parts — 132
  - Health, eMTB, Theft, Etiquette — 132
Prep for the Trail — 134
Glossary & Lingo — 142
My MTB Top 5 List — 144
About the Author — 145
Acknowledgements — 145

Location Map

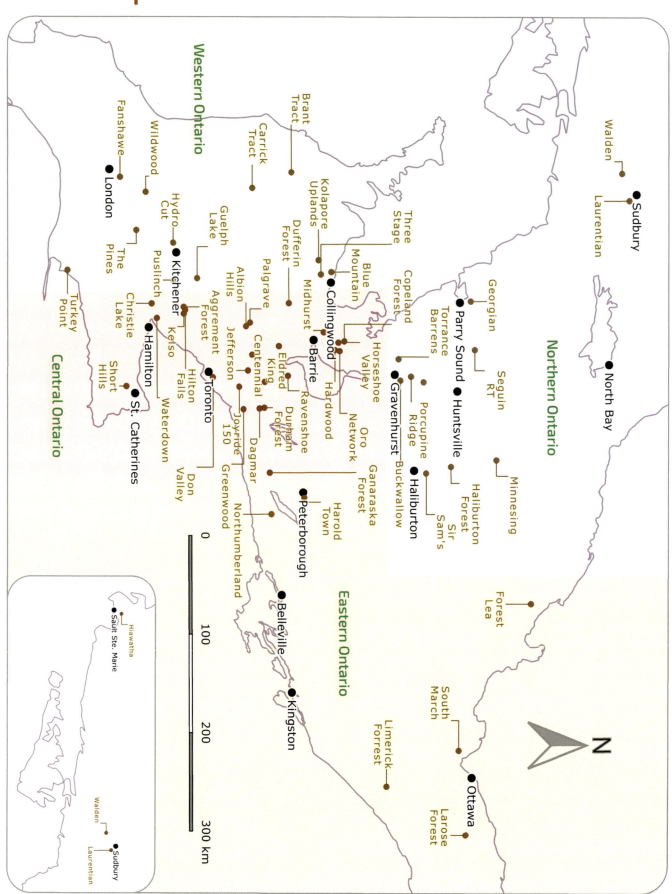

4 *Best Mountain Bike Trails in Ontario*

Introduction

Greetings to all avid mountain bikers in search of new track to ride in Ontario. This guide has the **top 55 trail locations in the province** for you to discover and enjoy. Get ready for a wild ride—your adventure starts now.

This is the MTB trail guide I always wished for. It's organized to be a quick read so you can **research less and ride sooner.** It's chock-full of info. I keep the reading short, informative and entertaining. And finally, for the first time, all trail locations have **detailed maps!**

Anyone who is fit and owns a reliable mountain bike will find trails to enjoy in this book, which includes info for all skill levels. I give advice and suggest suitable, **easy trail areas for beginners**. Other ride locations are strictly for more **experienced riders** who go hard and love challenging terrain.

There are 55 trail networks spread across Southern Ontario, and every one of them is different. You **might be surprised** at the variety. This book will help you experience more MTB adventures in Ontario than you thought possible.

The Spirit of the Ride

The origins of mountain biking go way back to cyclists wandering down dirt paths in search of adventure on old, rigid iron bicycles. Their desire to explore trails unknown likely led them to terrain that their not-so-steady bikes couldn't manage in any kind of comfort.

Those were the days, when it was low tech and heading out on a ride was a **free-form adventure.** With just a rumour about some magical trails out there, somewhere, in **the pursuit of MTB happiness** we went.

The evolution of MTB riding over the last 40 years has certainly changed and given us bikes that can **make us feel invincible** on the trail. But that **free spirit and curiosity** to explore the wild and be one with nature lives on. Off we still go, in the hopes that the drive there and the ride for the day will be a fruitful one.

While writing and making the maps for this book, I reflected on the **origins of MTB culture.** I had to stop myself and realize that this book, as accurate as I would like it to be, cannot and should not be perfect. Beyond the fact that trails change over time, riders don't need or wish to have everything spelled out for them.

What would be left of the **spirit of MTB self-reliance and discovery** if I added every detail and trail imaginable? Never mind the work involved to compile it—seriously, the book would never get published.

Why Write the Book?

It all started after a decade of seeking out new MTB trails to ride. I like variety. Finding accurate and complete information was iffy; most websites to this day are **crowd sourced** and only as good as what users wish to post. Opinions on trail conditions and descriptions were diverse. **Who to believe?**

Frustrated, I launched the ontariobiketrails.com (OBT) website in 2013 and started posting my own reviews, and it just grew from there. I wanted to give a single voice, a **balanced opinion** that readers could trust and use to compare other trails.

I have ridden every one of these MTB locations once, if not many times, in my 20 years before reviewing it. They all are recommended to deliver at least a few

Best Mountain Bike Trails in Ontario

good hours of riding enjoyment. This naturally will vary with a cyclist's ability, fitness level, what you are looking for, and the weather conditions.

So with that said, the objective for this book is to entice and inform you to make quick choices as to what locations suit your style. Using the list of stats, the map with squiggly lines and the brief trail review to establish the lay of the land, you can **choose your own adventure**.

The review is a brief commentary on what the trail experience might be like for you. I touch upon what I saw and enjoyed on the trails, and any not-so-pleasant aspects.

Keep in mind that riders' tastes in this sporting activity are broad. Some like it fast and flowy while others want an endless technical challenge. Many stay away from rocky rides, whereas I love them. There are those who like the comforts of a resort experience and purists who seek out rustic woodlots with few amenities but track to get lost on.

Publishing the Book

Publishing this book was a long ride down a double-diamond track. I got bucked a few times, but I made it to the end, intact. It certainly was a crazy ride with many surprises and obstacles.

I am semi-retired and booked off the beginning of the year to combine the text, maps and photos into a layout I could offer to you as a guidebook.

It started off on time, but things moved slowly. Subconsciously, I guess I knew it would be a monster. I found a great editor and started rewriting and updating all the trail reviews. I added a few new ones and omitted others that were fun to ride but just not on **my "A" list.**

Then COVID-19 came to Canada. No problem in terms of the book; I was at home on my computer anyway. Ah! but then it brought new distractions. My wife and teenage son were now working from home, then the stock market crashed and I was fixated on the drama.

What also started to happen was that key information I needed to update my reviews was disappearing. Official trail and club websites began hiding info to discourage anyone from thinking of going there during the pandemic. Emailing and calling became unreliable, as everything was shutting down. But I stayed on the proverbial MTB and kept pedalling.

In the end, it was the rendering of trail maps that took months—and hundreds of hours—to do. With 55 locations to make maps for, finding and parsing GBs of map data, adding GPS tracks, styling the base map with contour lines and hill shading was a huge learning experience and a **massive undertaking!**

Maps have a significant amount of visual information. It's an art to make sure all the lines, colours and text do not collide into a jumbled mess. I am humbled at what it takes for pro mapmakers to create accurate and coherent maps.

I take a lot of photos when I ride, but I knew I wanted other action pix too. That took time to source out, but I found some nice ones, all taken by Ontario photographers.

Recently I was excited to hear there is finally a MTB club forming in **North Bay** the NBMBA. I know of three ride locations I would love to post, but not until that club gets them approved, my friends. We all know of "illegal" loops out there; those will remain a secret.

I respect the wishes of any private MTB trails not to publish their whereabouts. **Kingston MTB Club** has such a place and you can certainly join to find out where.

My apologies to **Thunder Bay**. I hear there is good riding in **Trowbridge Forest** (Shuniah Mines), but the day I was to go, it was a killer heatwave and the beer was tasting pretty good.

And sadly, upon inquiring at a local bike shop on the status of **Macaulay Mountain**, out in Picton, I was persuaded to not to include it in this book. Seems it needs a lot of love. I hope some of you reading this can resurrect it.

I never planned to write this book; it just happened. I enjoy picture taking, looking over maps, discovering new trails and, of course, riding my MTB. Once I sorted out how to lay out the book and print it, the bike wheels were in motion.

I hope you enjoy the guide and find what you were looking for. After 30 reviews, I really had to get creative to have them sound different and entertaining. How many ways can you talk about a toaster? By using some MTB jargon and bits of odd humour, I think I've kept it a fun read.

Enjoy reading about these trail locations and then **actually ride them.** Promise!

At some point, you have to publish your book knowing that there will always be other trails left out. Perhaps a consideration for the next edition.

Any **feedback is welcome** to improve this guide and inform our MTB community. Send any comments, better GPS tracks, or suggestions for new MTB locations to review, to **staff@ontariobiketrails.com.**

And you can certainly **post your own Ride Review** at the bottom of any OBT trail page. We all want to know how your ride went.

For 20 years, I have been mountain biking, and **I still love it**. I wear a **permanent smile** every time I go out on the trail. Now that I'm in my early sixties, I have to tone it down a bit, but the joy of the ride is still within me.

My greatest thrill would be to know that you too have developed a passion for mountain biking and have helped in your own way to maintain and grow this wonderful sport.

With that, I would like to **thank you for paying for your copy** to support me and your cycling community. I thank you for caring, making it happen and funding my beer fridge.

Keep Crank'n! - Dan Roitner, Senior MTB Statesman

The MTB eBook

Since hardcopy books have no web links to further your trail research, I include a **free copy of the eBook** when you buy a paperback edition. Use the eBook version as a portable PDF copy on your phone or tablet. Just follow the instructions on the last page to find out how to access the eBook.

Best Mountain Bike Trails in Ontario

Using This Guide

Definition of Trail Listings

On every map page, there is an info list. To help you use this guide, I explain how to interpret my remarks and read the maps.

Address – At the top of the page is a street address (if there is one) in blue that will take you to the main parking lot to get to the trailhead. On the right of the page are the longitude and latitude coordinates of the main trailhead itself. Handy to plug into a mapping service on your phone or a GPS unit to find your way.

Length – All trails are in kilometres and rounded up. The length is approximate and refers to the total amount of singletrack, usually including other wider dirt paths, that makes up a good ride. Of course, that is subjective and I leave it to you to decide by reading the review.

As for determining the total number of kilometres, this became tricky. I compared numerous sources, and everyone had a different number. Some added the total length, while other clubs/resorts added the total amount of loops, which can give a higher amount. Some places even exaggerated; gracious me!

Regardless, all you need is enough to make it an enjoyable visit. And with MTB trails, it's not always about the distance, it's the quality of the ride that matters. Ten kilometres on a rock-infested track is a highway to hell. You would not want it longer.

In the end, I took everyone's info, including my own, to arrive at as accurate an estimation as possible about the percentage of the type of trail/path and access roads you may encounter at any given location.

Hiking Trails % – Narrow dirt paths, the width of one person, running in rather straight lines that hikers have made, even up and down hills. These usually take the shortest way across.

Singletrack % – Narrow paths similar to hiking trails but designed for cyclists, ideally along interesting topography. Trails meander and flow, in no hurry to get anywhere, and are cut to create less erosion and provide more challenge.

Access Paths/Roads (Doubletrack) % – Paths as wide as a car. They may have two worn tire grooves made by park rangers' or loggers' vehicles (though seldom seen). Many are Nordic ski trails in the winter.

Unless stated otherwise, consider all trails **two-way traffic**. Stay alert.

Elevation – What would a mountain bike ride be without hills? All locations have them, but how much do you want? I describe briefly the general **upward slope** of the land and any extra-nasty hilly bits you may encounter.

Terrain – This covers a lot of ground. I mention the general **soil base** of the paths and what to expect on your journey. You decide what you are willing and able to navigate. Some areas are rather **sandy**, others are littered with **stones, logs, roots**. How much can you tolerate—or let me rephrase that, how much fun can you endure?

Some like a fast ride on a smooth track with big berms, others want to gingerly thread their way through a minefield of boulders. Everyone has their preferences.

Along the way, the brave (and the foolish) can enjoy the added thrill of any natural or constructed obstacles and structures available. I will mention any stone, wooden, metal item —**boardwalks, ladder bridges, skinnies, ramps, jumps, teeter-totters**, or natural boulders and rock ridges to play on. (This is definitely not road riding; this so much cooler.)

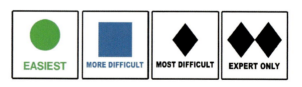

Skill – I use a simple three-level skill rating system: **Easy, Intermediate, Advanced**. Trails are rated at the **minimum skill level a bike rider needs** to be able to enjoy and be safe on those trails.

Skill is **not based on the distance** one can travel. I leave it to you to judge how far you can cycle around and get back.

8   Best Mountain Bike Trails in Ontario

Maps – If there are paper maps handed out at the gate (less frequent every year), a map board at the trailhead, and/or signs posted on the trails, I will comment.

At one time maps were hard to come by, but new technology has made paper maps less important. **GPS mapping apps** on your phone or other devices now make MTB rides more accurate, safe and predictable. (As an old-timer, I am not sure this is always better. Does it take the edge off the ride experience?)

Traffic – Though a mountain bike ride is usually a **solo** or **small group** experience in a large forest with space for all, one can occasionally see others. I list the typical encounters you may have beyond other MTB riders coming at you (or from behind you). Some locations have many hikers and dog walkers, plus slow-moving families with little ones on the trails.

I may mention possible (occasional, if at all) meetings with **ATVs, dirt bike**s or **horse riders**. These recreational riders have their own pathways. You might share paths or cross over their routes briefly. In the winter, when **Nordic skiers, snowshoers** and **snowmobiles** are active, some locations are closed to MTB riding, while others allow riders to share some paths with skiers.

Whenever you pass pedestrians, skiers/snowshoers or horse riders, please slow down! Be sure they see you and let them pass. Ask riders if their horses are comfortable with seeing mountain bikes. They could get spooked and dash away or kick you.

I'd like to say I have seen lots of **wildlife** in Ontario; that would be neat. But no, only the odd rabbit, pheasant and a few deer leaping away. A chance encounter with a **moose** or **bear** is possible the further north you go.

Facilities – Most ride locations are nothing more than **trees and trail** with public parking in a lot or along the road, and maybe an outhouse. You may find a **rain shelter** and a few **picnic tables,** that's it. I'll comment on any **local amenities** like **food (ice cream!), tap water or toilets** that are close by, plus extra frills like **bike rentals, repair shops, lessons,** or **swimming** and **camping/lodging** options.

Highlights – A short list of what you might see and experience on this route that is **scenic, interesting or unique**. Some spots may be only lots of greenery whizzing by.

Trail Fee – The cost of a trail pass. Most locations are **free!** But please support your leisure activity to sustain and improve trails if asked. This pays for services, upkeep and insurance for clubs and resorts. (And give back a little in some way, maybe volunteer to make the wheels go round.)

Phone – Some locations have a general phone # for info; many do not.

Website – Links to "official" government or related management websites if found. The **eBook links** will take you there and in the hard copy book, searching the **title names** online should do it.

Similar Trails – Other trails listed in this book and on the **OBT website** for you to compare and try. Though all are different, some similarities exist between these and the trail reviewed.

Local Clubs – Links to regional **bicycle clubs** that may ride this location—maybe a mountain bike club or a road cycling club with a MTB group in it. Check them out, socialize, learn a few things and find new places to roam.

Access (Directions) – This is the location of the bike ride and a few tips on how to get to a **parking lot** and to **find the trailhead.** Some locations have an exact address, others have do not.

I may add directions on how to get there, BUT... truly, with the convenience and accuracy of **online mapping services**, I leave it to them to get you there by searching the address or geographic coordinates at the top of the page.

My OBT website also can give you directions. The page with the specific trail review will have a feature to plot your route. The **flag on the site map** is where the main trailhead is, which usually has parking.

There may be other entry points mentioned. Signage at some of these places is at a minimum, or further down a side road, so keep your eyes open.

Bike Trail Map – I made these maps. It was a LOT of work and shows more detail than anything before it. But it does not aim to show everything. It's a guide for riders to get **a quick sense of what there** is and how the trails run, a way to dream of trails to ride and to figure out **how to get around.**

Note: these are a general rendition. Although they are as accurate as I could make them, they are only as good as the data I could use (more about that at the back of the book). **Do not rely solely on them for your survival.**

Best Mountain Bike Trails in Ontario

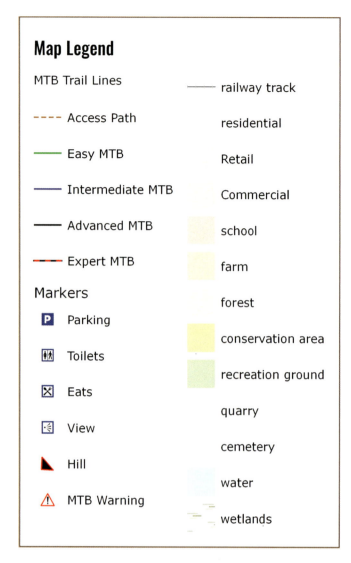

It's impossible to know or list **every trail** and **every trail name**. I used many resources to compile this data: my memory, GPS tracks, those from friends and clubs, websites, books, Ontario government surveying... Literally **gigabytes of data**.

And maps have **only so much room** to cram all the trail lines and text names, so some may be omitted. Some locations have **no names**—or **numerous names** for the same trail. I gave up and left those empty for the time being.

Trail lines are **colour coded** and use conventional MTB skill rankings. Some locations rank their trails ONLY based on their own area, which may exaggerate the difficulty (i.e. they may rank their most difficult trail as a black-diamond, but compared to other trails throughout the province, it's really a tame blue).

I have tried to give a more **balanced average rating**, ranking each trail against Ontario's other MTB locations. It's subjective, and certainly no Ontario black-diamond will compare to a double black-diamond run in BC or Utah. But it's **a good benchmark** for you to base other trail maps on.

Green lines are singletrack Beginner routes that are **basic, easy** and **safe for all**. They provide a good introduction to those trying out the sport and a great way for the rest of us to warm up. They're usually **not long in length** or hilly in nature, and they may offer a few **roots and rocks** to manage on a **smooth soil base**. Some wider **access roads** and **hiking paths** are also good for easy riding, and I made those green lines as well.

Brown dashed lines are other access roads and hiking paths—in my opinion they're not that entertaining, but still bike friendly enough to get you around.

Blue lines are singletrack for your Intermediate, average, **seasoned MTB rider** who is comfortable in the saddle and fit enough to take on **longer loops** and **steeper inclines**. There will be more and larger rock and root encounters and rougher terrain, along with **some obstacles** for you to enjoy and challenge yourself with along the way. These could be log rollovers, rock gardens, boulders, wooden boardwalks, skinnies, ramps and/or small dirt jumps.

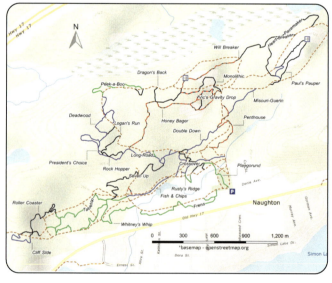

Black lines are **black-diamond** runs that call for **Advanced** riding skills. Experienced riders will appreciate these trails where **climbs get steeper** and so do the descents. Trails are faster or more gnarly with more frequent, **larger and more difficult** obstructions to manage. Any added, jumps, stunts and tricks built en route need good coordination and faith in your abilities.

Black and red dashed lines are **double black-diamond** runs (or **Pro Lines**) that only the best, most experienced riders on equally good bikes should dare venture to try. Most serious menacing stuff is on downhill runs and up north on the rocks of the Shield. High-end thrills and/or potentially high-stakes spills.

Map Legend

Symbols – These are the four key points riders want to know: **where can I park, are there toilets, can I get food and drink and is there anything worth looking at?**

 – a few suggested parking locations

 – location of toilet /outhouse

 – nearby food stores or restaurants (which have toilets, so I do not mark this twice)

 – scenery, lookout, there is something here worth checking out.

The **N symbol** on the maps points to **true north,** not magnetic north. The **distance scale bar** is divided in metres.

Contour Lines
– Being able to read contour lines on the maps can give greater insight to the elevation changes hill shading shows. Each beige contour line represents a **five metres** change in elevation.

The thickest lines are at every **100 metres** with **25 metre** increment lines half that thickness. Numbers on the contour lines display at every 25 metre intervals. **Numbers face into the slope of the hill as it rises.**

Review
– After riding each location, I write a general description of the ride experience based on what I believe a **typical mountain bike rider** may wish to know, considering all the different kinds of terrain and tastes in riding. I focus on the **main features** that that trail system has and any shortcomings worth noting.

It's a quick summary that elaborates on a few points listed on the other page, enough for you to decide to check it out or pass. None of **my opinions** are influenced or funded by anyone, just saying...

I encourage you to **add your own comments** after a ride at the bottom of any **OBT website review**. Tell us what you think of the trails there.

Photos
– Most of the trail photography was taken by me. I have added images from a few other local photographers to round out the book. Shots are of the trail environment and some scenery, too.

All the images in the reviews are **very authentic, taken at those locations.** There was limited space on the page for more pics. If you want to see more photos, head to the OBT website for a peek.

Getting good images of the trail is a challenging pursuit. **Staging a location shoot** with riders would be ideal. I was a pro photograbber for many years so at times coming up short pains me.

But I am there first to enjoy the ride. So getting a good exposure in a **dark forest** or on a **high-contrast** sunny day is a trick. Photos with just endless trail get boring real fast, so to **show scale** I wait for a rider to fly by or have my son or me in the shot.

And that should be plenty to get you started...

Finished our Sudbury swamp run

Best Mountain Bike Trails in Ontario

Central Ontario

Agreement Forest – MTB Trail

9475 Guelph Line, Milton　　　　　　　　　　*Trailhead -*　43.49951050, -79.99881512

Length – 38+ km

50% MTB singletrack
30% hiking trail
20% doubletrack access roads

Terrain – Generally flat, a few small hills, slopes east down to creek

Surface – Smooth dirt trail peppered with stones, some gravel, mud patches, limestone rock/boulders aplenty, boardwalks, all slippery when wet

Skill – Advanced, Intermediate (there is a bypass option on most harder routes)

Traffic – Light traffic, mainly MTB riders, hikers, dog walkers; in winter there are Fatbikes, skiers, snowshoers

Trail Pass – Free

Facilities – Small parking lots, three locations, amenities nearby in town

Highlights – Rocks and more rocks! Endless technical challenges; super-fun on a **Fatbike** in the winter

Trail Maps – None on trails (on purpose, to keep it natural), but plenty online

Phone – None

Website – HAFTA (Halton Agreement Forest Trail Association)

Similar Trails – Porcupine, Buckwallow, Laurentian, South March

Local Clubs – HAFTA (Halton Agreement Forest Trail Association)

Access – There are three small parking areas:

9475 Guelph Line: long gravel driveway, no sign at street level (Mohawk Racetrack is kind enough to allow overflow in their lot)

Two entry points at Sideroad 10 & Fourth Line Nassagaweya

Two areas for cars on the far side of the forest along Sixth Line Nassagaweya, north of Campbellville Rd.

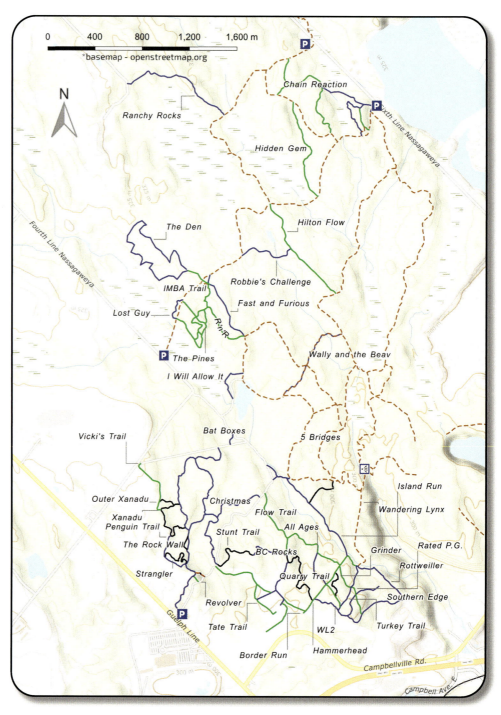

12　*Best Mountain Bike Trails in Ontario*

Review:

As with many secret riding haunts, the **Agreement Forest** area has become increasingly popular over the years and has matured into a legit MTB destination. This is a **technical rock riders' paradise** that will challenge the best and dismember the reckless.

This area near **Milton** is part of the **Niagara Escapement** and as such is littered with limestone rocks and boulders. You can't farm it, it does not drain well, but it's a perfect space for mountain bikes to roam.

This well-treed forest has a hydro corridor cut through it and a few access roads. No signs are posted, so finding your way to the sweet stuff is a bit of a mystery.

Meandering around **38+ km** of MTB cut trails and a few old hiking paths could be an adventure you seek. Most will access maps online. The **Halton Agreement Forest Trail Association** (HAFTA) MTB club website has some of the best descriptions of each trail any club has posted.

With the help of **IMBA**, HAFTA has applied great enthusiasm in building and maintaining some really enjoyable loops. The **2.3-km The Den** trail is a recent addition that's sure to please you rockhounds.

Nearly all of the **61 trails** in here feature rocky sections and **wooden structures** that you can nimbly work your way over or around. There's a constantly changing array of rock and twisty trail for the advanced rider to enjoy, and for added kicks there are plenty of **wooden ramps, log skinnies and hops to play on.**

Natural stone structures abound, with drops and rock gardens to master and climbs **requiring goatlike abilities.** Occasionally you will come upon car-sized boulders left behind from the last ice age, perfect for scaling up and over (some may consider them obstructions, LOL).

The **Rock Wall** is aptly named: it's a long, lumpy highway of stones left over from farmers clearing the land. Other favourites of mine are the **Boundary Trail A, BC Rocks** and **Hammerhead.**

If you're an **Intermediate** rider learning your way, you may find it a tougher going, but fear not, most nasty spots have an **easier bypass / ridearound** if you need to bail.

Now, not everything in here wants to bash you about. There are more mellow, faster trails like the **Pines, Burnt Out Car, Rated P.G.** and **Flow Trail** that let you open up.

From **Guelph Line Rd.,** the terrain is flat, sloping down into a valley where **Sixteen Mile Creek** runs. This not overly hilly area does have a few short climbs and switchbacks.

Actually, the level ground produces a fair number of soggy wetlands and mosquitoes, too. Some of this area has boardwalks and, though most of the trail is rock, there are pockets of mud.

Your **expensive dual-suspension** bicycle will finally earn its keep in here. And I strongly suggest you **wear armoured padding** for this spin. Also, pack well for any bike repair or safety issues, as traffic is light in here.

I am told it is actually **busier in the winter**, with **Fatbikes** following a marked loop. Seems the lack of hills is the draw and the snow covers much of the craggy parts.

The best rock riding is in the **Agreement Forest,** where trails continue north seamlessly for many more kilometres of similar terrain. **Hilton Falls Conservation Area** is on the east side (you need to pay to play here) and some nice track can be found scattered further in among the wide hiking paths.

This area is **one of Ontario's toughest** rocky, technical places to ride—and has no monster climbs. When your skills and gear are ready, prove yourself and take on this wonderful MTB playground.

Best Mountain Bike Trails in Ontario

Central Ontario

Albion Hills – MTB Trail

16500 Hwy 50, N of Bolton

Trailhead - 43.92741206, -79.82297388

Length – 50 km

40% MTB singletrack
30% hiking trail
30% doubletrack access roads

Elevation – Rolling medium hills with open grass fields, some steep climbs, nice switchbacks; gnarly bits abound

Terrain – A few sandy spots and rocks with assorted wooden bridges, ramps; the smooth soil can be very muddy and greasy after a rain

Skill – All levels; best for Intermediate MTB riders

Maps – Paper map at gatehouse; numbered signposts

Facilities – Parking, bike wash, washrooms, showers, snacks, pool, camping, and limited Fatbikes for rent

Highlights – Well maintained, Black race trail, lots of variety, chalet, plenty of camping

Trail Pass – $6.50

Hours – 9 am – 4 pm, weekends to 5 pm

Phone – 905 880 0227

Website – Albion Hill Conservation Area

Similar Trails – Durham Forest, Palgrave, Hardwood

Local Clubs – HAFTA , Caledon Cycling Club,

Access – Enter the main gate at 16500 on Hwy 50, north of Bolton. Drive 10 minutes to the parking lot by the chalet; main trail starts south, up around the bend, and then splits.

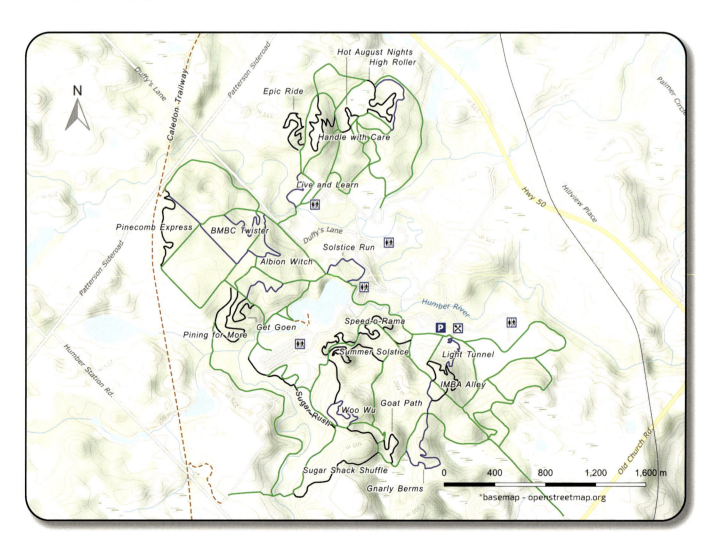

Best Mountain Bike Trails in Ontario

Review:

Albion Hills Conservation Area is a **top MTB destination** on the northwest side of **Toronto**, popular due to its proximity to the big city and all-round variety of track and amenities. A combined **50 km** of single- and doubletrack runs are sure to satisfy everyone.

It offers a **well-cut variety of trails** through a forested area of wide x-country ski paths with lots of additional twisty MTB singletrack loops.

The terrain has a **little of everything** and, as the name implies, it has **hills!**

Most of this course flows well, with **bridges, steep climbs, twisty track,** open fields, and a scenic cliff view onto the old pond, which is now drained.

Most of the riding is in the shade of the woods with one length across a field on the other side of the **Humber Creek**. In the spring it can have **biting bugs** around the wetlands, so keep moving.

Recently a **few route changes have made it even better.** I always enjoy doing **The Goat Path** and **Pinecone Express**.

One can work up a good sweat doing the **Black 20-km race course** (if the markers are still up), which Advanced MTB riders will love.

As with any area that is so **popular** and hosts races, the trails are getting beaten up. The base of smooth clay soil is getting wider and roots are starting to get exposed, making it a bumpy ride in sections.

Full amenities make the **trail fee** a bargain. As a park, AHCA has **camping** right at the trailhead and decent services to change, shower, swim, wash your bike and have a snack by the chalet. A perfect spot to camp and ride.

You may want to check on race events before you go. There is one on the summer solstice weekend and likely others every year. A backup is to ride **Palgrave** up the road.

The **switchbacks** are a blast to ride and the **log rollovers, rock drops,** and **rock gardens** (with optional easy bypasses) spice it up to make it never boring.

Various loop lengths, shortcuts and skill levels give you options to end your visit when you run out of gas. I found difficulty ratings are a little exaggerated.

Not the best place to learn mountain biking. By staying mainly on the easier-access road paths, you can train those legs on the smaller climbs.

At the gatehouse, when you pay, take the **paper map,** as map boards seem not to be posted except at the chalet. Sure, the trails are marked well with numbers, but without a **map for reference** you may get spun around.

This **top spot gets busy** on warm weekends! Get out of the city, make your way there for the exercise, the challenges or just as a recreational ride you will certainly enjoy.

Best Mountain Bike Trails in Ontario

Central Ontario

Centennial Park – MTB Trail

14859 Jane St., N. of King City

Trailhead - 43.96843178, -79.56306683

Length – 5 km

100% singletrack MTB trail

Elevation – 20 m vertical, flat on the beginner section, drops down into a hilly valley out back.

Terrain – Smooth soil base, sandy spots, a few roots, field stones, slippery after it rains, some poison ivy

Skill – Easy, best for beginners

Traffic – MTB riders, races

Maps – New map board and signs posted; not big enough to get lost

Facilities – Parking lot, outhouse, picnic tables, shelter, bike repair station

Highlights – Super flowy runs, great place to learn

Trail Fee – Free

Phone – None

Website – None

Similar Trails – Midhurst, Christie Lake, Coulson's Hill

Local Clubs – York Mtn. Bike Assoc. - YMBA

Access – Drive north up Hwy 400, exit onto Hwy 11 (King Rd.); head east then north on Jane St. Just beyond 16th Sideroad on the east side is the Centennial Park driveway - 14859 Jane St.

It's easy to miss; look for the tall communication tower on the hill. Parking is beside it.

Ride east beyond the parking lot map board and pick either direction to go in.

Regardless, you will likely ride it all both ways.

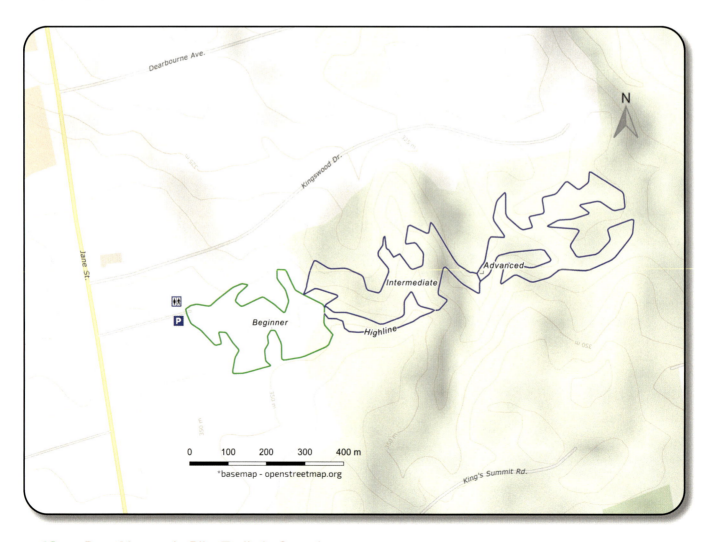

16 *Best Mountain Bike Trails in Ontario*

Review:

If you are learning to mountain bike in the **Toronto area**, then **Centennial Park** is the place you need to go to hone your skills.

Just north of Toronto, beyond **King City**, this area is the perfect spot to gain experience safely without overdoing it. You can enjoy an **easy ride** that's **not too long**, with **no surprises** to send you over the bars.

I am going to assume you are fit, but new to mountain biking, and your MTB is worthy of the demands of the trail.

With that said, these loops here are built (and rated) just right for someone's **first year** of MTB action.

Centennial has **three loops** that join one after the other. This is an **excellent trail design** that introduces the rider to an easy **Beginner** loop with flat, smooth terrain and wide banked turns to warm up on.

Further in, it gets more challenging as you head down into a valley. Here the **Intermediate** and **Advanced** loops twist over hill and dale and are sure to please. Don't let the word "Advanced" intimidate you; it's not. Frankly, it's no harder than the Intermediate loop, which is actually a tad hillier.

The terrain in this area is hilly, but the switchbacks surprisingly take you up with **little effort**. This somewhat sandy place unfortunately now has exposed tree roots from years of tire wear and rain. Roots are the only remotely tricky feature here, beyond a few old decaying logs and the odd fieldstone.

There is one more short section left called the **Highline** along the top of the valley. There are a few signs to point your way, but it's impossible to get lost in here.

What makes this such **a terrific ride** is that the routes were **cut specially for MTB riding.** These are not repurposed hiking trails. This is the kind of singletrack that winds and flows endlessly, **going nowhere in a hurry**, that regular riders love.

And here is where I want to invite not just the newbie crowd, but all seasoned MTB riders, to indulge.

Yes, the riding is sweet, but alas, it's over in no time if you crank it. With the whole circuit consisting of **a mere 5 km**, most will be left unsatisfied after once around. So **ride it the other direction!** And now you have **10 km**.

When I led group rides here, the problem was where to go after riding it twice? Unfortunately, there is not much close by, so you will have to drive about 25 km to **Albion**, **Palgrave**, **Coulson** or **Jefferson** to get your fill. Each will be a harder ride.

Centennial isn't just for beginners: there are **weekly summer races** (Tuesdays) and MTB clubs regularly ride here. This small woodlot northwest of the town of **King City** is perfect for riders of any ability who have limited time. Come on out for a **quick blast through the woods** after work or before weekend chores.

Best Mountain Bike Trails in Ontario

Central Ontario

Christie Lake – MTB Trail

1000 Highway 5 W, Dundas

Trailhead - 43.28036452, -80.03156658

Length – 16 km

60% MTB singletrack
20% hiking trail
20% doubletrack access roads

Elevation – None (well, almost), small mounds, gently slopes up from lake

Terrain – Smooth, sandy soil; a few roots; easy log hops; no rocks; closed when muddy

Skill – Easy beginner territory

Trail Pass – Car + driver $15, extra passenger $5, a little pricey for what there is

Facilities – Parking lot, washrooms, picnicking, swimming, canoe rentals

Highlights – Perfect for beginner MTB riders and family outings

Trail Maps – At trailhead only – marked posts

Hours – Sunrise to sunset (closed when muddy)

Phone – 905 628 3060

Website – Christie Lake Conservation Area

Similar Trails – Centennial, Guelph Lake, Dufferin Forrest

Local Clubs – HBMBA - Hamilton Burlington Mountain Bike Assoc.

Trailhead – From the SW parking lot, head south across the bridge over the Christie Reservoir to the map board, then head into the woods.

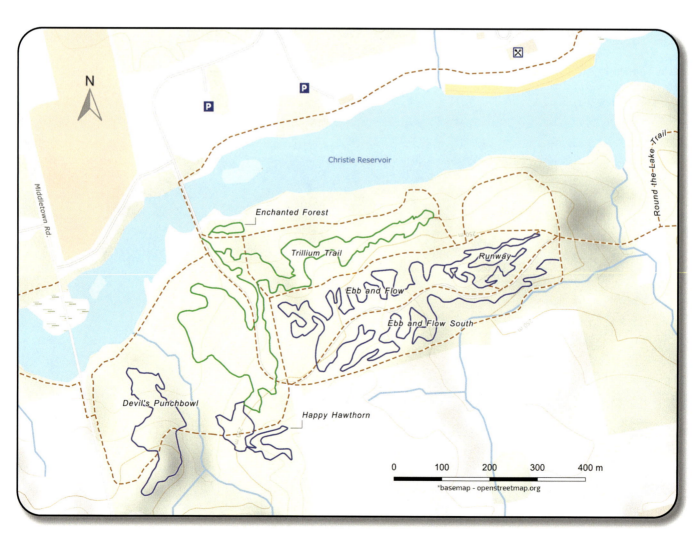

18   *Best Mountain Bike Trails in Ontario*

Review:

Christie Lake Conservation Area, just north of **Hamilton,** is ideal for the **beginner mountain biker**. The trails here are easy, well designed and safe for anyone to ride.

You will find a very **flowy sets of loops** on **smooth soil**, with **little elevation** and few rocks.

The active local trail-building community has made great efforts to create a **twisty, gnarly trail** through the pines. There are a few nice berms to bank on, and easy log rollovers added, too.

The 2.5 km **Trillium** loop is super-easy and level. The only challenges beginners have to contend with are some roots.

Weaving through the rows of pine, the **Ebb & Flow** trail, about 3 km long, is where the best twisty, fast fun is.

Out on the back end, the popular (and most difficult) loop is **Runaway**. This trail is short, with a few tricky dips and mounds where you can play with gravity. **Devil's Punchbowl** has some steep pitches as it does a circle. Both trails are rated **black diamond**. What? Seriously not!

One can blast through these twisty loops faster to make it more of a challenge, but since the trails are open to **two-way traffic**, be cautious for young riders coming the other way.

There are about **10 km** of trails here, with about **8 km cut for singletrack**. The rest are straight doubletrack hiking path. You can ride around the lake (reservoir) to add another **5 km** to that total.

With that said, you might have already guessed that this place **does not challenge** or strike fear into the heart of any **seasoned mountain biker** looking for excitement.

But it does serve as a good location for bike riders looking to **try out the sport** without getting frustrated or hurt.

It's a very **family-friendly ride**, as I have seen little ones riding it quite easily. Moms and dads, bring your kids and get them into mountain biking early!

As for the **entrance fee, I found it pricey** compared to some other Ontario MTB areas (Then again, how much did you pay for your bike ?!!)

Consider spending some time by the lake after your ride to make the most of the entrance fee. You can swim, fish or go for a paddle. There's also a nice disc golf course.

New loops are reportedly in the works that may improve and expand the riding opportunities here.

This little-known trail system is **worth trying once** and, while tame for thrill-seekers, it certainly offers a pleasant and varied ride for those getting into mountain biking.

Best Mountain Bike Trails in Ontario 19

Central Ontario

Copeland Forest – MTB Trail

1201 Ingram Rd. & Line 4 North, Oro-Medonte   Trailhead –   44.58707295, -79.68274757

Length – 60+ km

30% MTB singletrack
40% hiking trail
30% doubletrack access roads

Elevation – Level area by wetlands sloping to long climbs on the east side, large hills

Terrain – Smooth trail base of clay and sand; leaf-covered sections; roots; bridges; field stones; slippery when wet

Skill – All levels, from easy, flowy track to steep DH runs

Traffic – MTB riders, hikers, dogs, horses, Fatbikes, snowshoers, XC skiers

Maps – Basic info posted at trailhead; no trail signs; use a map app

Facilities – Parking lots; eats and lodging; bike repair at Horseshoe Resort, which has DH runs on their ski hill

Highlights – Long, speedy descents; endless trail; natural and rustic; wildlife

Trail Fee – Free

Phone – None

Website – Copeland Forest Friends

Similar Trails – Three Stage, Durham Forest, Kelso

Local Clubs – SCMBA

Access – Take Hwy #400 north to exit #117; head east on Horseshoe Valley Rd. W. (Simcoe County Road 22); then choose:

1 – Head north on Penetanguishene Rd. (Hwy 93), then turn right (east) on Ingram Rd. In 5.5 km, you'll see a large parking lot on the south side at 1201 Ingram Rd., just east of Line 4. (Recommended start point.)

2 – Or continue eastward on Horseshoe Rd. W., then turn left onto 5 Line N.; head up the road to find three trailheads on the west side of the road, beyond the route gets rough. (Good starting point to get to the harder/fun stuff faster.)

3 – Or use the Horseshoe Nordic Centre lot at 1106 Horseshoe Valley Rd. W., across the road from the ski hill.

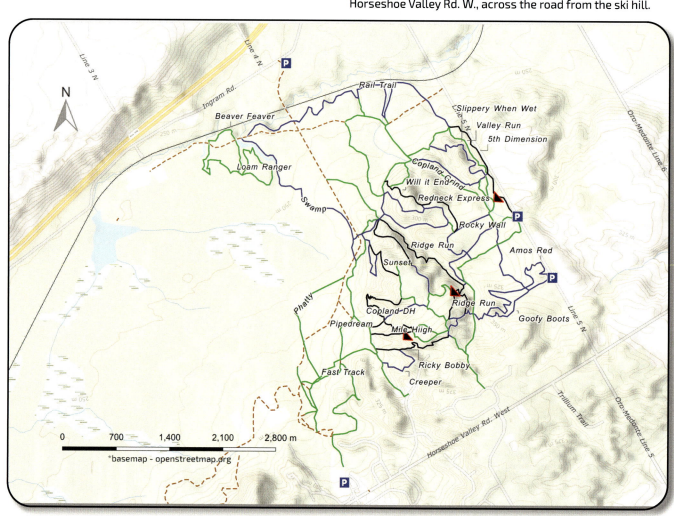

Best Mountain Bike Trails in Ontario

Review:

Copeland Forest is a **BIG ride** in many ways: large in size, enormous hills and over **60 km** of trails for you to explore.

It's a seemingly **endless MTB ride** that winds up and down slopes and across benched hillsides via twisty switchbacks and long, **speedy downhill descents**.

What you will find hidden within this extensive network are **log hops, ladder bridges** and **jumps**. There are also **rock gardens,** but otherwise, this area has just a few stones on the loops. The trails are smooth clay; some are covered in leaves and they are certainly slippery when wet. Other spots have plenty of sand to slow you down.

Oh, I didn't mention the other BIG thing here: the **marshlands** to the west, which take up more than half of this property. Trails skirting the perimeter are at risk of being swampy and buggy. This low-lying flat area slopes up numerous valleys to the east end of **Copeland**, turning into some **sizable hills**.

At about **130 metres,** the elevation here is one of the highest verticals at any MTB ride area in Ontario (excluding ski hills). Expect long climbs that will test your cardio and employ those blessed granny gears.

Ah! But with every painful grind up there is the **sweet payoff down**. Seldom do MTB riders in this province have such **long descents** to enjoy—so often, they are over far too soon. You can glide down a few of them for over a kilometre, so savour these ones, kids. And for the fearless DH junkies out there, there are a few **black-diamond runs** for your fix.

Enough with talk of hilly climbs. If you come in from the north side parking lot (best choice), across the train tracks, you'll find a series of **easier loops**, not flat, but not lung-busters either. There's lots of great riding through the trees on winding track over bridges, through water and muddy patches, too.

Coming in from the **Horseshoe Nordic Centre** car lot, past the golf course, is another easy start... the monstrous hills are to your left.

If you enter by the road on **5 Line North**, you can hit the popular, difficult and fast DH descents locals call **5th Dimension** and **Ridge Run**.

All this is under a mixed forest canopy with **few landmarks** to guide you—and to make it even more mysterious/confusing, there is little signage. With your focus on the tricky tracks and the greenery whizzing by, you'd better keep your sense of direction and should likely refer to a map app (not like we did in the old days, when we had to wander for days to find our way out, LOL).

In the winter, depending on the snow cover, there is some fine **Fatbiking** to be found. **Horseshoe Resort** runs a Nordic centre that rents Fatbikes. (They also offer summertime DH MTB riding on their ski hill.)

And need I say, in autumn, on a sunny day, the fall colours are spectacular.

Barrie, located 25 minutes south of **Copeland Forest**, is likely the best après stop for refuelling after your day ride.

Overall, **Copeland** is a **giant exhilarating maze** that will make you sweat and keep you wanting more. And likely you will be heading home happy no sooner than when your endurance level bonks out.

Best Mountain Bike Trails in Ontario   21

Central Ontario

Coulson's Hill – MTB Trail

3541 11th Line & Hwy 400, Bradford   Trailhead –   44.14920036, -79.64089111

Length – 13 km

35% MTB singletrack
40% hiking trail
25% doubletrack access roads

Elevation – One main large hill that slopes down to a creek valley on the north end, then goes back up slightly

Terrain – Smooth, firm soil; pine needles and leaves; log hops, bridges and structures; can be muddy; not good after a rain

Skill – All levels, best for Intermediate and Beginners to learn

Maps – None, a few trail markers

Facilities – Parking lot, outhouse maybe?

Highlights – Twisty, with many log hops; gets better at the back; relatively close to Toronto

Trail Fee – Free

Phone – None

Website – Simcoe County

Similar Trails – Dufferin Forest, Palgrave, Centennial Park

Local Clubs – York Mountain Bike Assoc.

Note - Hunting is allowed when in season, so wear some bright colours.

Access – Unfortunately, Coulson is right beside a bridge over the highway that does not have exit ramps.

From Hwy 400 northbound, exit on Hwy 88 and head east towards Bradford, then go north on 10th Sideroad, then west on 11th Line (Concession Rd. 11). There is a parking lot on the north side before the highway bridge. (It has been move further east in recent years.)

Any of the trails in from the car lot will make a good starting place for beginners except the SE corner has hilly tight switchbacks.

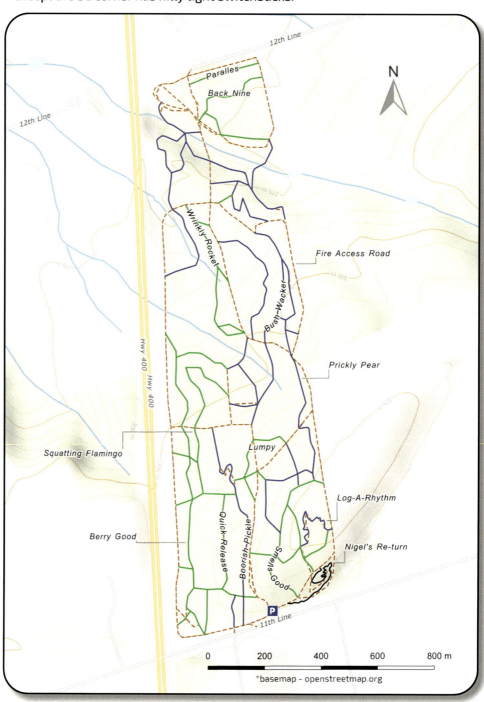

Best Mountain Bike Trails in Ontario

Review:

Coulson's Hill (Hodgson Tract) is a small but worthy woodlot to explore due north of **Bradford**. Well centred above Toronto and near **Hwy 400**, it has long provided me—and many other MTB riders—with a **convenient** spot to let loose for a few hours.

This small forest tract **packs in a lot.** From the parking area, the hill slopes down gradually to a small creek. Here you will find a few bridge crossings and a bank sloping up slightly, with a few minor loops, on the other side.

Suitable for any age or level of MTB riding, **Coulson** is made up of a patchwork of trails running every which way. Too small an area to get lost in, it has few directional signs, but there's no need of them: to get back to the car, simply head up the hill.

Now, posted trail names would help to sort out the **excessive shortcuts** and fragmented paths that can interrupt your pace. Stopping with your group to decide where to turn next gets tiring.

Or you can just go with the flow, knowing you will likely hit the same loops again ("Oh well...."), accidentally giving yourself more mileage here than the estimated **13 km.**

Every time I go there, I find new track. **It just keeps getting better,** even though it has suffered neglect and even the stress of rogue ATVs. There is definitely some MTB presence here: a local bike shop holds weekly races, and you will may find "illegal" wooden structures in there (some too homemade to trust).

My only complaint is the **hum from the highway** next to the area...so much for peaceful solitude. Yet there is plenty here to keep your attention and keep you smiling.

Circled by fire access dirt roads, this stand of mainly **tall pine trees** has fun-filled, twisty trails and long, **zippy flowy descents.** The trail surface is smooth clay with next to no rocks and oodles of **roots** and **log hops** to keep it interesting. They're perfect for beginners to **get the basics**.

Down by the creek in the **cedar grove** are a few **steeper segments,** but otherwise it's all easy going on the legs and you will likely climb **Coulson's Hill** several times.

The bottom west side near the highway is boggy, **perpetually wet**, and to be avoided, as is the area in general after it rains, when the trails get greasy.

Some Sportif riders would consider the area too small, too easy. Perhaps it is, but I have included it in the book for those of you who are **novice MTB riders** or in need of a **change of scenery.**

Certainly, for most, the ride will be thankfully longer than the drive you take to get here. After this trail outing, head south to **Bradford**, which is likely the best locale for an après munche stop.

Best Mountain Bike Trails in Ontario

Central Ontario

Dagmar – MTB Trail

1629 Concession Rd. 7, Goodwood

Trailhead - 44.01799856, -79.07476559

Length – 13+ km

90% MTB singletrack
10% doubletrack access roads

Elevation – A few valleys with moderate hills, open field between entrance and main ride

Terrain – Smooth, hard-packed soil base; some sand; gravel and round stones; log jumps, ramps, beams and rock gardens

Skill – All levels, but best for Intermediate riders

Traffic – MTB riders only

Trail Fee – Free

Facilities – No parking lot, no services for miles, pack what you may need

Highlights – Pure MTB riding with little filler; tons of variety; challenges; good times

Maps – Map board at trailhead and at major forks in the woods; decent signage keeps you moving

Phone – 416 661 6600

Website – Toronto Regional Conservation Authority

Similar Trails – Glen Major, Durham, Albion Hills

Local Clubs – Durham Mountain Bike Assoc.

Access – There is no parking lot by the trailhead. Parking lots are about ten minutes by bike in either direction at:

3 Rocks, 1030 Concession Rd 7

West Gate, 3559 Concession Rd 7

NO NIGHT RIDING

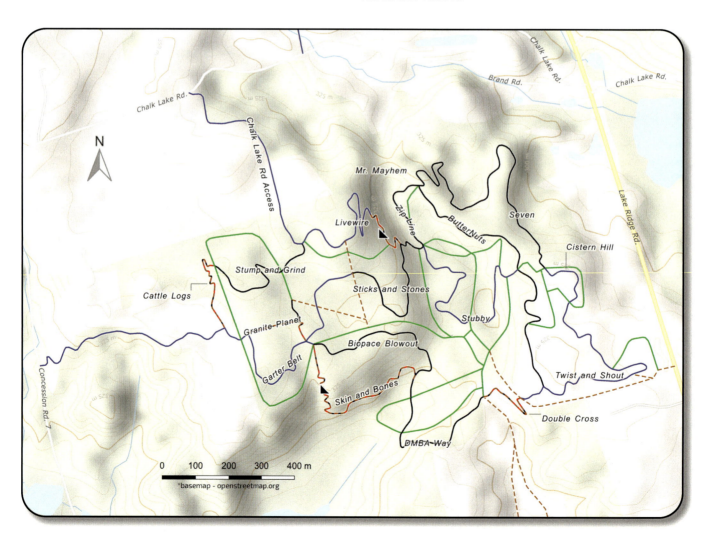

Best Mountain Bike Trails in Ontario

Review:

When **Dagmar North Trails** reopened in 2015, after about 10 years of uncertainty, the MTB community was all excited, and with good reason. These trails on Conservation land are mainly new **MTB-specific trails**, designed and cut for thrills and spills, and not resembling much of what was there.

Some are easy and winding for beginners, while others have **rock gardens, log jumps, ramps and beams** to keep the veteran riders entertained.

You'll never get bored or winded from too many hills; you may perhaps get a bit spun around if you're new to the area. Trails connect well and once you're familiar with them, it's **non-stop action.**

Even better, rarely do you have to ride doubletrack if you don't want to. As with any well-designed trail system, here you've always got a choice: you can pick the easy or the hard way through.

Upon entering the trailhead from the road, you will see a map board and a single trail. The fun starts right away, as you wind your way along a benched section in the woods to an open field.

Zipping through the tall grass of this field leads you to the first of many choices to make on your ride. You can go north and take on the **CattleLogs** trail for some trick **log hops** to exploit. Or be more cautious and enter the forest the other way—but there will be challenges for the meek in no time.

Further along, **Granite Planet** is a rock-infested trail and **Mr. Mayhem** is a large, challenging rock garden of **baby heads** descending into the valley; otherwise, most of the track here has a smooth base.

Easy, fun cruisers for more flowy speed can be found on the popular **Cistern Hill** and **Twist and Shout** sections. All routes are well signed, though I found the rating system a little exaggerated, as nothing here is truly worth a double black diamond!

I heard a new trail was recently cut here called **Skin & Bones**; it sounds dreadful. I can hardly wait to try it.

The **DMBA** bike club has done an **excellent job** of creating these singletrack trails. With the hard work of over 200+ MTB volunteers + donations, the Toronto area has a new spot to ride.

Parking is unusual at this location: there isn't any available at either of the two entrances! You are asked not to park at the trailhead or on sideroads, SVP. Instead, pick one of the two lots for Glen Major and ride to the entrance (the south lot is closer). It's amazing how so much trail can be compressed in **one square kilometre** (similar to Ravenshoe) and still leave mountain bikers grinning with delight. **Thirteen-odd kilometres** of trail might not be much, but it's all about quality, not quantity, in our mountain bikers' heads.

Dagmar is a great asset to have on the east side of Toronto and is certainly now another favourite locale for many.

Need more time on your trusty bike? Ride north up the road and do **Durham Forest** or go across the road and take on the **Glen Major Forest.** You will soon see why this area has become an **east Toronto MTB mecca.**

Best Mountain Bike Trails in Ontario

Central Ontario

Don Valley – MTB Trail

Pottery Rd. & Bayview, Toronto

Trailhead -   43.68923502, -79.36284781

Length – 20+ km

30% MTB singletrack
50% hiking trail
20% doubletrack access roads

Elevation – Big hills; steep climbs; fast, long drops; the valley is about 45 metres in elevation and trails use all of that height; riverside trails are flat

Terrain – Clay; slippery when wet; some off camber; gravel, sand and mud patches; gnarly bits with stone and roots; log hops and wooden structures

Skill – Intermediate to Advanced

Facilities – parking lots, no toilets close by

Highlights – Best MTB riding in the city, extra trails cut beyond map, bridges under tracks, fast drops

Maps – Map board at trailhead (limited to Crothers area); adequate trail signage; use your GPS map app

Trail Pass – Free

Phone – 311

Website – City of Toronto

Similar Trails – Albion Hills, Durham Forest, Jefferson Forest

Local Clubs – Don Valley MTB on Facebook

Access – There are three main starting points for Crothers Woods:

- At the bottom of Pottery Rd. & Bayview Ave. west of the train tracks; parking is limited on busy days and it can be muddy

- In the Loblaws parking lot on Redway Rd., which has tons of parking (and is a huge grocery store with food and drink)

- On the north end: at the bottom of Thorncliffe Park Dr. access road; tons of parking

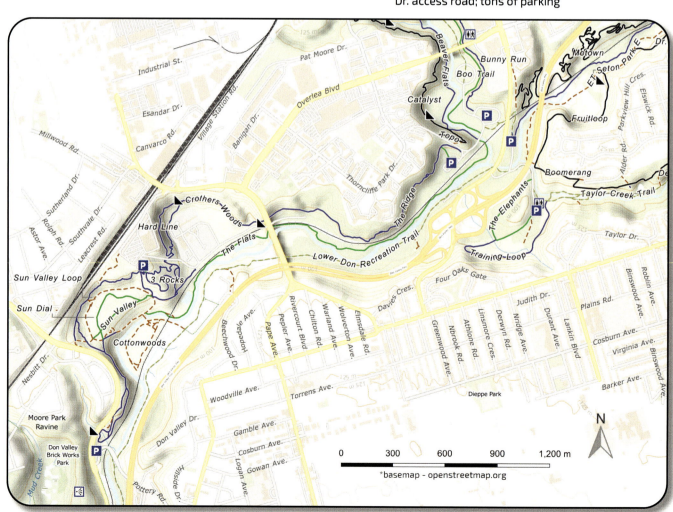

26   *Best Mountain Bike Trails in Ontario*

Review:

Down in the ravines of the **Don Valley**, in the middle of **Toronto**, is a worthy and convenient set of MTB trails to master and appreciate. Little else exists in TO to match the Don, and there is plenty here to discover.

Crothers Woods is the "city approved" area for us "crazies" to get our recreational kicks. Most of the routes traverse along the western slope halfway up the valley.

Full of **big climbs** to earn your **fast descents**, it may not be a long ride, but it will test you, thrill you and put you to work.

Over the years, these trails have been steadily improved with the help of **IMBA** and others dedicated to making what were initially hiking trails more of a **safe, flowing** trail system with **fewer erosion problems**.

New **switchbacks, wooden bridges** and **rock-armoured grading** were added to take on the frequent traffic this small city location has. More needs doing, but it's a good start.

The trail base is mainly **smooth clay** which is super-greasy when wet. With some of the trail off-camber, this will surely take you down. Give it a few days after a downpour, as muck puddles also form.

Along this fast ride are numerous **drops, log hops, skinnies, ramps, roots** and rocky bits: all welcome entertainment for the easily bored mountain bikers we are. There can't be more than **5 km** in the official area, but beyond **Crothers Woods** there is likely five times as much, built by local riders.

On the north end, where the **Ridge Run** spits you out onto the parking lot at **Thorncliffe**, there are two other trail options by the small bridge.

The first is to return back on the **Flats** trail along the **Don River**. This is an enjoyable, easy, level cruise through the tall grasses and riverside willows. Every year the path changes due to spring floods washing out the banks, so take heed the first time you venture in. A funky narrow wooden bridge takes you under the tracks and you are on your way down the sandy, winding path.

If you start itching, then you have been "kissed" by the **stinging nettle** bushes along this path. At one point, the trail comes up close to the train tracks. Though few trains run by, they are to be avoided (for LARGE, obvious reasons).

Midway along the river trail, you will encounter a **BMX ride park** made by locals. There are lots of dirt jumps and a pretty decent, if slightly confusing, pump track that MTB riders should try.

The second path option takes you north on either a moderate riverside route or up higher to **Catalyst**: a much harder, scary, technical benched singletrack. If you're game, this offers plenty of fun as it twists its way to **Eglinton Ave.**

The valley is full of hidden rogue paths peppered with questionable trail lines and structures, so be sure you are up to it. As a builder, after eyeing some of the wooden homemade structures, I caution you on their structural integrity... very dubious.

Unfortunately, the Don was a dumping ground for years and there is plenty of landfill with exposed brick, wire, metal bits and broken glass to maneuver around. So a flat is a possibility. Under the **Millwood Rd. bridge**, the metal wire cages holding in the stones look like perfect puncture villains, yet nothing has happened to me after dozens of passes.

As you cycle the Don dirt trails under the shade of the tall trees, there is little evidence of city life. You might almost think you were out of town. Only the occasional drone of the highway far below or the smell of the water treatment plant (you'll know it when you get there) tells you otherwise.

It's **a little country riding in the city** without fighting the traffic to drive there.

Best Mountain Bike Trails in Ontario

Central Ontario

Dufferin Forest – MTB Trail

937513 Airport Rd. Hwy 18

Trailhead – 44.21645441, -80.04785639

Length – 50+ km

35% MTB single track
40% hiking trail, horse paths
25% double track access roads

Elevation – Gradual slopes on most short hills; valleys on the far east end are deeper.

Terrain – Smooth, sandy base that drains well, horse-trodden areas, some very loose sand. No rocks here, and few roots or old logs to encounter.

Skill – Easy to Intermediate MTB riding

Traffic – MTB, hikers, horseback riders, Nordic skiers, snowshoers, snowmobiles.

Maps – Map board at trailhead, green tree markers on MTB loops.

Facilities – Large parking lot, outhouse, but no other amenities for miles around.

Highlights – Much endless single-tracks to explore. Very large and peaceful riding area. Deer may be seen.

Trail Fee – Free

Phone – 519 941 2816

Website – Dufferin County

Similar Trails – Ganaraska, Northumberland, Oro Network

Local Clubs – Team Van Go

Access – Just north of the Mansfield Ski area; park up the hill on the east side at 937513 Airport Road.

Most of the good trails run east and south from the map board.

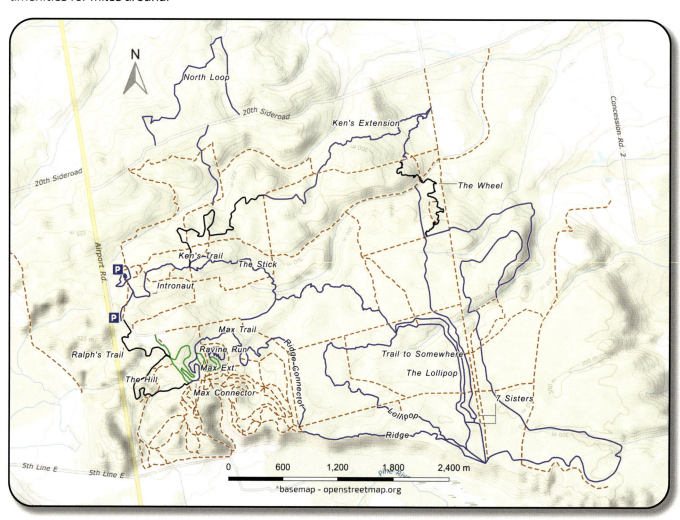

28 *Best Mountain Bike Trails in Ontario*

Review:

Dufferin Forest – Main Tract is one of the **largest MTB trail areas** in Central Ontario. With over **50+km** of riding suitable for **all skill levels,** it makes for an enjoyable mountain bike day trip for anyone.

This location is an easy **cross-country (XC) MTB style** of ride. Trails are fast and flowy on a **smooth, sandy base**. Hills **are gentle** at first with valleys getting deeper as you head further east to face more steep sections.

This **area drains very well**, so you can ride here at any time.

Recently I took a spin with a local club rider of **Team Van Go** to get an update on this **favourite MTB destination.**

Though he admits they are a little behind in the evolution of establishing distinct MTB loops, progress is being made and **it's looking good.**

I always remembered **Dufferin** as a ride where you can **get totally lost.** Trails after a few loops tend to look all the same and there were no signs to guide riders. At the trailhead, I saw a very busy, confusing map.

Recently, small **green markers** have been posted on trees for the designated MTB loops with a promise of **better map boards** and more of them are to be added.

Still, I recommend a phone **GPS app** to find the parking lot when the time comes.

Hopes are (when approved) to add a few log hops and structures to **liven things up.** But currently, there are few obstacles riders will encounter. There are **no rocks** here, either. **None!**

Naturally, then, these mellow trails make it **inviting for MTB beginners.** By the parking lot you will find a twisty loop winding back and forth among the rows of red pine as a fun **skill-developing course**.

We rode **two new trails** designed this year **SE** of the trailhead. (There is no official name or reference #, perhaps next year in an update.) One tries to be a more difficult hilly, twisty MTB track.

The other is a valley switchback (what I call a **Sidewinder**). Here the momentum from one bank carries you down and up the other bank, then back down and across again. In time, with use, it will find the right line and flow.

Intermediate Park style riders can certainly venture in here and ride the many access dirt paths and roads. One minor problem may be encountered. I found a few sandy roads so chewed up by horse hooves that only **fat tires** could manage them.

Thankfully, **horse riders** now have their own designated routes, which lessens the damage to our MTB trails. Slow down and use caution when you spot horses; some get spooked by our metal ponies.

As always, if you frequent this location, pay for a club membership or volunteer your time on trail maintenance. There are some **exciting new trails planned** by this small, dedicated club.

Efforts are made in the **winter to groom Fatbike** loops when possible.

An hour north of **Brampton** on **Airport Rd., Dufferin** is situated in the country near no sizable towns or services, so pack well.

Paths run in all directions, forking out for you to explore and possibly **wander off for hours**. So set your pace, get some exercise in, and **keep smiling** all the way.

Best Mountain Bike Trails in Ontario   29

Central Ontario

Durham Forest – MTB Trail

3613 Concession Rd. 7 & Hwy 21

Trailhead - 44.05037437, -79.09238093

Length – 40 km

50% MTB singletrack
50% doubletrack access roads

Elevation – Rather large hills and valleys (by Ontario standards) at the north and south end; more level in the middle

Terrain – Smooth soil, a few rocks and roots, some gravel, sandy on north end; drains well after a rain

Skill – All levels, but best for Intermediate and Advanced MTB riders

Traffic – Lots of MTB riders, hikers, dogs, Fatbikes in winter along with snowshoers & Nordic skiers

Maps – At trailhead and a few in the interior at junctions and MTB loops

Facilities – Parking lot, and outhouse; no food or water close by; can get busy on weekends

Highlights – Lots of variety for all levels; fast, gnarly and hilly track; new MTB trail cut and ramps built

Trail Fee – Free

Phone – 905 895 1281

Website – Lake Simcoe Region Conservation Authority

Similar Trails – Glen Major, Dagmar, Albion Hills

Local Clubs – Durham Mountain Biking Assoc,_- DMBA

Access – Drive up **Brock Rd.** in Pickering from **Hwy 401.** Go east on **Hwy 21** to **Concession 7** for the paved route.

Park on the side of the access road. Past the large map at the gate, most riders head south or east to start a ride. Go north to start the grand MTB tour.

An alternate gravel road route leads from the south coming up Concession 7 from Hwy 5. This passes the Glen Major and Dagmar trailheads on the way.

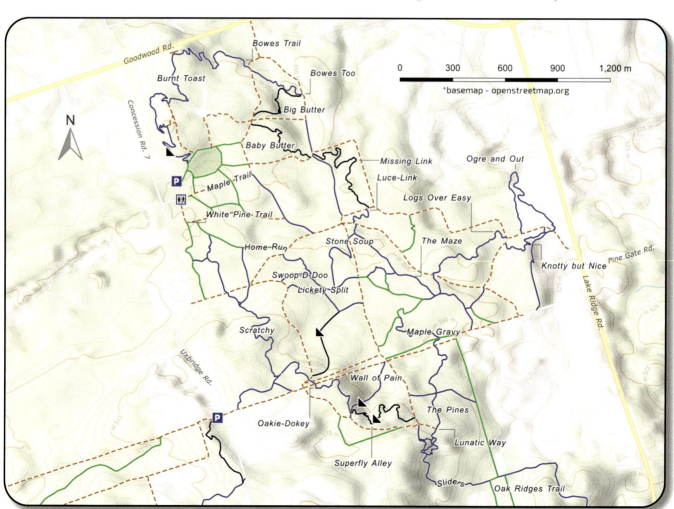

30   *Best Mountain Bike Trails in Ontario*

Review:

One of the **top rides** on the east side of **Toronto**, the **Durham Forest** has **40 km** of **bike trails for all skill levels**. This large, popular forest brings out many MTB riders and for good reason: challenges, variety and cardio.

Durham Forest has everything from wide, easy dirt access roads to hard uphill cranks and **fast, twisty** descents.

The terrain here is hillier at the south end and north side, which also has large patches of sand. The land flattens out more in the middle, where the easier trails reside.

While riding, **not everything flows together well**, and you might repeat a loop or get a bit lost. Does it sound like your typical MTB haunt? It is, but isn't that part of the fun? No worries, within minutes that will get sorted out. You cannot truly get lost here.

Personally, I find it hard to pick my favourite MTB runs, as they all have different qualities. But the **backside** of the forest is where all the sweet stuff tends to be.

For the grand tour, head north to the **Burnt Toast** trail to start your adventure. For a good workout, ride the Advanced **Baby Butter** trail into **Missing Link**.

For some easier **boardwalk** action, head further south to find **Ogre and Out**. Or fill your need for speed and get to the top of **Tower Hill** for a long bomb down.

There is plenty to like in **Durham Forest**—you just have to find it. A few map boards at junctions and trail signs at the entrances help, but I find there are not enough, so you may want to carry your own map.

Superfly Alley, the most **challenging track**, is on the **south end**, where the **most significant hills** are. If you reach ski chairlifts, you have definitely gone too far south!

For easy **beginner MTB riding**, there are **20 km** of main double-track access roads that cut straight across throughout the forest. Smooth soil and gravel are all you have to contend with, but you'll need to know there are a **few gradual hills** to conquer. These routes are wide and marked by posts with **Maple, White Pine, Red Oak,** or **Spruce** symbols.

Watch for hikers and dog walkers and, in August, for those delicious raspberries near the **Bell Tower** in the open areas that have been logged.

A very **active, large MTB club** maintains and updates trails in this area. Consider helping out. They have added new ramps and MTB loops for more thrills. (But no spills, please!)

Durham Forest is an excellent place for **Fatbikes** in the winter. Volunteers **groom 15 km of trail,** with even more you can try if the snow base is firm. Just stay off any cross-country ski tracks.

Not too buggy in the summer, the trails at Durham Forest drain well—but please **avoid when muddy** or **slushy** to lessen erosion.

Set your sights for **Durham Forest**. I am sure it will become a favourite for you, too. As for after-ride nibbles and drinks, little exists around here till you get close to **Uxbridge** or **Ajax.**

Need more riding? This area has tons. Simply head across the road, as a ride in the **Glen Major** forest or **Dagmar** can keep you crank'n for the whole weekend. **Wooo Hooo!**

photo - DMBA

Best Mountain Bike Trails in Ontario

Central Ontario

Eldred King - MTB Trail

16232 Hwy 48, Ballantrae

Trailhead - 44.06065693, -79.30789422

Length – 20 km (approx.)

30% MTB singletrack
30% hiking trail
40% doubletrack access roads

Elevation – While the trail has small to medium hills, the access roads are mostly flat; the singletrack can also be hilly

Terrain – The access roads are gravel, the soil smooth with some muddy spots and some very sandy stretches—watch out for horse patties!

Skill – Easy to Intermediate

Traffic – Bikes, hikers, dogs, horses, Nordic skiers in winter

Maps – A basic map can be found at the trailhead, but there is no other signage; the MTB track can be hard to find

Facilities – A large parking lot and an outhouse

Highlights – A lovely pond and dam that are fun to explore; plenty of sand for Fatbikes

Trail Fee – Free

Phone – 905 895 1281

Website – York Regional Forest, Oak Ridge Trail Association

Similar Trails – Ganaraska, Northumberland, Coulson's Hill

Local Clubs – Durham Mountain Bike Assoc. - DMBA

Access – Take Aurora Rd. going north on Hwy 48 to Markham Rd. to marker #16232, marked by an Eldred King Woodlands sign. Go down the gravel road and find parking on the west end.

The trail can be accessed in any direction from the parking lot. For most of the good riding, head in a southwest direction. Pond is northwest of the trailhead.

32   Best Mountain Bike Trails in Ontario

Review:

Eldred King Forest Tract, north of **Markham**, is a little-known, medium-sized area, **well worth trying at least once** for MTB riders. It's a great spot for **Beginners**, with over **20 km** of trail to explore.

And explore you will have to, as there is **no signage** beyond the map board at the trailhead. So use your phone map app or print one out, as routes run every which way.

Visiting the clearing by the **pond is a highlight** and a good spot for lunch, otherwise, the ride is not too hilly and almost all in the shade of interconnecting woodlots. That said, there is a **steep decent** at the far end of the the pond which is a bit of fun.

Getting to the **singletrack** among the access roads is the tricky part, as there are **no signs** and **few entry points**. But once you get in and ride around, you will be delighted at the amount of trail and the **great flow**.

Most of the **MTB runs** are on the **north half** of the map but some go into the **Hall Tract** and further south into the **Patterson Tract**. There are a few hilly spots that will keep it fun and challenging enough. Every time I go, **I find even more** twisty MTB trail.

Some of the side trails are carved out by **local horse riders**. You will know them, as they are more **straight** and **lumpy** from the hoof marks left behind. Not the best choice, but they could lead to better runs.

Unlike other ride spots I know, here you may likely meet a horse or come across **horse pies on the trail**, which in itself is a **technical trail obstacle** (LOL).

Note: When you see a horse, stop ahead and ask the rider how the horse may react. Some horses have never seen an alien mountain biker, and they may get spooked and throw the rider or kick you.

Also, expect to see **dog walkers** on trails near the parking lot and pond.

This mixed pine and hardwood forest is closed at times in the winter for logging. A few areas have **large swaths of sand** that are next to impossible to ride without an **unstoppable Fatbike**, unless it has just rained, which firms up the base.

The **sandy subsoil** found here is probably why it is not an all-round popular spot. As with many reclaimed forest tracts on the **Oak Ridge Moraine**, after farmers gave up the land, rows of trees were planted by the Ministry of Natural Resources and Forestry.

I have not checked out all corners of this forest tract. **Southwest** of the parking lot, it goes for a good stretch in many directions. At one point half way down on the west side, I came across an **archery range**. You're best to ride around it and not find a shortcut.

Some of these routes are **straight dirt roads**, others **sand traps** or **dead ends**. Still, MTB riders are carving out some good paths that warrant trying them out, though they may not be the awesome lines an Advanced rider seeks.

If you're like me and seeing an unknown trail **calls you to ride it**, then make your way to **Eldred King**. Find some new track and make it an **adventure** for a few hours.

I plotted on the map the trails I found the last time I was there. Send me any other tracks you find so I can add them too.

And mere minutes north on **Hwy 48** on the west side, is the **North Tract** for more to explore. Similar in size and terrain with more sand for the **Fatbike** dudes but less singletrack in there then Eldred.

Best Mountain Bike Trails in Ontario   33

Central Ontario

Ganaraska Forest - MTB Trail

10585 Cold Springs Camp Rd., Campbellcroft   *Trailhead -* 44.07475735, -78.50244011

Length – 100+ km

40% singletrack MTB trail
20% hiking trail
40% doubletrack access roads

Elevation – Gradual incline northward, with large rolling hills

Terrain – Smooth soil/sand, with some roots, fieldstones and gravel; watch for poison ivy on the shoulders

Skill – All MTB levels, best for Intermediate riders

Traffic – Never feels congested; MTB, hikers, ATV and dirt-bike riders, Nordic skiers, snowshoeing & snowmobiles, all have their own areas in which to play

Maps – A few maps at the trailhead; it has mainly doubletrack access roads for Nordic skiing, and the singletrack trails have a few signs. (Look for the IMBA Epic trail.) Use a GPS app for directions and backup.

Facilities – Parking lot, outhouse, bike wash and showers

Highlights – Tons of trails to explore and wilderness to experience; nice flow, long DH runs

Trail Pass – Day pass: Adults $12.00, youth $6.00

Phone – 905 797 2721

Website – Ganaraska Forest Centre

Similar Trails – Northumberland, Dufferin, Copeland Forest

Local Clubs – Peterborough Cycling Club, Cobourg Cycling

Access – Drive north 3 km from Hwy 9 (Ganaraska Rd.) to 10585 Cold Springs Camp Rd. and then on to the gatehouse for the Ganaraska Forest Centre. The trailhead is across the field from the parking lot, on the north side by the map board. North side has a few entry points – Bottom of Elgar Drive, Millbrook ride west on the Deyell Detour gets you in. Or east off the south end of the Glamorgan dirt road.

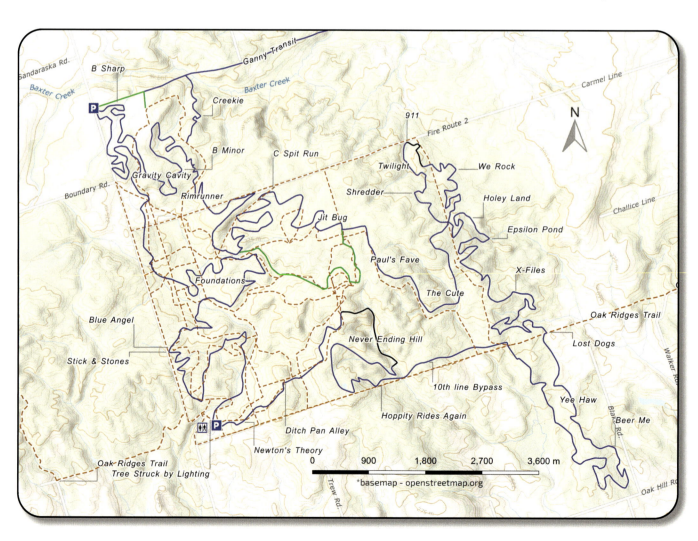

Best Mountain Bike Trails in Ontario

Review:

Ganaraska Region Conservation Area (aka "Big G", "The Ganny") is likely **Ontario's largest bike trail** area with **100+ kilometres** to explore. This huge, multi-use recreational trail system covers a wooded, northward-sloping terrain.

If you want to **ride forever**, deep into the woods, this is the place to be! **Cross-country distance cyclists** will love it. Downhill fly boys (and girls), too.

photo - Mike Stiell

The main paths are wide dirt access roads that take you over some of the largest hills found at any MTB location in Ontario.

Though usually not steep **inclines**, they will be **longer climbs** then most Ontario riders are used to. Once you pay in sweat to get to the top, the descents are a joy to bomb.

The main access roads, which are used for cross-country skiing, have colour-coded signage. As for the smaller MTB loops that cut in and out of these paths, not so much. You can get rather lost, as **this forest is extensive,** with few distinguishing features.

The south gatehouse hands out maps when you pay, so be sure to take one or use **GPS** if you wish to venture far. Cell coverage is spotty, but GPS will be fine.

Plenty of fun singletrack loops can be found, but are spread around over some distance. They flow well if the sand does not bog your tires down. Here and there are some twisty, gnarly sections to keep it interesting. I cannot recall many wooden structures or rock outcrops in here.

The International Mountain Bike Association (IMBA) lists Ganaraska as one of the **top rides in North America**, and you will find three IMBA-designed loops at **15 km, 30 km,** and **60+ km.** And even a **100 km** loop from Paul's Dirty Enduro Race can be conquered, though it's not that well marked. These combine singletrack runs with ATV track.

Indeed, it is an *epic* ride by **Ontario standards**, but nothing compared to the insanity of BC or Quebec downhill runs.

Coming in from **the north end** you'll find some of the best twisty track up that way and flowy **long DH runs,** too. A recently I had a chat with a busy trail builder from the **Peterborough** club who mentioned a new exciting trail called **Creekie**...on my list.

Ganaraska Forest is divided into three sections: **bike riding** in the **central part**, with motorized **ATV** and **dirt-bike riding** on the **west side.** (You may want to explore that area, for large berms and dirt jumps)

Fatbikes would do well here, and in the winter, though they are not allowed along Nordic ski tracks, to my knowledge.

The **east side** has **horse riding** and even more trail ... which I have not yet ridden.

photo - Northumberland Tourism

Be careful of vehicles, and since hunting is allowed in April. May and November, **wear bright colours**.

For **beginner mountain bikers,** this is a safe spot to ride with few technical surprises, just long hills to crank up.

Watch for **thorny raspberry bushes** and **lots of poison ivy** by mid-summer. They can close in on you, making it a challenge not to get whacked. Pick spring or fall to avoid these nasty plants. Okay, the raspberries are **tasty**, too.

I should add, that as far as MTB trail fees in Ontario go, at $12, Ganaraska is a tad pricey for what there are by way of services, so you may want to stay a while....

Book the whole day off and make your way out; there is plenty to like and trails to ride for all!

Best Mountain Bike Trails in Ontario

Central Ontario

Greenwood – MTB Trail

Church St. N & Concession Rd. 5, Ajax

Trailhead – 43.90100768, -79.07519319

Length – 20 + km

40% MTB singletrack
40% hiking trail
20% doubletrack access roads

Elevation – Flat on ridge, deep ravine, short hills, some steep paths

Terrain – Smooth soil, slick when wet, sandy spots, gravel in the old pit

Skill – Beginner to Intermediate

Traffic – MTB and recreational cyclists, hikers and dogs.

Maps – Map board at some trailheads, a few signs (but many trails have none)

Facilities – Three parking lots, outhouse (maybe), food and drink, lodging south in Ajax

Highlights – Large area to explore, lookout, creek path, potential to be awesome

Trail Fee – Free

Phone – 416 661 6600

Website – Toronto Regional Conservation Authority

Similar Trails –
Eldred King,
 Northumberland,
 Jefferson

Local Clubs –
Durham MTB Club

Access – North of Ajax at 2075 Church St N., a gravel road. Use the first car lot; the second one up the road is mainly for dog walkers.

Or drive further and turn right at the next road (Concession Rd. 5) and park in the north lot at the bottom of the hill by the creek for the other ride area (under development).

The main park entrance to Greenwood at the south end of Greenwood Rd. is not the closest entry point to good trails, but could be also used.

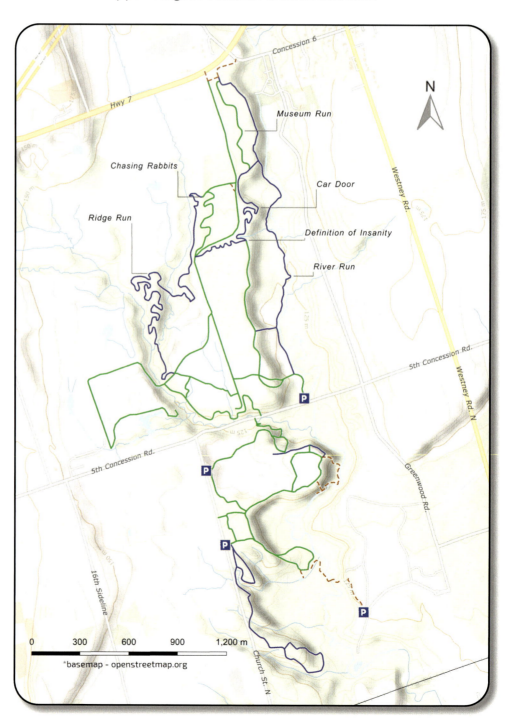

36   *Best Mountain Bike Trails in Ontario*

Review:

The **20-plus-km Greenwood Conservation Area** trail system is one of those bike rides made up of a mix of random hiking paths, old farm roads and MTB track cut by the locals.

Nothing is organized or connects with much sense, yet you can have a bit of fun exploring the lot. Why then added this to the book? ... For two reasons.

#1 All the riders who live just south of here in **Pickering**, **Ajax** and **Whitby**, and who would enjoy this convenient opportunity to get out and ride.

#2 It needs some LOVE! It has the potential to be more than a patchwork of unapproved, homemade loops and stunts.

Greenwood is just one of many locations in **Ontario**, some secret, that need proper direction for the sustainability, safety and growth of our sport. I get into this more at the end of the book.

Strength in Numbers: Plans have been approved and drawn to improve and add MTB track. Yet the **DMBA** bike club still needs able keen builders to make it so. Where are you?

Here is what you will find in Greenwood: **forest** and **river paths, boardwalks, open fields, steep valley inclines** and an old **gravel pit.**

The best riding is on the **south side** of the **Church St. N.** entrance and then **north of the gravel pit** and beyond.

Heading down into the valley, to **Brougham Creek**, may not be worth it. The riding has not been as good since the creek bridges were washed out by a flash flood.

Heading south, things start off easy on smooth clay hiking paths that family cyclists use. Beyond, you might find **hidden** singletrack on the SW side. That's what we MTB riders like and it's a favourite of mine, but **is it cool, legit?** I'm not sure.

In here, I have certainly seen **unapproved structures** built, including ramps, jumps and even a two-level spiral. By now they have been removed, then likely rebuilt... and again demolished. The cycle will continue, people, till the landowners are on your side.

The trails **north** go across and around the **gravel pit / dog park** (avoid the poop). Don't miss the cliff lookout on the east side of the pit; it's quite a view.

Still further north, across **Concession Rd. 5,** is a large plot of land **under development** which has a few nice runs that you will need to sniff out to enjoy. Currently a few map boards and signs get you around, but not many.

Unfortunately, these two areas do not (yet) connect well and you likely will have to ride the **Church St. gravel road north** to get there. A third tract of land to the west is also being developed. It all appears to be progressing slowly, or has this project stalled?

From that north-end parking lot on **Concession Rd. 5,** there are long, straight old gravel / dirt roads that take you in. One such path **curves west up the hill** to an open field, and beyond to a ridge that has around **3 km** of respectably twisty singletrack. Other routes were rather boring access roads.

Another option is to **follow the creek** trail first; it goes north along the bank for a good while. It's a pretty trail among the ferns and cedars, cutting close to the edge at times. Every year erosion will change this route slightly. At some point, you'll have to hike-a-bike up a set of **long, rickety stairs** to get out of there.

So there you have it: **Greenwood** is a decent ride, close at hand, with potential. Get organized, talk to **DMBA**, and **give back** by taking on this project. It's an amazing opportunity to be involved in the restoration and proper management of this area and to be part of sustainable trail design for maximum future fun.

Make this a destination worthy of talking about and move it up from my **B List** to everyone's **A List**...for Amazing!

Best Mountain Bike Trails in Ontario

Central Ontario

Hardwood – MTB Trail

402 Old Barrie Rd. West

Trailhead -   44.51798879, -79.59175678

Length – 85 km

60% MTB singletrack
40% doubletrack

Elevation – Slopes northward, lots of short hills, some steep on the advance tracks.

Terrain – Loam/sandy mix, roots, leaves, fieldstones, bridges, skinnies, jumps, teeter-totter, pump track, obstacles training area

Skill – **All levels**, but best for seasoned riders with good legs

Traffic – MTB riders, **Fatbikes**, Nordic skiers and snowshoers in winter, no one else

Maps – Good signage on trails; no fear of getting lost

Facilities – Parking, large chalet, change rooms, bike wash, pro shop, repairs, rentals, lessons, camps, racing

Highlights – Full-service facilities, beautiful new chalet, challenging trails, excellent technical sections, lookout to the south

Trail Fee – Adults $16, students $13, kids $11

Phone – 1 800 387 3775

Website – Hardwood Ski and Bike

Similar Trails – Dagmar, Albion Hills, Hydro Cut

Local Clubs – Hardwood Next Wave, SCMBC

Access – Drive north on Hwy 400 past Barrie, then exit to Forbes Rd./Simcoe 11. Head east about 9 km, road becomes Old Barrie Road W.

Entrance on north side at 402 Old Barrie Rd. West. Beyond gate are two large parking lots.

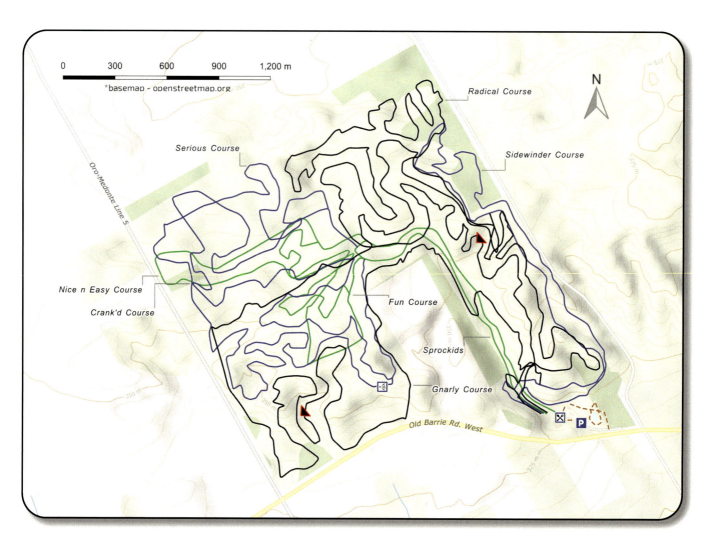

Review:

Hardwood Ski and Bike has long been a **premier MTB destination** for avid cyclists. The challenges and choices in trail routes, the many **race events** and the **full-service amenities** make it a popular choice.

Here is another area that has packed in a ton of trail in a relatively small plot of land. There's about **85 km** of trails going every which way, yet the excellent colour signage means I've never gotten lost here. Routes are all **one way** and use both single and doubletrack sections to keep you moving, and the trail difficulty ratings are accurate.

This area sloping north and is **fairly hilly**, so you will be asked to do short climbs repeatedly, and steeper ones if you take the expert way.

The base is smooth, dark loam mixed with leaves and sandy sections, some well worn. Occasional tree roots and fieldstones add extra interest. Wooden, stone and metal bridges, ramps and **jumps—some substantial**—test your skills. (Most all of these offer an easy ride-around if you'd rather not chance it.)

Hardwood has designed **11 customized routes** they call **courses**. Rated from beginner to superhuman, they wind around, creating some excellent riding. The easy ones are a few kilometres in length; most other routes are about **10 km** long.

To give beginners a taste of mountain bike action, the **Nice n Easy** and **Fun Course** fit the bill, offering short loops and gentle inclines on wide paths, with no obstacles to be seen.

With more climbs and structures to play on, the **Serious** and the **Crank'd** courses welcome the average (and above) MTB rider. If you need more mileage, the **22 km Venture** course heads further north for more twisty, fast fun.

For some leg burn'n climbs, quick dives and a myriad of technical challenges to max out on, the hyper and fit take on the **Gnarly, Sidewinder, Radical** or **Wilderness** courses to conquer or be crushed

You can also do the official **Pan Am Trail** (this challenging loop is the legacy from when Hardwood hosted the 2015 Pan Am Games MTB events) for added punishment.

To be certain you will run out of juice at **Hardwood** before you run out of trail. Lines cross countless times, so you can easily pick another course or head back to the chalet to recover.

Hardwood also has a **dirt pump track** and a **wooden obstacle** course to practice on. So there is lots to keep you and the kids entertained.

The bugs are not too bad by mid-summer, but you may smell an odour in one area on a hot summer day; it's coming from the dump, which, unfortunately, is just next door.

Hardwood, one of the few commercial MTB locations in Ontario, is a 20-minute drive north of **Barrie**. A recent fire prompted them to rebuild the chalet and it's BIG and beautiful! There's now a larger lunch area, a pro shop and changing space. A temporary food truck outside caters to the hungry 'til the next building phase adds a cafeteria space.

Originally started decades ago as a Nordic ski centre, Hardwood, like many other locations, has integrated MTB activities in the summer.

It has become a focal point for training and racing on Wednesday nights, and it hosts many weekend races and events. Lessons and kids' bike camps are offered. It's one of the few places in Ontario where you can actually rent a MTB on site; be sure to book ahead.

Fatbikes are welcome to share Hardwood in the winter, as this spot turns into a cross-country ski destination when the snows come. Fatbikes ride the **Phatty** trail and along Nordic routes.

Unlike most MTB locations, where you have to rough it, Hardwood has the all the **comforts** and **conveniences** (for a price) if you want them. For anyone thinking about **trying mountain biking**, all the way up to **racers training**, this is the place to be. A visit here will satisfy all.

Best Mountain Bike Trails in Ontario

Central Ontario

Hilton Falls – MTB Trail

4000 Campbellville Rd., Milton

Trailhead - 43.50634094, -79.96377713

Length – 18 km MTB + 17 km access roads = 35 km

35% MTB singletrack
35% hiking trail
30% doubletrack access roads

Elevation – Small, rolling hills; level around falls

Terrain – Smooth soil, muddy spots, gravel, rocky roads, rock gardens, limestone outcrops, drops, boardwalks, bridges

Skill – Intermediate to Advanced (MTB beginners use the gravel roads)

Maps – At trailhead and on some intersections (but not for all trails); going too far in could get you briefly lost

Facilities – Parking lot, toilets, snack bar, picnic tables

Highlights – Crazy-gnarly rocks, reservoir, Hilton Falls with old mill ruins, fall colours

Trail Fee – pay at gate: Adults $7, kids $5.25

Phone – 905 854 0262

Website – Hilton Conservation Area

Similar Trails – Agreement Forest, Kelso, Three Stage

Local Clubs – Halton Agreement Forest Trail Assoc.

Access – Hilton Conservation Area, 4000 Campbellville Rd, Milton

From the large parking lot, head past the gatehouse up the gravel road on the right. Give it some speed: the first climb is a good one.

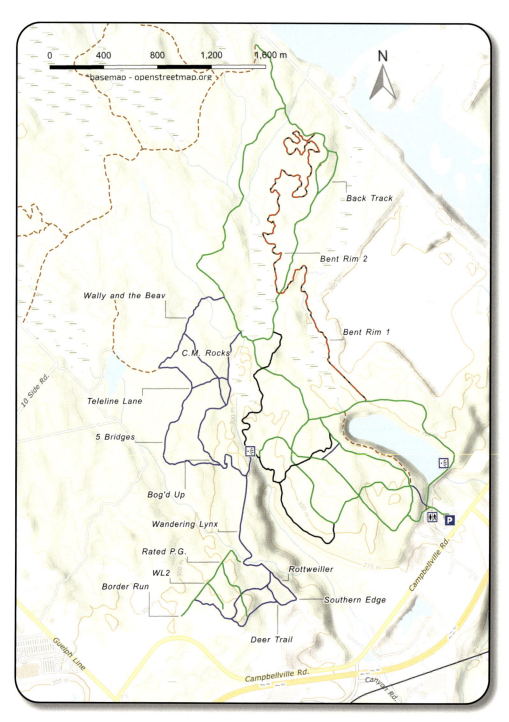

40   Best Mountain Bike Trails in Ontario

Review:

Hilton Falls Conservation Area near **Milton** has diverse terrain ranging from easy access roads to trails for **hardcore mountain bikers** who love **rock**.

You will find everything from gravel **roads** that take you in and around the **reservoir** to **insane rocky sections** that only **experienced riders** with **dual-suspension bikes** should dare.

I would consider this area a **harder ride** than **Kelso**, across the valley. (Yet not as popular, wonder why?) You may wish to wear padding and armour if you are an aggressive MTB rider.

There's great fun be had here on the park map's **blue loops**; the **Five Bridges** trail and **Wally and the Beaver** are favourites.

The brown **Wandering Lynx** trails are a good ride, too. Expect plenty of **rocky limestone outcrops** to navigate, **wooden bridges** to cross and **log hops/ roots** coming at you aplenty. Yet the pace has enough easier gaps of smoother terrain spaced between to maintain the **pursuit of MTB happiness.**

Not so much on the **infamous** double black diamond **Bent Rim Trail.** Even with a **full-suspension bike**, the **long rock gardens** are **ridiculously hard** to clear. Too much walking and cursing! Maybe it's possible on a (electric) **29er**? Ride at your own peril — **I warned you!** (Naturally, you will have to check it out, LOL)

A for beginners is to stick to the main gravel roads on the map. Easier—but not effortless—with lots of **rocks** and **ridges** on these access roads. And the roads by the reservoir have some **sizable hills** for you to overcome.

Consider packing a lunch to eat at the falls. Definitely visit the **ruins of an old mill** at the **waterfalls,** which are the highlight of the park. This becomes a **beautiful area** in the fall season when the colours are out.

A curious thing about this location. Being on the **Niagara Escarpement**, and perhaps because of the change in elevation, it has given me **wacky weather.** On sunny days I have been surprised with hail, snow and sudden downpores. Just saying, pack an extra jacket.

When you start, take the right-hand **trail** from the parking lot to avoid an **even steeper climb** going the other way.

This area brings in a lot of hikers, children, dogs who tend to head to the the falls area. Otherwise there are few peole elsewhere.

Signage is decent, but there is a chance **you may wander** beyond them and then a **GPS map app** comes in handy. I am not sure they still give out paper maps at the gate. This practice is not so common anymore.

Beyond the official ride area, the hiking trails/ roads extend northward up along the **6th Line** as part of the **Bruce Trail** and westward past the **Wandering Lynx** trail system.

Yes! There's more **rock mayhem** beyond… into the **Halton Agreement Forest** trail network you go.

photo - Paulo LaBerge

Best Mountain Bike Trails in Ontario 41

Central Ontario

Horseshoe Valley - DH MTB Trail

1101 Horseshoe Valley Road, Barrie   *Trailhead -* 44.54780250, -79.67279993

Length – 15 km

90% MTB singletrack
10% doubletrack access roads

Elevation – 80 m vertical, hill sloping up is shaped like a horseshoe, grades are not crazy steep

Terrain – Clay/sandy base, roots, fieldstones, rock gardens, big berms, ladder bridges, skinnies, drops, dirt jumps, ramps

Skill – All levels – best for Intermediate learners

Traffic – MTB riders, hikers and tourists – open daily from 10 am to 5 pm

Maps – Online; posted trails use a numbering system

Facilities – Parking lot, chairlift, bike rentals, repairs, food, lodging, water sports, golf, skiing

Highlights – Good introduction to DH riding, hilltop view, many other services

Trail Fee – Lift ticket $29/day

Phone – 705 835 2790

Website – Horseshoe Resort

Similar Trails – Blue Mountain, Copeland Forest, Sir Sam's, Kelso

Local Clubs – Simcoe County Mountain Bike Club - SCMBC

Access – Drive north from Barrie on Hwy 404 and go west on County Rd. 22 (Horseshoe Valley Rd. W.). Park near the ski hill on the south side.

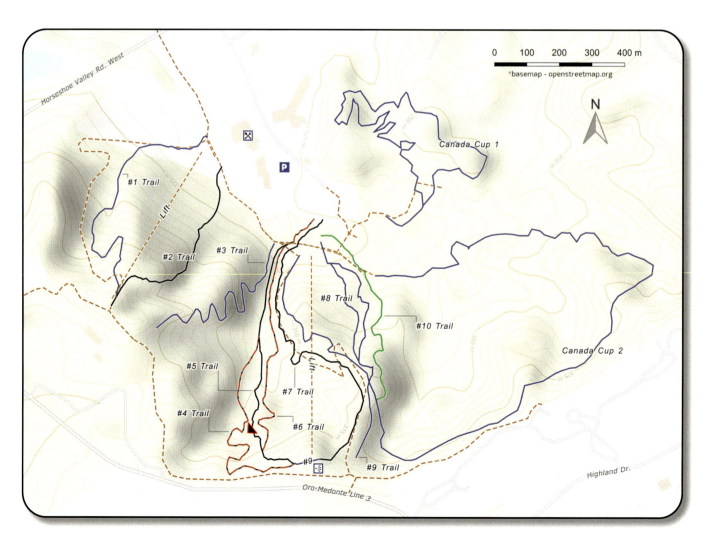

42   *Best Mountain Bike Trails in Ontario*

Review:

North of Barrie, **Horseshoe Valley Resort** has a **downhill bike park** that's introduced many a rider to the thrill of gravity runs. Though short in height and smaller than most North American DH parks, it has a good following and delivers plenty of thrills for all.

As **Blue Mountain's** baby brother, it's a good fit for those interested in trying this style of mountain biking. Cheaper and **closer to Toronto**, it is a great training ground for riders who aspire to take on more epic jumps,

longer bombs and steeper slopes eventually.

The **high-speed six-person lift** takes riders to the top of this ski hill in no time and **eleven runs** offer a little something for every skill level. With only **80 metres** of vertical, you know going down will be over in a few minutes—just do more. Trails have no names, just numbers (this seems rather dull compared to all the creative trail naming I've seen).

Since trails are designed to introduce mountain bike riders to downhill runs, you can try things out using your current MTB, if it's decent and well built. Certainly, any MTB rider with a few years in the saddle should not have a problem doing the **Beginner** and **Intermediate** #1, 3, 8, 9 and 10 trails. These runs coming down through the woods are full of **berms** and **small jumps**, ideal to practice on and build up your courage.

Moving on to the steeper **black-diamond territory**, trails #2, 4, 5, 6, and 7 include more serious jumps on your way down and it might be wise to beef up your gear for these more extreme exploits. **Bike rentals** can be booked, or a mechanic is available if you've been too hard on your own iron horse.

If you plan to open it up, a **full helmet, DH bike** and **pads** are in order so you can enjoy the speed, take the pounding and maybe spare yourself some knocks.

Horseshoe's staff **trail builders** have listened to their riders and have made **changes for the better** every year. Routes have been altered and tweaked with more runs, which equals more mileage, too. No longer do trails # 4, 5, 6, 7 converge into one path halfway down to spit you out at the bottom. Each of these favourite runs now has its own **separate line**.

Staff water down the dry tracks to keep the dust at bay, as this soil has lots of **sand** in it. Keep in mind that too much speed on the **berms** could result in you washing out.

While you're here, you can take on a little **XC riding** in the woods on the east side, where you'll find two old Canada Cup race loops to give your legs a workout. It's an **Intermediate** MTB ride with a mix of hills, roots and gnarly bits to add variety to your day. **Canada Cup 1** trail is about **2.2 km** and **Canada Cup 2** trail climbs the big hill and heads down it, too at close to **3 km**.

But most riders are **here for the speed** and rush of the vertical runs. If it's been a few years since you've been here, things have changed and improved.

For more vertical pursuits nearby, head to **Copeland Forest**, just moments away and across the road, or **Three Stage** by **Collingwood**. The riding is free on these trails, but you'll have to earn your downhill, as there are no lifts.

Horseshoe Resort is a **full-service** vacation playground. You can extend your stay for eats or a sleepover, or take in many other sporty summer activities while you're here: there's a water slide, wake park, golf, ziplining, treetop treks…

In the winter, **Fatbike riders** gather at the **Nordic ski centre** across the road to commence their frosty adventures.

Best Mountain Bike Trails in Ontario 43

Central Ontario

Jefferson – MTB Trail

1245 Bethesda Side Rd., Richmond Hill Trailhead - 43.95141357, -79.42100316

Length – 12+ km
30% MTB singletrack
50% hiking trail
20% doubletrack access roads

Elevation – Slopes slope up from Stouffville Rd. to a plateau with another valley on the north end; some steep sections and ridge lines

Terrain – Smooth soil, patches of pure sand, tight turns, a few old log hops and structures

Skill – Intermediate to Advanced

Traffic – Bikes, watch for hikers and their dogs

Maps – New map boards have some wide trails on them; MTB trails not signed

Facilities – Limited parking; use Bethesda lot

Highlights – Central and close to Toronto, new twisty track, trails are finally legal

Trail Fee – Free

Phone – 416 667 6600

Website – TRCA – Oak Ridge Corridor

Similar Trails – Centennial, Midhurst, Durham Forest

Local Clubs – York Mountain Bike Assoc. - YMBA (a chapter of DMBA)

Access – Parking is limited – access is from Stouffville Rd. on two small driveways or along Bayview Ave. northeast of the bridge.

There's a large lot on top end at 1245 Bethesda Sideroad.

I am told eventually Stouffville Rd. will be widened and new car lots will be made.

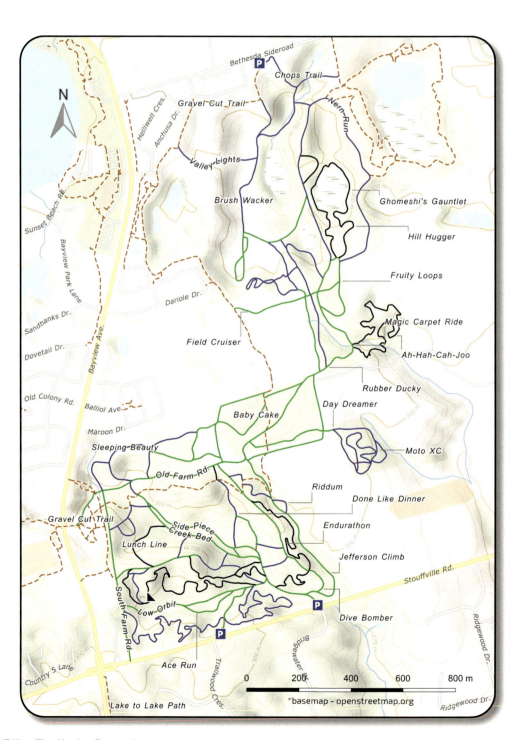

44 *Best Mountain Bike Trails in Ontario*

Review:

Jefferson Forest on **Stouffville Rd.** is like an old friend you keep visiting; they keep changing, and so do the times. For me and many others in **Toronto**, this has long been the **closest little bit of heaven** to let loose on our trusty steeds.

Situated just off **Hwy 404**, north of **Richmond Hill**, it feels the **pressures of urban sprawl**. What was once an unknown **patchwork of woodlots and fields** on a dead-end road many years ago has morphed many times over the 20 years I have been there.

First came the **Bayview bridge**, then a new subdivision that wiped out our favourite entrance. Recently a **gravel path** was cut through the middle of the forest and now yet another neighbourhood is being built.

Gone are the motocross bikes that would tear up our track; here come the dog walkers and strollers.

Some of this change is progress. An area that used to be wild, with an uncertain future, has now been taken on by the **TCRA** and the **York Mountain Biking Association (YMBA)**, a MTB club.

As of 2020, it has finally been given the blessing: **it's officially legal to MTB ride here.** Although the forest's status is likely to continue to change, let's assume there will still be good riding for years to come.

As for the current riding experience in there: **it's a mixed bag.** There are some fine, **long XC trail lines to bomb down** and a few **gnarly, twisty sections** here and there. Most of the expert hilly track is in the **SW corner** of the property. Some paths are just old hiking routes or dirt roads from years ago when there was a homestead here.

Trails go pretty far back, reaching between farmers' fields and homes. Where the area levels off in the middle, it makes for an easier twisty, fast ride with a few quick dips.

Local riders always seem to be cutting new trail and building illegal wooden structures, only to have these removed by the "authorities" over and over again. This should settle down now that **there is a plan** and troops to deploy.

There's talk of **trail signs and maps** in the works, as well as trail repairs and maintenance (contact the club to help out). These should help mitigate the erosion issues that **Jefferson Forest** has had to endure over the years. The plan is to keep 90% of trails that are currently there; any trail expansion is a far-off future possibility.

The wide, mellow **Gravel Cut** path has been recently cleared through the forest, and to me it feels like it spoiled the wilderness feel of the woods. But that's me being a little selfish. It is a handy connector if you want to head west for a **XC spin on gravel** along the **Oak Ridge Corridor**.

The **fall colours are beautiful,** and in the spring, when the **trilliums** come out in carpets on the forest floor, it's enchanting.

This **central location close to Toronto** was once called "Mosquito Coast" 'cause there can be a few down in the valley.

There are plenty of places around to grab a beer and bite afterwards to reflect on **how lucky we are** to still have this spot to let loose.

Best Mountain Bike Trails in Ontario

Central Ontario

Joyride 150 – MTB/BMX Park

150 Bullock Dr., Markham

Features - XC MTB wooden elevated 800 m trail with log rollovers, rock gardens

Two pump tracks, skinnies, ramps, bridges, logs, a few rocks
Jumps – lots! Foam pit plus rails, ledges, steps, quarters, resi

BMX quarter pipes, wall rides, spines, drop-ins, bowls
Dirt jumps outside

Elevation – Flat warehouse floor with wooden ramps, catwalk circling the area and lots of bridges

Terrain – Everything is hard if you fall (except the foam pit): cement floor, rock gardens, wooden ramps; there are dirt jumps outside

Skill – All levels, some advanced skinny ramps and crazy jumps

Traffic – Lots of BMX riders zooming and jumping, MTB riders, too

Maps – It's a small area, so you don't really need one

Trailhead - 43.87740855, -79.27314591

Trail Fee – $17 to $28 (for anyone over 6 years old; depends on when you visit); and one-time registration fee five bucks

Hours – Mondays to Thursdays: 3 pm to 10 pm; Fridays to Sundays and most holidays: 10 am to 10 pm

Facilities – Parking lot, food, change rooms, toilets, bike repair, rentals & storage, pro shop, party room, ride camps

Highlights – Not weather dependent, late nights, a winter destination, lots of challenges for all

Phone – 905 294 1313

Website – Joyride 150

Similar Trails – Sunnyside, ROC, Ashbridges Bay

Local Clubs – Defiant MTB Group on FB

Trailhead – Magic purple door, north side of large parking lot

Directions – East on the 401 or 407 to McCowan Rd., head north, turn right on Bullock Dr.; ride park is at 150 Bullock Dr., Markham, north of Toronto.

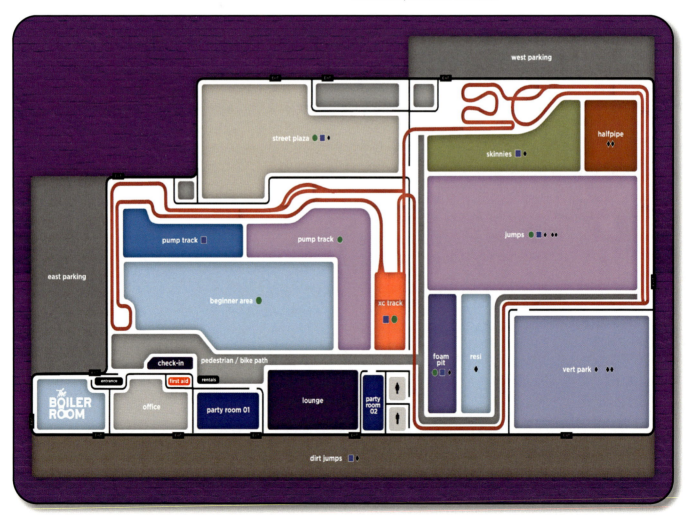

Best Mountain Bike Trails in Ontario

Review:

Out on the edge of Toronto, **Joyride 150** is of the few indoor bike parks in Ontario (and likely the best). This **BMX / MTB ride park** in a converted large factory space in **Markham** has a little bit of everything to please everyone.

Designed and built well, it invites riders of all skill levels to try out its offerings and to learn, **improve and move up to the next level.**

The space is full of **wonderful, wacky structures**—a playground for kids on wheels of all ages, even 40-year-old kids (ahem).

When you enter this purple-painted building (love the colour) everyone needs to sign a waiver at the desk. Management has put a lot of thought into properly managing safety concerns. All riding is one way and there are guardrails and padding on poles. But this is still a building full of metal fixtures and hard concrete or wooden surfaces. Helmets are required, and I recommend **elbow and knee pads** and bike gloves. Helmets and pads can be rented.

Depending on your discipline, warm up on the **two pump tracks** or ride the **elevated wooden XC ramp** around the outside wall: a few loops should do it.

This track has numerous, though brief, tricky technical **stone and wooden features** to keep you interested.

Then move on to whatever tickles your fancy, whether it's just for fun or you have a weak skill in need of training. The beginner zone by the desk starts newbies off on **super-easy ramps and skinnies** that are barely off the ground… and I mean inches.

If you are beyond that, the next building features tons of seriously challenging **ramps, logs and skinnies** to play on for hours, all crammed onto the floor space.

Not your thing? Then **jumping** must be in your system, and they've got plenty of ways to catch some air. If you are new to this or have a trick that needs testing, attempt it first in the **foam pit**.

Then go nuts in the **Jumps, Vert Park** and **Halfpipe zones**. The **Resi** and **Street Plaza** areas give you even more daring feats to nail as you tempt fate on the **rails, ledges, steps and quarters.** Wheeeee!

Started about 10 years ago as a novel idea, this indoor bike park has succeeded in building a following, and has even expanded.

A few years ago, **dirt jumps** were added out behind the building. It's not a huge area but it is real dirt and lots of fun unless there's been a recent rain, then it's closed (sad face).

Prices are not cheap, but then, neither is your bike. **Joyride's** hours cater to the after-school / work crowd late into the night. Lessons, parties, kids' ride camps, and women's-only events are held here, too.

A mechanic is on site to fix your [whatever] and they have nearly 100 bikes to rent out.

In the winter, **it's chilly** in this big box, so you need to make your own heat. And then in the summer, **it can get toasty.**

It's not as scenic as a ride in the woods, but it's a great way to **hone your riding techniques** on a bad-weather day or in the winter. When you or your kids need to let loose and the rain/snow is coming down, here is where to get it on.

Best Mountain Bike Trails in Ontario

Central Ontario

Kelso – MTB Trail

5301 Steeles Ave W, Milton

Trailhead - 43.49635792, -79.92312393

Length – *22 km*

40% MTB singletrack
30% hiking trail
30% doubletrack access roads

Elevation – Slopes down to the edge of the ski hill, then 75 m steeper descent to bottom

Terrain – Smooth clay base, gravel, rocky limestone outcrops, fieldstones, muddy patches

Skill – All levels; best for Intermediate – Advanced MTB

Traffic – MTB, hikers on the Bruce Trail, Fatbikes ride on top in winter, hill closed for skiing

Maps – Paper map at pay booth, plenty of signs on the trail

Facilities – Parking lots, outhouses, lessons, races, picnic tables, lake swimming, camping

Highlights – Fast trails down the ski hill, views over the cliffs, rocky terrain, wooden structures

Trail Fee – Adults $7, kids $5.25 (good for same day ride at Hilton Falls, too)

Phone – 905 878 5011

Website – Conservation Halton

Similar Trails – Hilton Falls, Agreement Forest, Three Stage

Local Clubs – HAFTA - Halton Agreement Forest Trail Association

Access – Preferred parking for trailhead is at the top of the ski hill, which has most of the loops, though you can also park at the base.

Take 401 to Hwy 25 south towards Milton. Go 4 km west on Steeles Ave. (Halton Regional Rd. 8) Drive up the hill to 5301 Steeles Ave. W. and Old Bell School Line, gate and parking on north side. Base of ski hill main gate is at 5255 Kelso Road, Milton.

Hours: Mon. - Friday 8:30 am – 4:30 pm; weekends 10 am – 4 pm. Kelso is often closed if trails are muddy, so check before heading out.

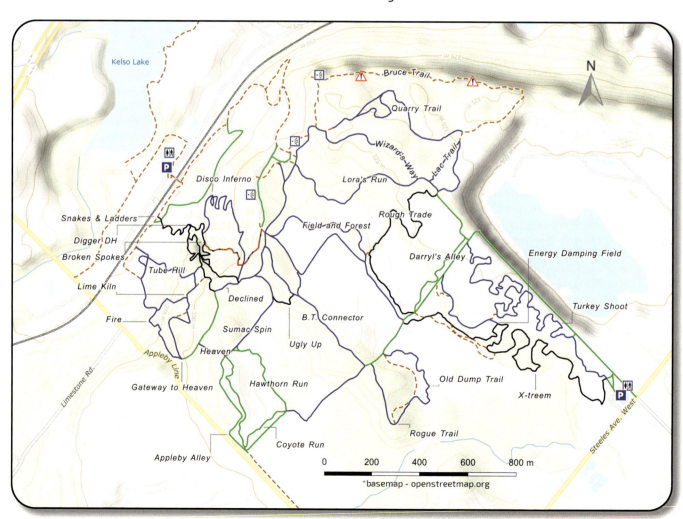

48 *Best Mountain Bike Trails in Ontario*

Review:

Kelso Conservation Area near **Milton** is a popular **MTB hub** that offers variety in terrain and challenge, with a downhill for thrills.

Perched on the **Niagara Escarpment**, it includes several main loops at the top of **Glen Eden ski hill**—plus a few heading down the hill—and claims to have **22 km** of trail.

The preferred place to start your ride is to **park at the top**. Or park at the main gate at the base of the hill and start first with a climb.

From the car lot on top, the trails start off the right way, heading down on the **2.3 km Turkey Shoot** run. Loved by all, it twists its way along through rows of trees and open patches of grassland with the occasional cluster of **limestone rock**, likely gathered by farmers a century ago.

This spits you out onto an **old farm road** which leads to a grid of easy, straight paths around overgrown farm fields. Nothing special here, but good to speed along XC-style and warm up.

Eventually you'll reach the forest line, and here it gets better again. More **rock piles, gnarly moments** and some **wooden structures** challenge (or then again, entertain) the better riders while they're cruising along these wooded paths. These trails are often a little wider than they should be, since the area gets a lot of traffic. You will see little that is tight singletrack.

As you get closer to the edge of the escarpment, the rock count increases and so does the degree of descent. At some point, you will need to make the big decision: **head down the hill or ... not?**

Most pick the black-diamond **Snakes and Ladders** descent (75 m) for a twisty, fast blast to the bottom. DH riders love it. It's steep but **not rocky**, so keep calm, keep your butt back and hold on to the bars.

If you prefer to go down with less fear as you grip the brakes, look for the **Fire** or **Lime Kiln** trails on the far west side, which are a bit more gentle. Watch out, though, because some use these trails to climb back up.

Disco Inferno is another way to go: either climbing up on switchbacks across the open ski hill or for a quick boogie down.

Once you're at the bottom of the ski hill, the unpleasant reality is the grind back up it. A chairlift would be ideal, but none runs in summer (I wonder why?). So either crank up the gravel service road on the east side or find another trail up.

Once at the top, now you know how much reserve power you have in your pistons (your legs) to try it again.

Check out other corners of this location to find any **log hops, rocky bits or skinnies** and do the **Rough Trade** loop, a favourite for some good climbs.

Save the best for last: on your way out, you must take on the advanced **2.2 km X-treem** trail to get your fill. It's **rocky, twisty** and full of challenges to take on (or pass for another day). **Rock drops, ladder bridges, berms** and sizable **wooden jumps** to grab some air... if you dare. This is an exciting technical ride that flows down from the car lot, but you can ride it up with not too much effort.

Kelso is closed any time these hard-packed trails get wet and greasy, so call first if in doubt. Recently a new **6.3 km** winter **Fatbike** loop has been added.

View beautiful vistas from the cliffs... but stay away from the edge, it has claimed lives.

At the base of the hill, there is a lake, beach and activities others can do while Mum or Dad escapes for a run or two... Just saying it's an option.

For whatever reason—perhaps it's the buzz of the downhill, the jumps or the race events— Kelso fills up with riders on any sunny weekend. And while it's popular, and plenty of the riding is decent, I find the other half of the trails here a little **too mellow, uninspired** to be desirable MTB track.

For those like me who need more and **better rock action**, may I recommend **Hilton Falls** and next door, the king of rock & roll: the **Agreement Forest**. You can see them right there, across the valley, calling you.

Best Mountain Bike Trails in Ontario   49

Central Ontario

Midhurst – MTB Trail

#1331 Hwy 26, north of Barrie

Trailhead – 44.44900349, -79.76454464

Length – 28 km

35% MTB singletrack
45% hiking trail
20% doubletrack access roads

Elevation – Southern length of area is level. Slopes quickly down to creek on north side

Terrain – Smooth soil base, large sandy areas, occasional rocks and boulders, lots of log hops and wooden structures

Skill – Easy to Advanced

Traffic – MTB and pleasure cyclists, hikers with dogs (watch for poop), ATVs, snowmobiles in winter

Maps – None; little signage; closed-loop system makes it hard to get lost; locals can point the way out

Facilities – Parking lot, outhouse, bike repair station at Admin Centre

Highlights – Wooden structures, fast runs, log-hopping gauntlet, train bridge

Trail Fee – Free

Phone – None

Website – Barrie Community Sports Complex

Similar Trails – Dufferin Forest, Glen Major, Northumberland

Local Clubs – Simcoe County MTB Club - SCMBC

Access – Two suggested parking lots and entry points: at the very large Barrie Community Sports Complex, or in the rear parking lot of the Simcoe County Administration Centre. The trail network can be also accessed from Nursery Rd.

The trailheads are not well marked, so you need to park near the forest and seek out the most likely path.

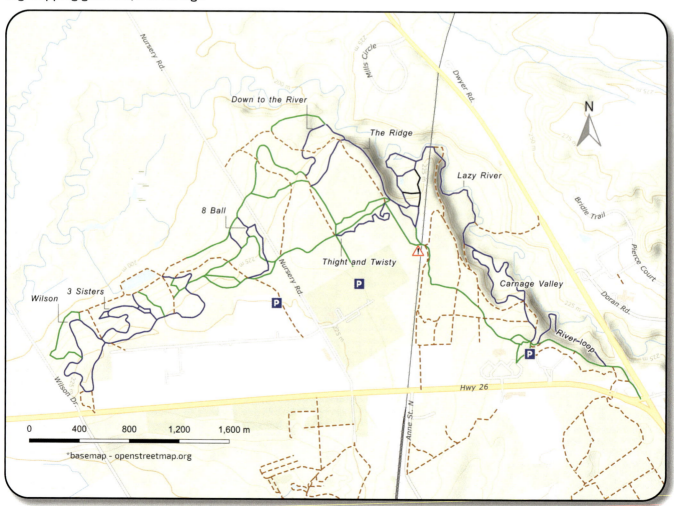

50   Best Mountain Bike Trails in Ontario

Review:

The **Midhurst** bike trails just north of **Barrie** offer a real **mix of terrain** worth discovering. Here you will find old hiking trails with a few new singletrack MTB loops.

The woods have a **variety of structures, large glacial rocks, jumps** and **log rollovers** to keep things interesting.

Many of the trails are hiking loops, but there are occasionally some decent MTB side trails that are a challenge to ride.

The trail system basically has an **upper route** and a **parallel lower trail** running by the pond and **Willow Creek.** Numerous side trails connect down the hill from one to the other. I did find some **fast DH runs** for a twisty MTB rush, though brief.

When you get to the pond/lake (when does a pond become a lake, I wonder?) you can ride around it. That seems to be the limit of how far you can go north.

Tight & Twisty is a short singletrack, in the middle off these woods, a gauntlet of **log jumps/rollovers**, the most I ever saw coming at me in 15 minutes of hauling it. Oh, what fun!

Eventually, there are train tracks and sideroad crossings that will slow you down a bit on what is otherwise a fast ride. Find the trail where the train crosses over the creek—it will take you down under the span of an **old bridge**.

On the east side of the tracks, the main trail opens up and gets **very sandy**. You'll have a chance to try a collection of **formidable ramps**.

You will find **boardwalks, skinnies, teeter-totters** and **jumps** of all sizes. These really add some spice to the menu. (Note: There are some other old wooden structures I would not trust.)

At the far end, one of the best singletrack loops, **Carnage Valley,** zooms you down to the creek and then makes you work your way up.

There are a few homemade signs, but no official map or signposts the last time I was there. Regardless, you can spend a few hours here riding the fun stuff without getting too lost.

Look out for **dog walkers** (and poop) and family hikers on weekends. ATV riders may venture nearby, but they have their own trails north on **Nursery Rd.** (which you could check out, hint hint).

I would think **Fatbikes**, Nordic skiers and snowmobiles are in these woods during the winter.

Though not on everyone's radar, this spot is worth checking out for any keen mountain bike riders looking to do something different for half a day. You'll see why **Midhurst** is a long-time **favourite for locals**.

Best Mountain Bike Trails in Ontario   51

Central Ontario

Oro Network – MTB Trails

280 Bass Lake Rd. E., Oro Station   *Trailhead – 44.55302098, -79.59520983*

Length – 65+ km

60% MTB singletrack
30% hiking trail
10% doubletrack access roads

Elevation – Moderate elevation changes; a few short, steeper switchbacks and descents

Terrain – Flowy, smooth sandy/loam base, fieldstones, berms, ladder bridges, a few log piles and boulders to roll over or jump and the odd rock garden

Skill – Intermediate (the sweet spot)

Traffic – MTB, hikers, joggers, dogs; in winter you'll see Fatbikes, snowshoers, Nordic skiers, snowmobiles

Maps – Info at trailheads, small post maps – print map mailed when you join SCMBC

Facilities – 9+ parking lots, outhouses (maybe), tune-up stations

Highlights – Endless XC trail, creek bridges, large boulders, MTB mecca

Trail Fee – Free

Phone – 705 726 9300

Website – County of Simcoe

Similar Trails – Dufferin Forest, Turkey Point, Northumberland

Local Clubs – Simcoe County MTB Club – SCMBC, FB page

Access – The "Hub," east of Oro-Medonte Line 7 at 280 Bass Lake Rd. E., is the trail & social epicentre.

I counted another six more parking/trailheads that connect to this trail network, plus two separate loops to the east that do not connect: the Schumacher Tract climb at 866 Bass Lake Side Rd. E. and the Breedon Tract loop at around 2100 (or so) Line 9 N., north of Old Barrie Rd. E.

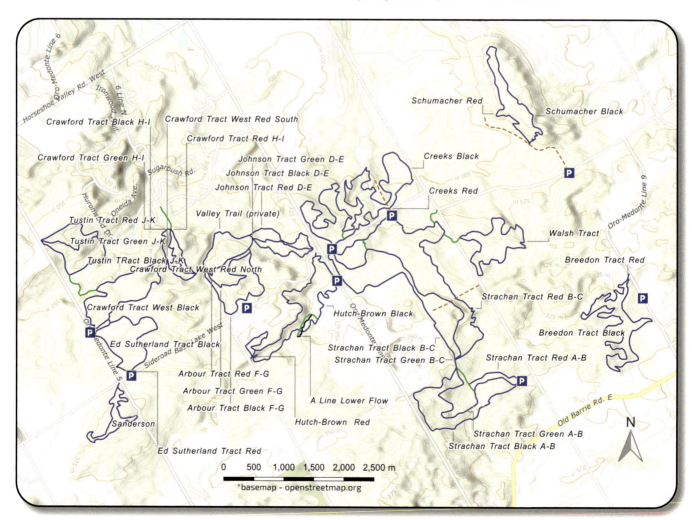

52   *Best Mountain Bike Trails in Ontario*

Review:

The **Oro Trail Network** encompasses a large wooded area between **Barrie** and **Orillia**. I estimated **65+ km** of loops, as much as any **XC MTB rider** could wish for to zoom around in one day.

What brings mountain bikers back to **Oro** is not only the number of trails available, but also how all of it is at a comfortable **Intermediate** level. You can expect a pleasant day of easy climbs and flowy descents.

The majority of the singletrack is a blend of smooth sandy soil and some gravel, roots, and small fieldstones. It is not as bumpy as it sounds and seldom has any surprises or awkward terrain to navigate for the average rider. It's perfect for a slower family outing as well.

Out in the middle of these back roads, riders park at the **"Hub."** Most of the loops emanate from this point, but there are two others not directly connected that you can also explore.

As for the journey through the bush, you won't come upon ancient temples or majestic fjords, it's just lots of greenery with a few minor sights.

On the **3.3-km Welsh Tract** ride, we found a rock garden and, further down, a **homestead foundation** made from the same round stones. See if you can spot other farmhouse ruins or stone walls on your trek.

Occasionally there are ramps up **large boulders** left over from the last ice age, or **log piles** that can give you liftoff for some air.

If you take notice of your natural surroundings, you will be traversing through numerous forest tracts, each in a different logging cycle, from **regrowth to harvest**. Some areas are more open, with younger saplings (and raspberries!); other wood lots have mature stands of shady, green wilderness.

Down on the popular **9-km Creeks** loop, bridges and log paths keep you out of the wet, black muck. Twisting through the cedar grove is a little different than the vegetation on the trails higher up.

In the last decade, much has been done to improve and expand the quality and length of trails in this area. The Simcoe County Mountain Bike Club **(SCMBC)** calls **Oro** its home base and its members have been key in the development and stewardship of these trails.

The trailhead signage here is minimal, no large maps. An old red and black colour scheme, with paint swatches on the trees, is used for the trail lines (this is not a difficulty rating). Tiny club trail maps are posted on poles. Some are missing, but new ones are in the works.

When you join the club, you'll receive a custom map in an email; otherwise, you'll want to turn on your favourite mapping app to stay on course. Most loops are a few kilometres long with few shortcuts, so picking the wrong way will cost you time and energy.

Nearby **Copeland Forest** and **Hardwood** are not that similar to **Oro**, with more challenging, and excellent MTB rides worth checking out.

These parts see plenty of snow, which means the **Fatbike** enthusiasts will be out roaming in the winter on 20+ km of mellow track. Grooming is done on parts of it when possible.

Thanks to the quality and amount of great trail here, **Oro** has become **one of Ontario's MTB meccas.** It has produced its share of local top racers and even finds some MTB enthusiasts retiring close by.

For a day trip—or longer—it's the **ideal escape**: trade your city obligations for freedom on the open trail with your trusty stallion and a few good riding mates.

Best Mountain Bike Trails in Ontario

Central Ontario

Palgrave – MTB Trail

17580 Duffy's Lane, Palgrave

Trailhead - 43.95106352, -79.85931112

Length – 22 km

70% singletrack MTB trail
20% hiking trail
10% doubletrack access roads

Elevation – Rather hilly on the singletrack MTB trail, but it flows well; not as much climbing for wider forest paths—riding counter-clockwise is easier

Terrain – Smooth soil with some sandy spots and gravel, can be muddy; a few roots and rock piles; log hops, structures and berms

Skill – Intermediate

Traffic – Typically bicyclists and hikers; quiet during the week and light on weekends

Maps – Found at trailhead; signposts along the route, but I felt they were too varied

Facilities – There are three parking lots, but I recommend the Duffy Lane entrance

Highlights – Picturesque ponds, the longest continuous singletrack loop in the area

Trail Fee – Free

Phone – 416 661 6600

Website – Toronto Regional Conservation Authority

Similar Trails – Albion Hills, Glen Major, Dufferin Forest

Local Club – Caledon Cycle Club

Access – Drive north **11 km** past **Bolton** on **Highway 50**—just beyond **Albion Hills**. Turn west on **Patterson Side Rd.**, and then north up to **17580 Duffy's Lane** for **2 km**.

Look for the parking lot down the road, on the right and just past the curve.

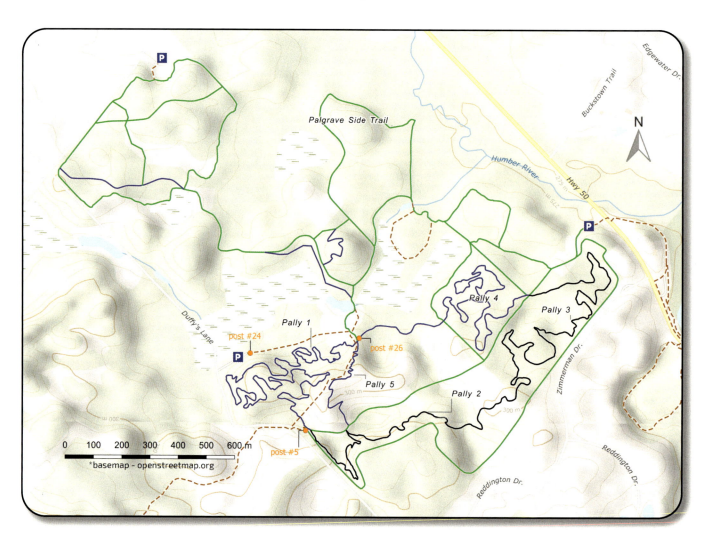

54 *Best Mountain Bike Trails in Ontario*

Review:

Palgrave Forest offers MTB riders near **Toronto's west side** some extra trail in which to let loose. This somewhat secret spot has plenty of **long** and **hilly cross-country-type** tracks to really get your legs burning.

This intense, fast **cardio ride** consists mainly of one continuous loop. I find it keeps getting better over the years, as racers have cut better trails and signs are now popping up to clarify what was once a somewhat confusing forest trail. (Although at times it still is.)

The terrain consists mainly of black loam soil that does get a little muddy/slippery after a rain. There are also a few **sandy patches** of subsoil.

Due to tree farming, much of the forest is straight **rows of pine** mixed with native trees. As a result, there are some open areas, as well as a pond.

Expect plenty of **winding climbs**, but you'll be rewarded with quick bombers down (making this place a favourite!).

This continuous, uninterrupted trail is unusual, as most **MTB areas** have trails which intersect too frequently. Here, once you get going, you rarely have to stop to sort out which way to turn. Amen!

With switchbacks and berms, most of this **mega-loop** flows well. I recommend you ride it **counter-clockwise**: it's easier and flows better. A few simple **structures, rock piles,** and **logs** keep it interesting, with alternate easy outs if you are not up for them. Just don't get too cocky, as there can be new features that could surprise you.

An **easier ride** in the woods for **beginners** would be to stick to the wide and straight old hiking paths, which will give you about **9 km** on the **Oak Ridge** and **Bruce** trails that are not so demanding on the hills.

The scenery is pleasant, but nothing more than endless trees in a green forest. It's certainly a **quiet, empty** place on weekdays.

Numbered posts have recently been added, and although you may get turned around you'll never get lost.

In the northeast quadrant of **Palgrave** there are signs of **old cross-country ski paths** you could also explore. However, these routes are not on the map and are rather overgrown—but isn't that part of the fun?

From the parking lot, the ride can start beyond the gate five minutes down the access road on your right. Some riders choose to start in on this giant loop by heading south around the bend on Duffy's Lane.

This location is very similar to Albion Hills, and a good alternative when Albion gets too busy. Make your way here for some serious enjoyment and exercise soon!

The official start and end points of the trail are a bit odd. Head 5 minutes up the access road beyond the gate, trail on the right. (From the parking lot (post #24 on the map board), you can ride straight to #26 along the route.)

Perhaps a better starting point is to ride down the road (Duffy's Lane) around the bend to post #5, where you will find a map board. From there you can start a more logical loop.

Best Mountain Bike Trails in Ontario   55

Central Ontario

Ravenshoe – MTB Trail

22612 McCowan Rd. and Ravenshoe Rd.

Trailhead - 44.20925007, -79.36464639

Length – 17 km

50% MTB singletrack
30% hiking trail
20% doubletrack access roads

Elevation – A flat, square forest tract with lots of small and medium climbs

Terrain – Loam, sandy spots, some gravel; can be muddy; super-twisty track; many log jumps and ramps, plus access roads

Skill – Easy to Advanced

Traffic – Popular MTB spot on weekends, a few hikers and dog walkers. Trails are two way; most ride them clockwise

Trail Pass – Free

Facilities – Limited parking, two lots, no outhouse (there should be)

Highlights – So much gnarly track in such a small area. Flowy trail and new boardwalks!

Maps – Map board at trailhead with signposts at loop entry points.

Phone – None

Website – York Region

Similar Trails – Dagmar, Albion Hills, Puslinch,

Local Clubs – York Mtn. Bike Assoc. - YMBA_(a chapter of DMBA)

Trailhead – Most riders enter where the map is, on McCowan Rd. side; another entry point is on the northwest side.

Directions – Take Hwy 404 north to where it currently ends at Ravenshoe Road (Regional Rd. 32), drive east 9 km to McCowan Rd., then go south for 600 m. Parking is on the right at #22612.

The corner parking lot at the northwest of the tract, at the corner of Ravenshoe and Carley Rd., is also a good starting point; it's not as popular and likely not full on weekends.

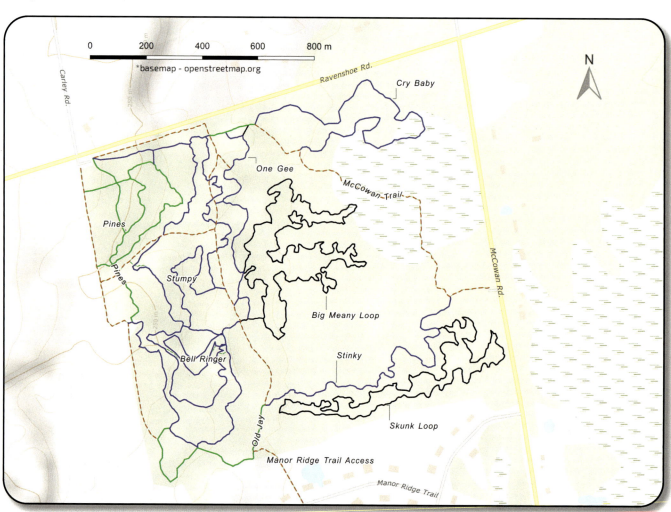

Best Mountain Bike Trails in Ontario

Review:

Ravenshoe, as MTB riders affectionately call it—it's officially called the **Brown Hill Tract**—offers a lot of thrills packed into just a 1-sq-km woodlot.

It's truly an exercise in how much twisty, gnarly trail can be squeezed into such a small space. Amazingly, most of the nine loops are somehow one to three kilometres in length.

The trail builders certainly made an effort to pick some of the craziest, zig-zagging insanity they could conjure up, and it works!

This is totally a technical ride. Beyond the twisty track are log hops, some large and boardwalks to maneuver. Some boardwalks are nice and skinny, the way we like them. Many of the wooden structures have been replaced, after many years of precarious use, by a dedicated lot in the DMBA club.

Most of the trails are a slow ride, more for the **technical types, not for speed demons,** though there are moments when a quick blast down a slope or heading along the access roads will get you moving.

You'll find the elevation is flat, barely changing 'til it goes up on the west side. It is though still lumpy terrain where trails go up, over and around these mounds while negotiating the trees and root clusters. Many quick 90° pivots, 180° turns and wriggles through narrow tree gates will keep you focused.

The level areas are super-muddy when it has rained, and greasy to the point you could fly off your pony. Here, where it does not drain well, the mosquitoes are going to feast on you if it is a wet summer. Up by the pines, the soil changes to a sandy base that can slow you down.

Some of the paths are getting a little wide from **too much love**, but most are holding up well. Though with such a compact trail, riders are taking shortcuts too often. Naughty! This leads to some confusion as to which way to go. Ample signage helps with that.

The hardest (= best, most fun) runs are **Big Meany** (2.6 km) and the 2-km **Skunk** loop. They are super-gnarly, but not as impossible as when they were first cut. I have noticed that over years of riders cutting their own lines, these trails have become easier.

The Skunk is one of my **top ten trails** in Ontario. I keep trying to clean it and I just can't without dabbing (that means putting my foot down). If you try it, just remember: it used to be much harder!

Actually, everything here is worth riding: **Stumpy, Cry Baby, Bell Ringer**...they're all great singletrack trails that you'll wish went on longer.

In the spring, before the leaves come out, there are masses of trillium flowers to behold.

Some of these trails have been here for more than 20 years, and this has become a **favourite destination** for many Toronto-based riders, including myself. I have been here so often, and it **never gets boring**. Come on out and test your worth against **Ravenshoe**. You'll be back.

Best Mountain Bike Trails in Ontario

Central Ontario

Short Hills – MTB Trail

Pelham Rd. and Gilligan Rd., St. Catherines   *Trailhead* - 43.10833677, -79.28708799

Length – 48 km

30% MTB singletrack
40% hiking trail
30% doubletrack access roads

Elevation – Hills and yes, they are short! And some are mean. Level riding in the valley or on top of the escarpment

Terrain – Loam, sandy, muddy spots, stones, gravel, pavement, bridges, water crossings, some tasty hidden singletrack

Skill – Easy to Moderate

Traffic – MTB riders, lots of hikers, tourists, horses

Maps – Signs for hiking trails, and the two park loops directions may be unclear. Bring a map

Facilities – Parking lot, outhouse, no services at the provincial park

Highlights – Scenic, lookouts, waterfalls, bridges, dam, old mill, Brock University.

Trail Fee – Free

Phone – 905 774 6642

Website – Ontario Parks

Similar Trails – Don Valley, Guelph Lake, Fanshawe

Local Clubs – Short Hills Cycling Club, FB page

Access – There are many possible parking locations in the area. The favoured one is at Short Hills Parking Lot A, at Pelham Rd. (Regional Rd.69) and Gilligan Rd.

Or you can park at the mill, at 2749 Decew Rd., or on the university grounds.

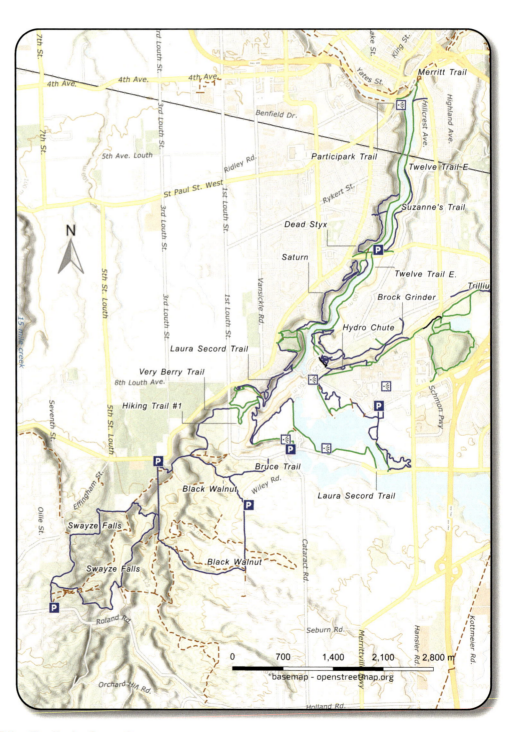

58   Best Mountain Bike Trails in Ontario

Review:

Down south of **St. Catharines**, the **Short Hills** trail network is an easy-flowing **cross-country MTB tour**. With about **48 km** of off-road riding, this long route is a collection of different paths and constantly changing scenery.

When riders refer to **Short Hills**, they usually mean not only the provincial park by the same name, but also the trails heading north around **Brock University** and down the **Twelve Mile Creek**.

It is an enjoyable, scenic ride through forests; across fields and **bridges**; by **waterfalls and dams**; and through a creek valley into suburbia. It has views of the city and tourist spots to visit – the historic **Morningstar Mill, Decew** and **Faucet Falls** and the university grounds.

It's also a jumble of trails and paths that connect with little signage to keep you on track. Parts of it are the **Bruce Trail** and **the Laura Secord Legacy Trail**; other sections are non-descript short MTB lines you can have fun on. Few are technical or require a full-suspension MTB.

Starting in the **Short Hills** park, there are only two large loops: the **5-km Black Walnut** and the **6-km Swayze Falls**. Both are a mashup of dirt and gravel hiking trails and old farm roads crossing fields and weaving thorough woodlots. Each has a **60 m climb** on them; the Walnut route seems harder.

Leaving the park and heading NE, you have two options: picking the easy track running the along the creek valley or the other are on top. Here you could split the ride into two parts or only do one.

Option 1: Following the creek on the left bank past the hydro dam for about **5 km** down the now wider creek/river. This easy dirt path will turn into a mellow paved park path that runs along the water's edge. Ah! but hidden up in the trees along the bank are moderate, fun singletrack lines to be discovered.

When you get near the **406 highway**, take the pedestrian bridge across the water to double back on the other side of the creek for more of the same.

The other choice requires climbing to the top of the **Brock Escarpment**. This way can involve visiting the mill, taking pictures of the waterfalls, and cycling around the reservoir and the university grounds. I consider this the touristic, more scenic route, with some paths so tame they're downright civilized.

It is a bit surprising that an area as populated as the **Niagara Peninsula** has little to MTB ride, but for more kicks, you'll have to head to **Dundas Valley** or **Turkey Point**.

I do not think mountain biking is a priority in these parts; you will encounter many **more hikers** than cyclists on the route. Slow down, let them know you're coming and give them space. (A bear bell or bicycle bell might help.)

When you go, enjoy this XC outing, visit the old mill for ice cream and play the tourist for a moment.

Afterwards, **St. Catharines** has a slew of pubs where you can quench your thirst and fill your belly.

….And allow me to remind you that there must be 20 wineries within 10 km of this ride where you can go for a tasting or lunch as well.

Best Mountain Bike Trails in Ontario   59

Central Ontario

Waterdown – MTB DH Trail

Waterdown / Hamilton

Trailhead - 43.32293686, -79.90097204

Length – 25+ km

30% MTB single track
50% hiking trail
20% double track access roads

Elevation – Since this is part of the Niagara Escarpment, trails tend to be steep trail near the top and then they level out with smaller valleys below.

Terrain – Mainly smooth soil which can be slippery if wet. Clusters of rocky limestone located mostly near the top. Some sections have gravel, tall grasses, log hops, roots and a few wooden structures. (Note: some do not look well built; bridges are getting old and unstable.) Downhill ramps and jumps.

Skill – Best for Intermediate and Advanced MTB riders.

Traffic – Mainly hikers and dog walkers; not many riders.

Maps – No signage for MTB riders, so use a GPS app. Some markings for hikers on the Bruce Trail.

Facilities – Parking. Food and services are close by in the town of Waterdown or Hamilton.

Highlights – Not busy, endless XC MTB trail, DH runs and beautiful fall colours with a few lookouts too.

Trail Pass – Free

Phone – None

Website – None

Similar Trails – Three Stage, Copland Forest, Kelso

Local Clubs – True Grit Cycling Club

Access – Not the easiest place to find. For an Intermediate MTB ride, park on Rockcliffe Rd. by the small parkette, then take the gravel path leading down the hill.

For more Advanced MTB and DH riding, enter behind the Wal-Mart by Hwy 6 & Dundas St. E. or the path off Grindstone Way.

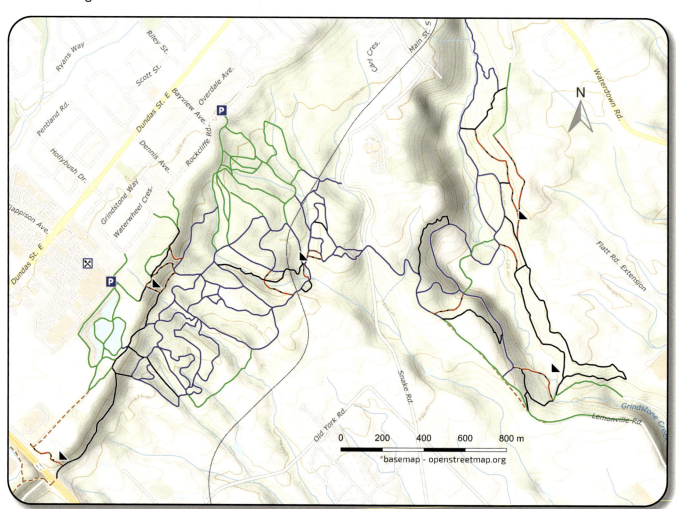

60   *Best Mountain Bike Trails in Ontario*

Review:

Next to **Hamilton**, and below the town of **Waterdown**, MTB trails meander for **25+ km.** Mountain bike riders will have plenty to explore, test their skills on, and put their climbing gears to use.

Clappison Woods, aka **Rockcliffe** or for some the **Black Woods**, is a forested area on the side of the **Niagara Escarpment** offering mountain biking in its raw form.

Tons of trails crisscross every which way through valleys, up crests, and down across creeks in all directions with **little signage** to sort them all out.

The paths in here were first cut by hikers, and as such go in rather straight lines with a few crazy climbs (that you may have to walk). Signs of new track designed for MTB fun occasionally appear, and even some **Downhill** action can be found.

In general, the **Expert track** is on the west side of the escarpment, but there are pockets of rocky technical riding elsewhere, too. The terrain is very hilly and rock infested closer to the top.

As the slope levels out towards the lake, riders will find less rock and more **smooth dirt track** to zoom on. But expect occasional roots, a few old log hops and wooden structures to keep it interesting.

This is a favourite spot for hikers walking the **Bruce Trail** (marked by white and blue swatches on the trees) and dog walkers. So watch for them, slow down, and share the trail, as you will find more of them than mountain bikes in here.

This forest area stretches in all directions, leaving you to discover (get lost – LOL) the many potential routes. Heading down towards the lake offers more riding in another "secret valley" once you **cross the train tracks** (with caution) and then yet into another valley beyond **Snake Road.**

Since this is a little-known place with **no MTB signage** (the local riders like it that way), you may want to pack a phone to **refer to a GPS map**. As every trail seems to look the same, you can easily get spun around riding the same routes over again.

Below the mall, **Downhill MTB** riders can blast down the 35-metre vertical on the **Ridgeline** run doing big jumps. This is one of the few places to practice this in Ontario.

It gets rather slick in here and muddy after **wet weather.** By October the trees put on a show of **fall colours** and you can start to see the lake. This leaf cover on the trail can get slippery and hide nasty obstacles you need to watch for.

With plenty of variety, **Waterdown** is good fun. You'll get in a day of MTB action, exercise, and exploration as you learn your way around on these interweaving trails.

Best Mountain Bike Trails in Ontario

Western Ontario

Blue Mountain – DH MTB Trails

108 Jozo Weider Blvd., Blue Mt., Collingwood   *Trailhead -*   44.50233751, -80.31289798

Length – 25 km

20% MTB singletrack
80% DH singletrack

Elevation – 220 metres (720 ft), easy descents to extreme verticals on ski hill slopes

Terrain – Clay/sandy base with limestone outcrops, loose stones, roots, off-camber sections, drops, bermed & twisty track, large dirt and wooden jumps, wood walls and bridge overpasses

Skill – Intermediate to Advanced Proline levels

Traffic – MTB riders, hikers and tourists at base and top of hill

Maps – Good signage at the trailheads, paper map available

Facilities – Full-service resort, bike & gear rentals, lessons, large base village for food and lodging

Highlights – Best DH ride park in the province, lift access, fast descents, jumps, extreme technical riding, lookouts

Trail Fee – Ride park + lift ticket, season pass available, expensive

Phone – 1 833 583 2583

Website – Blue Mountain Resort

Similar Trails – Horseshoe Valley, Three Stage, Copeland Forest, Sir Sam's

Local Clubs – Team Van Go, Collingwood Offroad Cycling

Access – The main parking lot for summer activities is at 108 Jozo Weider Blvd., Blue Mountain Resort, Collingwood.

You can park at the top (at 221 Swiss Meadows Blvd.) if you have a ride pass.

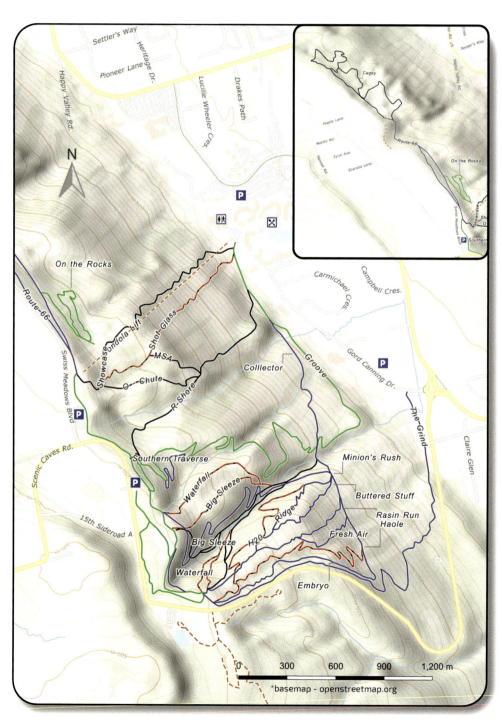

Best Mountain Bike Trails in Ontario

Review:

Downhill MTB riders who feel the **"need for speed"** come from near and far to **Collingwood**. The slopes of **Blue Mountain** bring **avid DH riders** for the best Ontario has to offer. Here you can taste a little bit of the action that otherwise can only be found elsewhere like the west coast or in Quebec.

Blue Mountain is a large ski resort on the side of the **Niagara Escarpment**. Just about **220 metres** (720 ft.) of vertical is all nature left us—hardly a mountain. Regardless, it's got plenty of thrills packed in for you to conquer, or break bones trying.

An open gondola takes you to the top in no time. Or haul yourself up on the long **2.3 km Grind** switchback, which can be done in 20 minutes. Though there are a few trails on the top to get you around, and the **3 km Cagey** loops at the far end are decent, everyone is here for the wicked descents.

There is one lift on the centre of the hill, yet all the DH riding is to the left. This odd setup requires riding over every time you reach the top...and then riding back across to the lift when you get to the bottom. The trails are well signed and accurate in the skill levels posted; you'd be a **fool to underestimate**.

Terrain is smooth black topsoil and, clay with **fractured layers of limestone** underneath. This stone is to be respected: loose patches, protruding rock shelves and drops keep things exciting. But there is even more, for **Advanced** riders...**grab some air** on the **large dirt jumps** and **wooden ramps** to test your form as you fly down the **Prolines** of **Haole** and **H20**. But first, you have to pass a **Freeride assessment** to get access to the magic kingdom.

The green **Groove trail** and blue Intermediate **Minion's Rush** have little to get you airborne; they're more about speed (if you wish it). Fast grades with wide, banking turns keep you moving and make for a good intro to either **Raisin Run** or **Embryo**.

Heading down any **black- or double-black-diamond** run requires skill, courage and commitment. Grades get extreme, while the track gets technical as gravity pulls at you. Pick your line, lean back and take it on; braking will have little effect on the loose stone and muddy patches. A popular, twisty, bermed track is **Showcase**, which nestles in the trees just right of the lift that takes you up.

It is quite common for riders to repeatedly **practise the same routes**, working out the difficulties and pushing their limits. Lift tickets are not cheap, nor is **Blue Mountain** next door to **Toronto**, so most riders make it a full day on the hill.

You could start out using your regular MTB on the slopes' green and blue runs (within limits). Wearing padded armour and a **full-face helmet** is a good call. Eventually, you will appreciate the control, comfort and abuse a tank-like, downhill-specific MTB will give you. Rent one a few times before pulling out the big bucks.

As the **largest ski resort in Ontario**, Blue has a full complement of services. You can rent DH bikes, gear, and padding; take lessons; or find a place at the hip ski village to eat and even stay overnight.

Since it's a few hours from Toronto you may wish to spend a night and ride the **DH** at **Horseshoe** or **Three Stage** for more MTB madness the next day.

After your **heroic feats** on the "mountain" face, find time to visit **Collingwood**, 15 minutes away. The area has become a major vacation and tourist destination, with plenty of patios, burgers and tasty beers to please.

However long you spend here, take a moment to gaze out when you get to the top: you can see far over the waters of **Georgian Bay** and beyond to **Barrie**.

Best Mountain Bike Trails in Ontario

Western Ontario

Brant Tract – MTB Trail

1300 Concession 12, Paisley

Trailhead -   44.23807271, -81.22121279

Length – 20 km

70% MTB singletrack
30% doubletrack access roads

Elevation – Flat woodlands, small gully, sloping river valley embankment

Terrain – Smooth soil, field stones, some gravel, roots, wooden bridges

Skill – Easy, great for beginners, some harder loops with climbs & tight switchbacks

Trail Pass – Free

Facilities – Large parking lot, outhouse, picnic tables, bench, shelter

Highlights – Good (and only!) MTB riding in the middle of nowhere

Trail Maps – At trailhead, mapped signposts at junctions

Phone – None

Website – MTB the Bruce

Similar Trails – Coulson's Hill, Christie Lake, Midhurst

Local Clubs – No MTB clubs in this area

Access - This location sits in the middle of farm country located just east of Bruce Road 3 at 1300 Concession Rd. 12.

Trailhead is east of the large parking lot by the map.

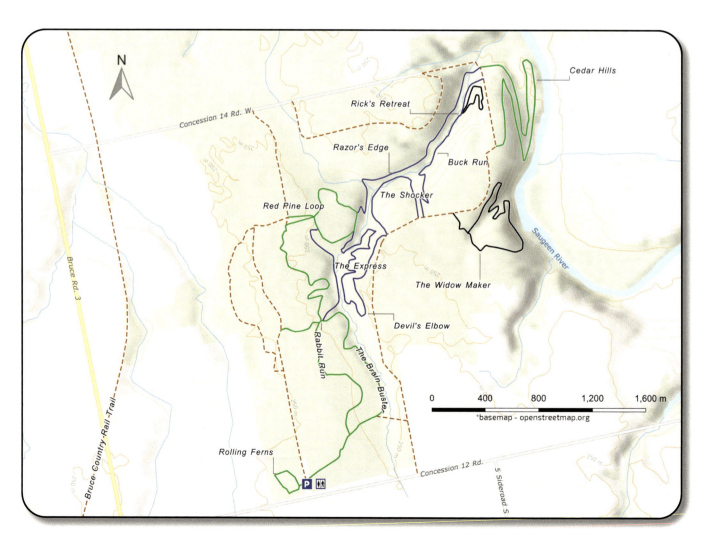

64   *Best Mountain Bike Trails in Ontario*

Review:

The **Brant Tract** sits in the middle of flat Ontario farm country **south of Paisley**. Although you might expect it to be boring, this trail system has some **surprisingly good mountain bike runs**.

Between hand-cut **singletrack** for MTB riding and a few riverbed gullies to vary the terrain, you get a sweet, fast ride, with nothing risky. This is a great location to **learn mountain bike riding**.

This woodlot is tree covered and **well maintained**. The **10 short loops** vary from **rolling, flat terrain** to some fine **twisty inclines** by the **Saugeen River**.

Starting off from the parking lot, the 2-km **Rabbit Run** and the 1.5-km **Brainbuster** trails offer a nice warmup, and they're a good intro for newbies. If you're more advanced, these may seem like tame, flat jaunts into the woods. You might start thinking, "What have I gotten into? This is too easy!".

But never fear, this trail system is designed properly, with the tougher stuff on the back end. That would be **Rick's Retreat**. It's rated as a red "Advanced" loop because of the climbs and tight switchbacks, but it's not actually that hard.

Advanced MTB riders need to seek out the 3-km **Widow Maker**, which loops you along the steep banks of the river. It's the **hardest/best loop** here.

There is nothing here for those who like the odd **log hop** or **rock garden**. These trails will not challenge you much on the technical end, they are pretty safe. Then again they're **perfect for beginners**. Lots of **boardwalks** and **bridges** keep it flowy and fun.

I found more bugs here then you would expect. Also, it can be very muddy with slippery clay if it has rained recently.

The signage is excellent. This is not a busy location, so pack tools and a tube just in case. You may find a few hikers and even horses on the **10 km** of extra access roads that ring the perimeter of the Brant Tract and farms.

Picnic tables can be found at the trailhead and along the route to give you and friends a reason to stop.

If you need more riding, there is a Rail Trail just west of this woodlot. The **Bruce County Rail Trail** runs across **Concession 12**. Used primarily by ATVs, it is a rough, flat MTB cross-country ride that goes on seemingly forever either way.

Although I feel this area is **not worth making a special drive from Toronto**, I'd definitely recommend checking out if you are passing through this area on your way up the Bruce Peninsula or to Manitoulin Island.

A side note: You can make this ride part of an adventure weekend with a paddle on the Saugeen R. in a canoe or kayak, which can be arranged by outfitters in Paisley.

Best Mountain Bike Trails in Ontario

Western Ontario

Carrick Tract – MTB Trail

45000 Huron Bruce Rd, Clifford

Trailhead - 43.97417970, -81.08014756

Length – 8 km

80% MTB singletrack
20% doubletrack access roads

Elevation – Short hills; flowy, bermed singletrack; switchback climbs; roots; tight turns

Terrain – Smooth soil with lots of gravel mixed in, tabletop jumps

Skill – Beginner, Intermediate

Traffic – Lonely place, only a MTB riders

Maps – At trailhead, signs posted at junctions

Facilities – Parking lot, outhouse, picnic table

Highlights – Well-cut, flowy track, an all-shady forest ride; not busy; and we saw a deer!

Trail Fee – Free

Phone – None

Website – MTB the Bruce

Similar Trails – Centennial, Christie Lake, Dagmar

Local Clubs – None

Access – South of the town of Mildmay, drive along Hwy 9, turn west onto Huron Bruce Rd. and proceed to #45000.

You can miss it easily. Look for a blue sign on the crest of a hill on the north side. Take the gravel road in to park your car.

There are two entry points from the parking lot: Johnny's Swamp of Doom trail on the west side or the gate at the Forest Access Road.

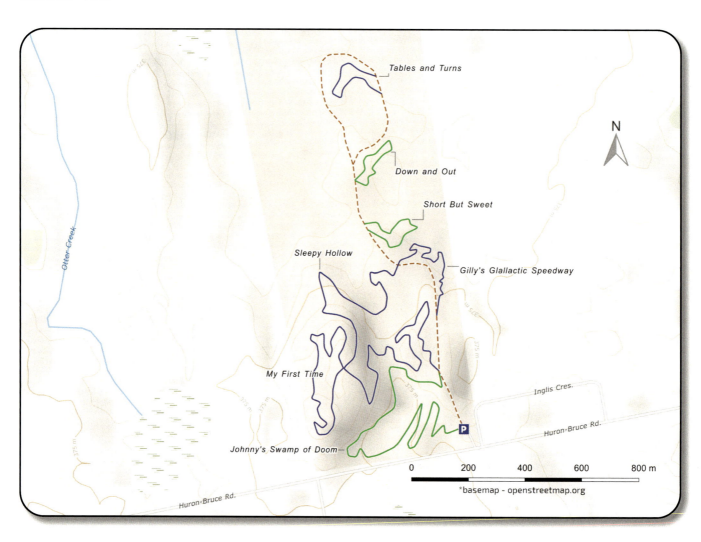

Best Mountain Bike Trails in Ontario

Review:

Treat yourself to a quick spin and a bit of MTB excitement on trails that **flow well and move fast** at the **Carrick Tract**. Out in the middle of nowhere in Ontario farm country, south of **Walkerton,** this small but well-made set of loops is well worth trying.

For years I gave little consideration to this location, thinking it was too small, so what could it offer? Yet when we finally rode it, I found the trails, though short, to be of **fine quality** and **well designed**.

At **8 km** in length, you could ride it the opposite direction for more mileage. If they added a few more kilometres of trail, this area would make it onto my **A list**.

This singletrack is **hilly** and has a lot of **stone aggregate mixed** in with the soil (which I suspect is left from the last glacier melt). Thus it likely fares well **after it rains**.

Hand built with mountain biking in mind, these loops **twist and turn**, with **berms** and **benched** trails. There are no structures or log hops to be found here, just **rooty sections** and plenty of small **stones**.

The trail starting west right from the parking lot is **Johnny's Swamp of Doom**, a **1.6 km** warmup beginner loop. It's a fun run, with little swamp, a few mosquitoes and thankfully not much doom. :^0

The feature trail in here is **Sleepy Hollow**, a harder, hilly, fast crank that connects with the **My First Time** loop. It then continues on **Gilly's Galactic Speedway** for a total of **4 km**.

A newly added loop at the back end, **Tables and Turns,** has a few simple **table jumps** built out of dirt, but they are small and harmless compared to those massive dirt track jumps you see in videos. Truly this trail should **not** be rated as **Difficult**.

Currently the map on the official website needs updating. The map board at the trailhead has a few **more short loops** to it than the map posted on the web page. Also, the trail lengths have been recalculated and are **now shorter.**

Carrick Tract is an oasis in the middle of endless flat farm country where there's not much else to mountain bike ride. Try it next time you are travelling through the area. I was **pleasantly surprised** how enjoyable it was, and I predict you will be, too.

Best Mountain Bike Trails in Ontario 67

Western Ontario

Fanshawe - MTB Trails

1424 Clarke Rd., London Trailhead - 43.03950321, -81.18162633

Length – 22+ km

*15% MTB singletrack
65% hiking trail
20% access roads*

Elevation – Flat sections with gentle, flowing hills

Terrain – The road is paved while trails are smooth soil, with a few rocks, roots and some gravel sections; watch for mud puddles after a rain

Skill – Easy to Intermediate

Traffic – Cyclists, hikers and dog walkers; not too busy

Maps – Found at trailhead; follow blue hiker markers

Facilities – Parking lot, outhouse, camping, swimming, park store, bike wash, boat rentals

Highlights – Fast XC ride, views of the lake and farm country, good camping

Trail Fee – Pay at gate – cyclists $8 if you ride in, or per car $14

Phone – 1 866 668 2267

Website – Fanshawe Conservation

Similar Trails – Wildwood, Dufferin Forest. Short Hills

Local Clubs – have not found a local MTB club :^(

Access – Entrance at 1424 Clarke Rd., London.

Go past the front gate to the first parking lot by the dam; trailhead is nearby at the treeline. If camping, the campgrounds have paths close by.

Parking also exists at Fisherman's Point on Rebecca Rd.

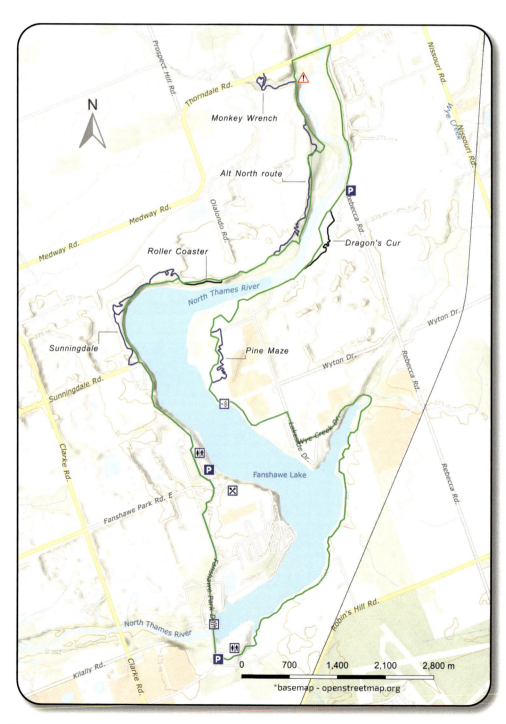

68 *Best Mountain Bike Trails in Ontario*

Review:

Fanshawe Conservation Area has a **large loop** that circles on the banks of the reservoir. This is an easy but long **cross-country style** ride at **22 km** just on the edge of **London**.

Most of the single track is a **hiker's path** that is rather straight with a smooth soil base and the odd root or rock. Inclines are short hills and not too steep for any seasoned rider to manage.

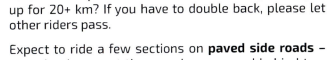

This is a **scenic ride** that is ever changing as you circle the lake (reservoir). This can be a **fast ride if you like it that way**, or a slower **family outing**, though **a bit long for kids**.

Follow the **blue-diamond hiker symbols** as you go around and you can't get lost.

Cyclists are asked to **alternate directions depending on the day** [clockwise on even-numbered days, counter-clockwise on odd].

What this loop does not have is a **shortcut**, so are you up for 20+ km? If you have to double back, please let other riders pass.

Expect to ride a few sections on **paved side roads** – over the dam, past the camping area and behind two golf courses. They are short stretches with few cars to contend with.

There are **four black-diamond side loops** (two are not on the map) that are a little bit harder and **cut the way MTB riders like**, with a few cool **structures**… but really not that tough.

By Ontario MTB standards, they feel like just harder **Blue** trails. Hmmm, sorry, guys, the **Canadian Shield** is black-diamond country!

The **Dragon's Cur** is twisty fun and the **best loop** while at the far end of the lake **Monkey Wrench** features **boardwalks, ramps, a swing bridge** and a trick water crossing. Don't get wet.

Expect to get mud on you and the bike as there can be a lot of **small mucky puddles** on the loop, even a week after it has rained.

I would **avoid the ride after rain or in early spring**. Would prefer more maintenance to fill these holes and a few more boardwalks over them, too…. please. There is a bike wash at the trailhead on the west side.

We found one **small creek crossing** to ride through, kinda fun, but don't take it too fast or your shoes will get wet. Again, after a rain, not so easy to manage for beginners.

There are a few picnic tables along the way: a good excuse to snack and take in the view.

The **camping here is excellent**, and you can rent a kayak/canoe to make it a weekend stay (no bike rentals).

If you are out this way, there not much choice to find decent riding trails. So this long loop is a welcome way to give you a **few good hours** on your steed.

Best Mountain Bike Trails in Ontario

Western Ontario

Guelph Lake - MTB Trail

7673 Conservation Rd., Guelph

Length – 20 km

50% singletrack MTB trail
50% hiking trail

Elevation – Gentle hills, with a high point in the middle that slopes down to both sides

Terrain – Smooth soil with a few rocks and rock gardens, occasional tree roots

Skill – Beginner to Intermediate MTB

Traffic – MTB, hikers, dog walkers, Fatbikes

Trail Maps – At the trailhead; there are a few signs on the trail, but they are not well laid out or numerous enough. Print your own map.

Facilities – A parking lot, with basic services in park's camping area.

Trailhead - 43.58760947, -80.27331620

Highlights – Enjoy a fast ride, a rock garden and lakeside views, including a dam.

Trail Fee – Free

Phone – 519 824 5061

Website – Guelph Lake Conservation Area

Similar Trails – Fanshawe, Wildwood, Palgrave

Local Clubs – Guelph Off-Road Bicycling Association - GORBA

Access – There are numerous entry points near the conservation area:

- across from the dam on 7673 Conservation Rd.
- by the river on 797 Victoria Rd. N.
- at the end of Kaine Hill Dr.

Best Mountain Bike Trails in Ontario

Review:

The **GORBA** trails, near the Guelph Lake Conservation Area offer **20 km** of relatively **mellow** bike trails, good for **beginner mountain bikers**. Any riders who are looking for **nothing too surprising** on their ride, and who are more into quick lines through the woods, will enjoy this route. You will also find plenty of loops along the way—over 30!

There is the **odd rock garden** and a few **tree roots** to manage, but most of the area consists of smooth, fast-winding trail through the pines, and it's not too hilly.

I found a few tricky side trails not listed on the map at the far end, but most of the **area is tame.** Hence, a good place to learn mountain biking.

My favourite runs at **Guelph Lake** are **Devil's Backbone** and **Snake Charmer** for the fast, flowy descents. And riding the harder **Phoenix** loop is twisty fun, too.

West Nile is a short, technical, bumpy, lumpy section by the water; it's made from river stones and likely the most challenging terrain here.

Fatbikes roam the woods in the winter here. This part of Ontario is not known to get too much snow to slow you down.

The local MTB club, the Guelph Off-Road Bicycling Association (**GORBA**), actively manages these trails, and they ask riders to stay off when conditions are muddy.

If you follow the **Speed River** down from the dam, the trail crosses **Victoria Rd.** There is more riding to be had beyond, although the trail now becomes a park path leading right into **Guelph**: mellow, but enjoyable.

I really wanted to love this place based on what I had heard, but felt **two issues need work:**

First, as I rode through this trail system with my son, I hoped for **more thrills**, but any man-made structures were few and old (decaying). I don't even recall any log jumps!

A refresh that includes some new features to enhance the MTB experience (boardwalks, bridges, rocks, logs or berms) would be a welcome addition.

Secondly, this trail system **lacks enough or proper signage** that logically guides riders through.

That said, you can't get too lost, but you may have to **stop at every junction** and determine which way is the best route. It becomes a bit of a guessing game, which is a tad frustrating as it interrupts your flow.

This area has enormous potential, and I hope they one day put some fun and challenges back in. Recent winter logging has changed a few routes, but not much else.

This trail has no fee, as it is not located inside the Guelph Lake Conservation Area, which is across the lake. However, there is also **good camping** there if you wish to make a weekend of it. The sandy beach and warm waters are perfect for an after-ride dip.

Best Mountain Bike Trails in Ontario

Western Ontario

Hydro Cut – MTB Trail

1522 Glasgow St., Kitchener

Trailhead - 43.42888170, -80.56339999

Length – 30 km

85% MTB singletrack
15% doubletrack access roads

Elevation – There are two woodlots separated by a field with hydro lines running up the middle; area slopes gradually up westward

Terrain – Smooth clay, mud patches, roots, the odd rock, grass field, bridges, structures

Skill – Most trails are Intermediate to Advanced (easier kids' zone by Glasgow lot)

Traffic – Mainly MTB riders and a few hikers. Bike travel is one way on singletrack loops; two way on main trail

Maps – Well marked with posted signs and a few map boards (could use a few more out at remote trail forks)

Facilities – Large parking lots, very close to malls & restaurants, etc., no outhouse at trailheads

Highlights – Regional hub, well-cut and -maintained MTB track with variety and ample challenges.

Trail Fee – Free

Phone – None

Website – The Hydro Cut

Similar Trails – Albion Hills, Dagmar, Hardwood

Local Clubs – Waterloo Cycling Club

Access – Main lot is at 1522 Glasgow St., Kitchener. Ride west from Glasgow lot for five minutes to enter the forest.

The other (perhaps better) access point is off 1974 Snyder's Rd. E. There is no sign and the side road looks like a driveway to a farm. Head down the hill across the tracks to the parking lot.

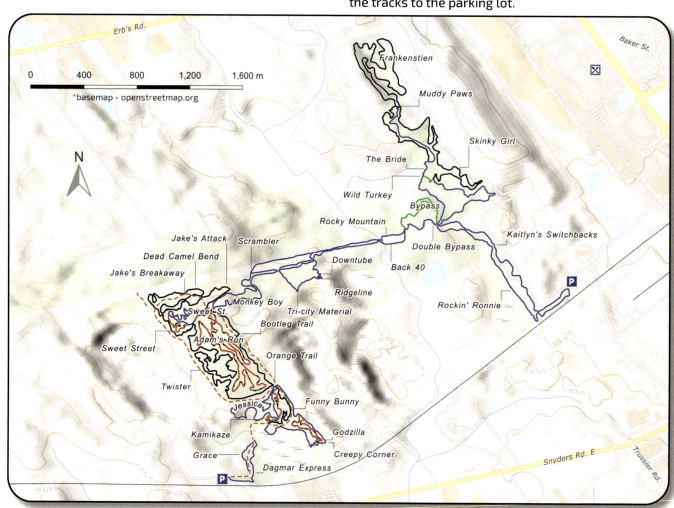

Review:

The **Hydro Cut** has some of the finest mountain-bike riding in Southern Ontario. With **30 km** of loops and as many trails, it is a **favourite destination** for many.

Situated on the west side of **Kitchener**, it also serves the cities of **Waterloo, Cambridge, Guelph** and beyond as a **central hub for MTB action**.

These **twisty, hilly trails** are in **two woodlots** connected by a straight, open trail section along a **hydro line corridor**.

Surprisingly, there are a lot of loops packed in here (like nearby **Puslinch**). And actually hillier than you would expect when you arrive.

The local club keeps a **well-maintained trail network** that flows nicely and has **moderate inclines** on a smooth clay base. There are few rocks, just an assortment of exposed tree roots.

The ride never gets boring. All loops are short in length (longest 2.4 km) with random **log rollovers, bermed curves, boardwalks** and **wooden** or **stone structures/jumps**.

There's plenty here to add interest and challenges that Intermediate or an Advanced rider will love....and more are being added all the time. **Grab some air if you dare!**

You can take **optional easy lines** around many features. If there's **no bypass at a trail entrance**, then consider it a warning by the builders that the trail ahead has more of the same and may perhaps be too hard for you to venture onto.

Being so **popular**, all singletrack trails are **one way** only. Trails tend to loop back to the same start points at **three different junctions** where there are map boards (there is generally good new signage throughout the area).

A few favourites are the flowy, fun runs on **Stinky Girl** and **The Bride**, plus the downhill rush on the sidewinder switchbacks of **Kamikaze**...watch the bottom.

The difficulty rating here is a little exaggerated by Ontario standards. (This is a tendency as you head further west in the province.) A **black-diamond trail** may have a few tough features to navigate, but it seems **Intermediate** to me throughout.

Two minor points to mention that shouldn't affect a great day of riding: the **mosquitoes** are really "friendly" and on the east end, you may catch a whiff of the local dump.

The area has an very **active, passionate** club membership that builds trails and posts many group rides (e.g. Monday Ladies Night). There has been talk of an expansion to adjacent woodlots... can you help, or volunteer?

If you have not been there lately, the crew have added more "obstructions" to play on and a new loop **Tri-city Material** into **Ridgeline** to **Downtube**.

Fatbikes are permitted year-round; it's best to use the **Snyder** entrance in the winter to get to the main trails.

The parking lots fill up on busy days. **Hydro Cut** is closed in early spring and after a good rain to reduce erosion. Check the status on the club website, just in case...Enjoy!

Best Mountain Bike Trails in Ontario

Western Ontario

Kolapore Uplands – MTB Trail

495428 Grey County Rd. 2, Ravenna

Trailhead – 44.42232025, -80.40652370

Length – 40+ km

90% hiking trail
10% doubletrack access roads

Elevation – Hillier on the north end, low wetlands on the south, a few steep climbs/descents in the valleys

Terrain – Smooth track with leaf debris; limestone outcrops and short drops; water and muddy patches; bridges

Skill – Intermediate – this is a XC-style ride

Traffic – Light traffic consisting of hikers, dog walkers, and MTB riders, Nordic skiers

Maps – Info board at the trailhead; good signage on ski trails printed map can be purchased online or at Ravenna General Store

Facilities – Parking lots, outhouse at main lot

Highlights – Wilderness, solitude, bridges, lookouts, rocky ride

Trail Fee – Free

Phone – 519 538 0283

Website – Kolapore Wilderness Trails

Similar Trails – Three Stage, Hilton Falls, Oro Network

Local Clubs – Collingwood Offroad Cycling Club

Access – The large main car lot is on the east side at 495428 Grey County Rd. 2, where the road bends. Cross the road to find the trailhead slightly south of there.

Also, easier trails are accessed south of here on Grey County Rd. 2 where the road bends again at Osprey Townline.

Metcalfe Rock parking lot at 415400 10th Line south of Sideroad 9 puts you somewhat in the middle of the trails area. Parking and trailhead are on the east.

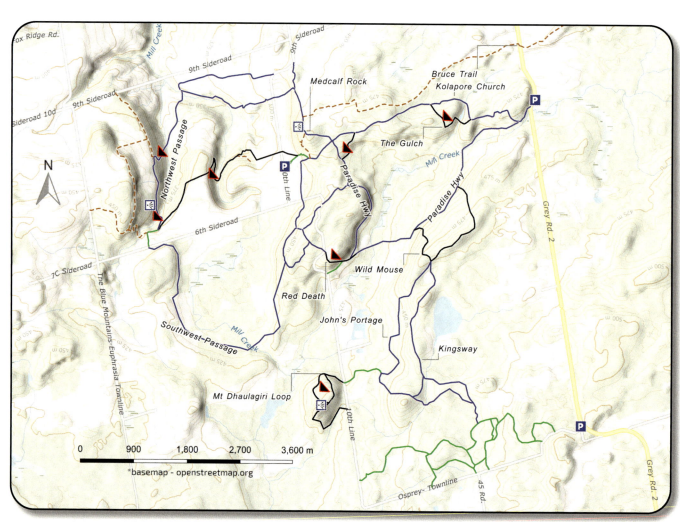

74 *Best Mountain Bike Trails in Ontario*

Review:

If you are looking for a **MTB XC wilderness adventure** in southern Ontario, **Kolapore Uplands** southwest of **Collingwood** will give you that experience. Enjoy hours of touring through forests on the rocky back of the **Niagara Escarpment** in peaceful, natural surroundings.

Numerous **forested loops** take you around **wetlands** and through clearings, over **many bridges,** and up and down valleys—some with steep grades. Much of this is on hiking trails or winter cross-country ski paths crossing over a number of side roads.

photo - Paulo LaBerge

Although you'll see a lot of trees, the area does offer a few **lookouts** such as the **Duncan Escarpment** and **Mount Dhaulagiri**. You'll have to work the granny gears before you can appreciate these views.

Kolapore offers a hilly ride on a smooth base with frequent **rocky limestone** encounters. Although it's **not super-technical** here, you'd better be agile enough on your pony to like the stony parts.

Much of the terrain may be covered with leaf debris. Take note that there could be **hidden rock crevices** under this floor covering that could suddenly tip you over.

This area is **suitable for any seasoned Intermediate MTB** rider capable of finding their way. There is signage (for skiers) at intersections to help you with navigation.

You should be **self-supporting** and prepared for the unexpected, since you may not encounter more than one or two other riders, or the odd hiker with their dog, all day. Also, it's a bit remote, so your **cell signal** may be weak in here.

The tributaries of **Mill Creek** create plenty of wetlands. Expect wet, **boggy areas** during a rainy spell or in early spring. This poor drainage makes it slippery and does promote bugs, so be ready. The **Southwest Passage** trail is usually a winter route and difficult to travel in the summer.

I recommend stopping at the **large creek bridge** for a snack break or even lunch overlooking the marshlands. That bridge and a few others have been rebuilt as they were in need.

Easier cycling loops can be found on the southeast corner of this forest if you are new to mountain biking or out with the family (and good with directions).

Kolapore is managed by a Nordic ski group whose volunteers put in many hours on trail maintenance and bridge replacement. Please consider supporting their efforts by buying their trail map (which is more detailed than mine).

Riding in here in autumn, when the **fall colours** are ablaze, is spectacular. **No Fatbikes** on the ski loops in the winter, please; use the Bruce trail.

Two hundred years ago, this area, then called **Paradise**, was home to sawmills and hunting camps. Eventually the name was changed to **Kolapore** after a city in India, probably by an early British settler with memories from there.

Your ride in **Kolapore** will likely leave you with fond memories of a **little slice of paradise**, too.

Best Mountain Bike Trails in Ontario

Western Ontario

Puslinch – MTB Trail

4343 Wellington Rd. Hwy 32, Cambridge

Trailhead – 43.42790094, -80.25897133

Length – 20+ km

60% MTB singletrack
20% hiking trail
20% doubletrack access roads

Elevation – Mixed terrain of flat and short hills on the east side; a few quick, steep climbs

Terrain – Gravel, sand and stony areas, fields, ponds; south side has more loam; some muddy spots and more trees

Skill – Easy (good for learning) to Intermediate, a few tough spots

Traffic – Busy on weekends with MTB riders and dog walkers near the entrance (watch for poop), horseback riders; best ridden clockwise

Maps – No map board or signs; a few tree blazes; lots of intersections can make the backside confusing, but you really can't get too lost

Facilities – Parking lot and nothing else—not even an outhouse!

Highlights – Plenty of variety, gnarly and fun, side winder (gravity switchbacks); Parabola trail rocks!

Trail Fee – Free

Phone – 519 621 2761

Website – Grand River Conservation Authority

Similar Trails – Christie Lake, Forrest Lea, Carrick Tract

Local Clubs – Waterloo Cycling Club

Access – Parking along Wellington Rd. 32 south of Hwy 401, 4343 Wellington Rd.

Head down the centre either way around the ponds, or take the 401 trail slightly further north toward the highway, get to the good stuff.

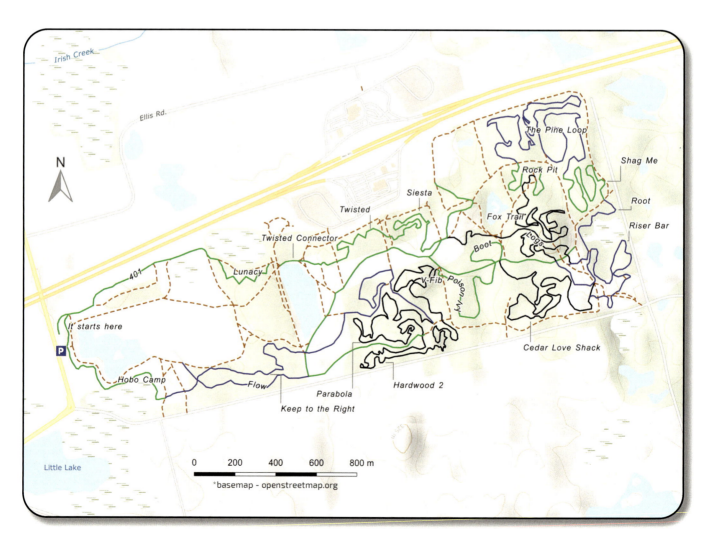

76 *Best Mountain Bike Trails in Ontario*

Review:

Puslinch Conservation Area is an excellent all-around MTB experience. Just east of **Cambridge** by Highway 401, it serves up **20+ km** of surprisingly varied and challenging trails to discover.

Riding here, you'll see why they say this once was an aggregate gravel pit to supply fill for constructing the highway. The hills are short and the **terrain has a lot of gravel**. I would think much of this is first to dry after it rains.

From the parking lot, the biking in either direction around the two ponds starts off as too easy. But just hold on, it gets much better once you're past them. Doing this area clockwise seems to be the better option.

Heading down the north side, you'll find stands of planted pine trees with the trail weaving in and out of them. Berms help

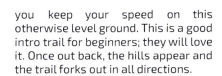

you keep your speed on this otherwise level ground. This is a good intro trail for beginners; they will love it. Once out back, the hills appear and the trail forks out in all directions.

On some of the climbs, you'll need plenty of steam going up and skill going down. The round stones and gravel act like a bag of marbles.

There are few signs in this moderate-sized woodlot, so take any path and explore until it ends at a sideroad. A map would be helpful, or just wing it—you will find your way back...eventually.

There is a lot packed in here and much of it is flowy and twisty, making the most of what little precious real estate there is.

Once you head back on the southern loops, you're totally into the hardwood forest and the soil base gets smoother. But that bliss won't last long, as there is still a bounty of random rocks and boulders to keep you busy. It's a little harder on the steep gnarly climbs, which might lead some to rate this as **Advanced** trail.

A straight hiking trail cuts through this area with excellent loops on either side. With little signage, you need to pay attention to where the fun trails start. One of my favourite rides in Ontario is here: the **Parabola**, an oval loop, technical yet fast, too much fun and all for free!

Another highlight is what I call a **sidewinder**; I believe it is on the **Fox** trail. This is where riders bank the valley back and forth repeatedly with little effort. With the right momentum and proper design, these gravity switchbacks are a joy to zoom through and are popping up everywhere.

Popular with local riders, Puslinch also has its share of hikers and their dogs, so near the entrance, note the poop surprises you may need to dodge. As a conservation area, it has no services and is still undeveloped. A short drive west, where you likely came in from the highway, you'll find all the amenities you could need in **Cambridge**.

Some complain about the drone of the highway behind the trees. I never seem to notice—too busy focusing on the trail and enjoying it with my chums.

Best Mountain Bike Trails in Ontario

Western Ontario

The Pines – MTB Trail

745751 Township Road 4, Woodstock

Trailhead - 43.17879061, -80.69506785

Length – 12 + 8 = 20 km

85% MTB singletrack
10% hiking trail
5% doubletrack access roads

Elevation – Flat by the river, short hills in the interior

Terrain – Smooth, sandy soil; lots of roots & pine needles; some gravel; muddy pockets; bermed, tight turns; log hops; bridges; new DH ramps and dirt jumps

Skill – Easy to Advanced

Traffic – MTB riders and mosquitoes (hiking is not allowed)

Maps – Trailhead map board, new signposts on trails

Facilities – Large parking lot, outhouse

Highlights – New downhill runs, more challenges, quiet, shady, best riding for miles

Trail Fee – $10 guest day pass, $35 yearly (pay on club's website)

Phone – 519 451 1188

Website – Upper Thames River

Similar Trails – Fanshawe, Wildwood, Christie Lake

Local Clubs – Woodstock Cycling Club, FB page

Access – Location is on a quiet country road out in farm country. Drive to 745751 Township Road 4, northeast of Woodstock. (The sign is hard to spot—it's small and up on a pole.)

Head north down the long gravel road to the parking lot. Trails start on north end from the map board.

Open year round and for night rides.

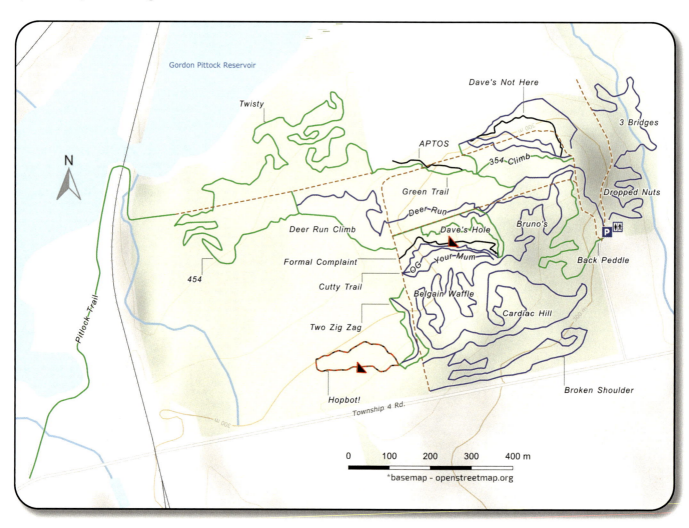

Best Mountain Bike Trails in Ontario

Review:

The Pines, near **Woodstock,** in the middle of central Ontario, is an oasis of fast MTB riding for all those in need of some cycling action. On the banks of the **Thames River** northeast of town, this woodlot has around **20* km** of twisty trail jammed into it.

The pine trees planted in orderly rows somehow gave the local bike club that manages this property the right idea: they snaked trails around the trees every which way for gnarly MTB manoeuvring with little straightaways or doubletrack to bore you.

This area is pretty flat, being by the river, with a **smooth, sandy trail** base that drains well and little rock to be seen.

A small hill in one quadrant gives a meagre **15 m** of elevation gain. It's still enough to tear through **Broken Shoulder** and **Cardiac Hill** to **Belgian Waffle's** fast and flowy loops, a favourite of mine.

Twisty has the flat, easy stuff by the river and is, as you might expect, serpentine. On the west side of the trailhead is a short, scenic loop called **Dropped Nuts** going into **Three Bridges** with...Ummm, yes, only rwo bridges, a rock garden and a large ramp to roll over a tree trunk—what fun.

Author's Note – At this point I had to rewrite the rest of this review for the book. At the 11th hour, someone emailed me with the news: spring logging had trashed the place, and most of the loops had been changed! What else could do I but drive there the next day to scout it out?

My original review went on to say how the riding was **pretty tame** and the few structures encountered were rather safe stuff. And the so-called **black-diamond** loop had humoured me with its lack of danger to dismount me.

Well, things have much improved, and local riders I met on the trail were excited! I can see why. There is now **danger in their lives!**

Woodstock MTB club members were busy building this spring (2020) and they took this opportunity to reroute many loops for the better. What little elevation they had has been maximized. Any riders into tricking out on some mean **DH jumps** can now take on a variety of **aerial feats.**

New lines have been cut through this woodlot with **faster and bigger berms** than ever. It was still somewhat a mess in there, with tree limbs and logs strewn about, so I can't comment on the flow and signage yet. It will need a few seasons for the tracks to settle in and to get permanent signs posted.

Trails mentioned earlier are still there, and now the highlight is the **mini-downhill runs**. At the top from left to right, the DH trails **Your Mum, OG, Cutty Trail,** and **Formal Complaint** get successively harder to master. You start off hitting the rollers and progressively get yourself onto some serious **gap jumps.**

Need more liftoff? I saw other jumps off the access road, and down the **Hopbot!** Then also find the short **Dave's Not Here! Man!** and **Artos** trails for chances to endo on the drops, gaps and tabletop jumps.

There is enough in here to crank it out for a few hours. All looks encouraging, they are making great efforts and the word is getting out. The **Fatbike** scene in the winter, I am told, is extensive. Grooming is iffy with the mild temps and less snow this far south, but it happens when possible.

Once a private club ride location, this has since been opened up to guests. Please **pay your way** online. The moderate fee supports maintenance and insurance to keep it all going and feed our MTB habit.

With little else for around for kicks, **The Pines** is a welcome MTB sanctuary that now features some appealing DH runs. It's sure to get you moving! Drop by on your way to **London** or elsewhere. It's just minutes away from where highways **401 & 403** meet and close to the town of **Woodstock** for a post-ride food and beverage stop.

*Currently there are **12 km** of remapped loops with **8 km** more planned by the end of 2020.

Best Mountain Bike Trails in Ontario

Western Ontario

Three Stage – MTB Trail

Side Road 6 & 2nd Line, Collingwood

Trailhead – 44.44141820, -80.30687663

Length – 40+ km

50% MTB singletrack
30% hiking trail
20% doubletrack access roads

Elevation – One of the highest points on the escarpment, this bluff drops down in three stages. The top area slopes to the edge of the bluffs, then drops steeply to a terraced level area, then descends to the base.

Terrain – Smooth soil base, random limestone outcrops, log hops, well treed, mud patch and slippery when wet.

Skill – Intermediate – Advanced

Traffic – Light MTB usage, hikers; winter sees Nordic skiing and snowmobile trail use.

Maps – Little signage, no map; one could get spun around and lost; use a GPS phone app

Facilities – Small parking lots; pack what you need

Highlights – Tons of good-quality trail, fast, flowy and gnarly rock, DH runs, lookouts, tasty apples

Trail Fee – Free

Phone – None

Website – Pretty River Provincal Park

Similar Trails – Agreement Forest, Kolapore, Copeland Forest

Local Clubs – Team Van Go

Access – From Collingwood, follow Grey County Rd. 19 southwest towards Osler Buffs ski hill; take 19 to the top of the hill. Moments later, turn south on 2nd Line, a dirt road. Drive south 'til you meet Side Road 6 and park where you can. Two trails going south get you in.

Or park west at the next intersection (at 3rd Line) and head south from there.

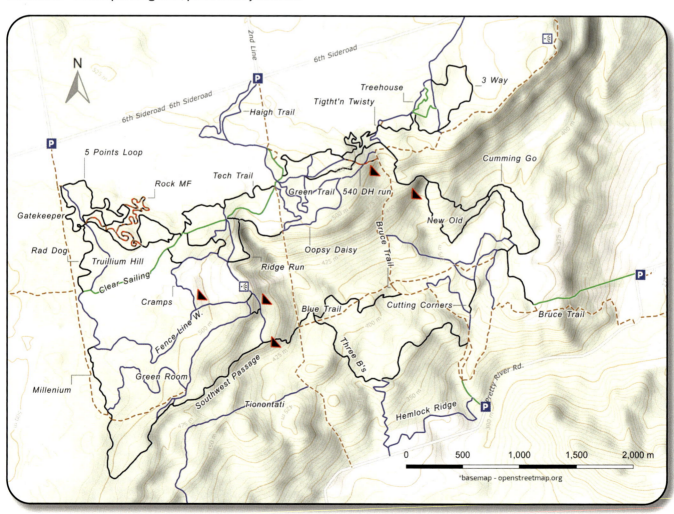

80 *Best Mountain Bike Trails in Ontario*

Review:

Up on the bluffs of the Niagara Escarpment, minutes away from **Collingwood**, resides **Three Stage**. This trail network within **Pretty River Valley Provincial Park** calls riders in search of that elusive **MTB zen**.

They call it **Three Stage** for the states of fulfilment achieved the longer you ride there. Somewhat plausible? It actually refers to the three levels of the hill.

Most of the **trails are on the top** of the bluffs; halfway down is the second stage, where the land levels out as a terrace, and then finally there's the bottom level, where a country road passes. More track is found on this plateau with fast downhill routes between stages. There is little to ride on the bottom.

Since this is one of the highest points on the escarpment, you can imagine there is a lot of climbing, especially if you take the downhill routes. For some, these seldom-found **DH runs** are worth the buzz.

Most are satisfied **staying at the top** exploring this large forest. The **40+ km** of trails here are wild, with little maintenance: the park is not operational, so you'll find no infrastructure or services. You are free to roam and get lost.

photo - Paulo LaBerge

For decades, this has been a quiet spot that only experienced mountain bikers should try. It's rustic, rugged, hilly and tons of fun. Some routes are hiking paths, while others were cut with MTB riding in mind. With no map and few trail blazes or landmarks to help you get around, it becomes an adventure.

Much of this is a mixed forest with a few open areas such as the orchard. In the fall, look for apples from the old trees. It's grown in over the years, so there are not many scenic lookouts left, but you will encounter limestone outcrops and see beautiful rocky cliffs.

Coming in from the main entry point at **2nd Line & Side Road 6**, there are two fun express trails. Pick one to take you into the middle of this twisty bowl of spaghetti. Starting on the **Green** Intermediate loops takes you eastward to get acquainted with the terrain.

Then, once you have found your groove—and if you're willing—circle around to the other half and find the harder **Red** trails, which are loaded with rocks.

The singletrack has its share of boulders and old logs to keep you focused. Some crevices are hidden by forest-floor debris. It gets ugly in here when wet, as much of the smooth path, made up largely of clay / loam / leaves, becomes slick.

Most of it connects and makes for a marvellous flowy ride that will make you work because **little of it is level.** Up and down you go all day, crisscrossing the top. There are some steep spots that are really tricky, off-camber stuff... and fast!

Sloping to the bluffs' edge, the hill quickly drops to down to the second stage, where more level Intermediate trails wind around two small ponds and wetlands. Note: Some sections heading down the cliff are extra-rocky terrain that only **rock fiends will love.**

The **Bruce Trail** cuts through this park and sees a lot of hikers, so be nice and yield to others. Some of their paths are off-limits to us.

By now, I hope you've gotten the impression of **Three Stage** as the kind of trail where you are on your own and should refer to a GPS map app to find your way out. All those hills are going to need good legs, granny gears and shocks for the rocks. If your balance is not the best, padding will spare you.

May you find **good karma** on these paths to joyous enlightenment and then find a patio in **Collingwood**. That craft beer will taste great over your tales of the trails with buds.

Best Mountain Bike Trails in Ontario

Western Ontario

Turkey Point – MTB Trail

Turkey Point Rd., Norfolk

Trailhead - 42.71165905, -80.34604988

Length – 75 km

60% MTB singletrack
30% hiking trail
10% doubletrack access roads

Elevation – Rather flat in some parts; a few quick inclines, then trail slopes down to a ridge by the lake

Terrain – Smooth, sandy soil; though dusty, it drains well. Little root or rock, a few log hops and bridges, plenty of twisty track and straight bombers

Skill – All levels; trails are rated harder than they really are

Traffic – Popular, room for everyone, watch for hikers

Maps – New signage; map boards and trail post numbers

Facilities – Parking lots, outhouse, camping and beach area

Highlights – Includes lots of trail variety, Carolina forest, Lake Erie is warm for swimming

Trail Fee – Free

Phone – 519 426 3239

Website – Turkey Point Provincial Park

Similar Trails – Oro Network, Northumberland, The Pines

Local Clubs – Turkey Point Mountain Bike Club, Facebook

Access – Parking at Mole Side Rd. (not a throughway) at Turkey Point Rd. and Charlotteville 1 Rd. to access the most popular trails; other trails can be accessed from the following parking spots:

- South end of Mole Side Rd. via Front Rd.
- Turkey Point Rd., East on Charlotteville 2 Rd. or
- Long Point Eco-Adventures on Front Rd.

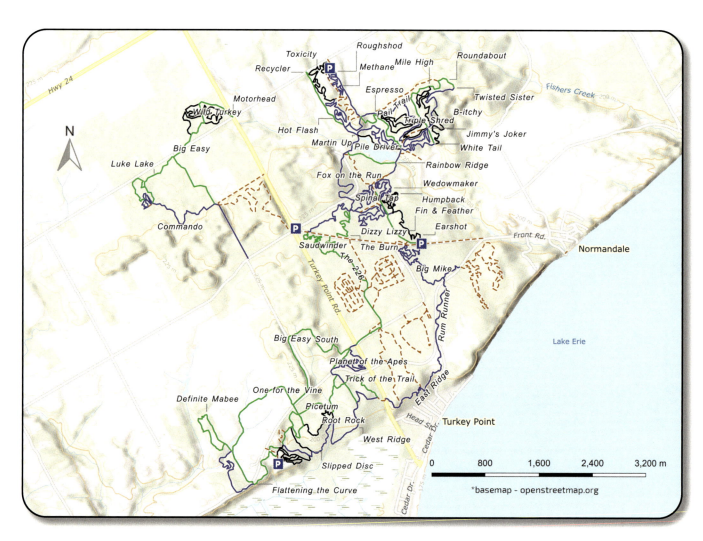

82   Best Mountain Bike Trails in Ontario

Review:

With claims of **75 km** of track on **72 different routes**, the Turkey Point area offers mountain bike riders tons of great riding action. The choices and locations will bring you back.

Down by the shores of **Lake Erie**, this location has **three areas** to crank through and discover. The terrain is generally **flat, sandy soil**, with the odd short, quick incline to mix it up.

A very passionate group of riders from the Turkey Point Mountain Bike Club cut and maintain this area. They make the best of the lack of elevation by **twisting and turning the trails.** Some spots get nice and gnarly, while others flow faster.

The terrain has a gradual slope to the lake where it meets a bluff that drops to the **beach** and **waterfront.**

As you boot around, you'll notice a distinct difference in plants and trees here in the southern part of Ontario. This is the northern edge of the **Carolinian Forest** and some sections have that **oak savannah** feel as you zip through a more open canopy.

Less ground cover to brush against is a good thing, because **ticks** (carriers of Lyme disease) and **poison ivy** are an issue to be aware of here. Stick to the centre of the trail when you ride. And always **check for these nasty critters after the ride.**

My starting point was the popular one at **Mole Rd.** and **Turkey Point Rd.**

Here we started in on the **Saudwinder** trail, working our way over and checking out **Dizzy Lizzy** and other winding loops to eventually take the **Humpback – Earshot – Rum Runner** trail combo southward to the lake.

Riding west along the edge of the bluff **Ridge trail** we cranked. It would be a little unnerving for a beginner to fall down the hillside, but in my opinion, it's not tough enough of a track to be designated a black diamond.

This area is part of **Turkey Point Provincial Park** that has **camping** and a **beach**, which you could certainly work into your visit.

There are other trails to be found in different forest tracts in the Turkey Point area. Heading further west, beyond the ridge, are loops that run through **Burning Kiln Winery** and **Long Point Eco-Adventures**.

Another area just **northeast** of where we started, uses part of an old landfill for some **harder runs**. Then, farther up in the **northwest quadrant**, there are a few more kilometres of singletrack for you to test.

If you are a member of the local MTB club, you have access to more **private tracks** to shred. So, this area has tons of sweet flowy track to try (second only to the **Oro Network** in Ontario).

The bike club also has an **active women's MTB riding program** that looks encouraging.

Make your way down one day. It gets **hot and dry** in these parts, so expect some dust, use bug spray to keep the bugs off and be sure to check for those ticks after your ride. **It's a joy to cycle** and the hills aren't that hard—it'll keep you moving and smil'n!

Best Mountain Bike Trails in Ontario

Western Ontario

Wildwood – MTB Trail

3995 Line 9, RR #2, St. Marys

Trailhead – 43.26837129, -81.06871107

Length – 25 km

30% MTB singletrack
50% hiking trail
20% doubletrack access roads

Elevation – Some small hills, gradual climbs along the banks of the dam, and a few long descents

Terrain – Mostly smooth soil, sandy spots, some gravel, roots, muddy areas, wood structures

Skill – Easy except for Hardwood loop, which is Advanced

Maps – At the trailhead by the gate; numbered post markers on the trail

Traffic – Cyclists and hikers. Note – On odd days, ride trail counterclockwise

Facilities – Parking lot, washrooms, bike rentals, bike repair station with bike wash, camping, swimming, and boat rentals

Highlights – Varied scenery, lake views, camping by the trail

Trail Fee – Day pass: Adults $8, kids $4, vehicle $14

Hours – From dawn to dusk; no night riding

Phone – 519 284 2292

Website – Wildwood Conservation Area

Similar Trails – Fanshawe, Minnesing, Orn Network

Local Clubs – Woodstock Cycling Club

Access – Wildwood Conservation is where **Hwy 9** meets **Hwy 7**; at the roundabout go to **3995 Line 9, RR #2 east of St. Marys.** The trail signs start at the highway underpass and dam by the gatehouse.

Helmets are mandatory on trails.

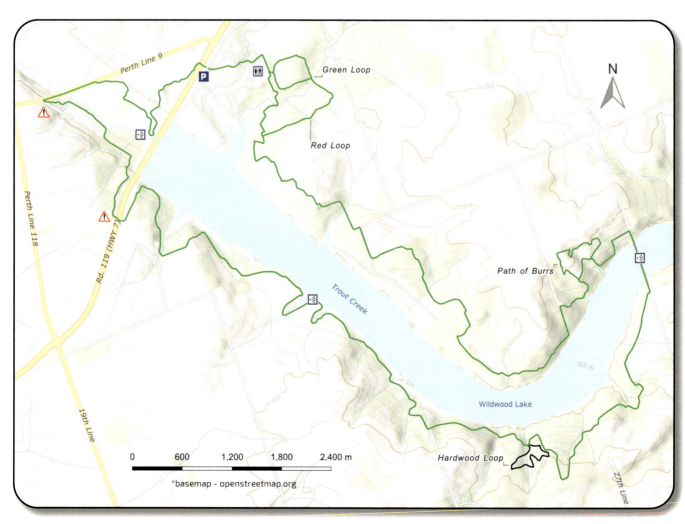

Best Mountain Bike Trails in Ontario

Review:

Wildwood Conservation Area offers **25 km** of **cross-country-type cycling** and two **MTB side loops**. This bike trail circles the Wildwood Reservoir, offering a variety of terrain and scenery. It makes a good outing for the day or a weekend. **Bike rentals** (both MTB and **Fatbikes**) are available at the gate, and they look decent.

Situated in the middle of **Ontario** farm country, Wildwood lies north of **London,** and 10 minutes east of the town of **St. Marys.** There is not much other trail riding to be had in the area, but this spot is worth a visit.

This trail offers a **fast-paced XC MTB ride**, and you can keep your pace going for most of it. However, there are also opportunities to stop and take in the view, picnic or sit by the water on the way. You'll encounter bridges, boardwalks and the **large dam**.

The terrain varies from a smooth soil or gravel base to lumpy roots, muddy patches and even a tiny creek crossing. Glimpses of the lake can be seen, though some of the trail takes you far from the shore.

On the **north side** of the lake, the path is wide **doubletrack.** There are a few rather long hills (which are fun to go down) with farm fields and cottages to see.

The **south side** is narrow **singletrack** that winds through a forest with some rooty sections. Here you will eventually find the **Hardwood Trail**. This loop is a must for the experienced MTB thrill-seeker. Pay attention, as there are skinny bridges with consequences and oodles of log jumps. Difficult to master, this section is the highlight of the ride.

The general flow of traffic **alternates direction** every day; on odd days it is counterclockwise. Plenty of signs keep you going so you can't get lost. Numbered posts help for map reference.

Unfortunately for some, this long loop has **no shortcut**. This means one must commit to doing it all or doing a U-turn at some point. The length may be a bit much for young kids and the unfit. (My son, who was 10 years old at the time, managed to do the entire 25-km loop with me, then slept quite well that night in the tent.)

Another option is to consider some **Bikepacking**: there are four backcountry campsites on the loop, and it could be fun to break up the journey with an overnight stay. It would be wise to reserve ahead.

There are three sections on this loop that briefly meet up with **car traffic.** From the gatehouse, there is a highway underpass to get to the base of the dam. The trail then takes you to **Hwy 9**, where you cycle on the shoulder long enough to cross the road bridge, and then dodge back into the bush at the **13th Line**.

In a few minutes, you will need to cross **Hwy 7**, which is busy. Beyond are happy trails for the next hour 'til you get to the far end. To cross the lake, there is a quiet gravel road at **29th Line** that also offers a panoramic view.

Be forewarned that the other side loop, **Field of Burrs,** is lame. Picture a mowed path through tall grass meandering on the side of a hill – why? There appears to be little to challenge or explore here. The lack of trail wear tells me others think the same.

Skip that detour and stick to the long trail loop, which is well worth doing. It's very similar to **Fanshawe** in many ways; both park areas are run by the same local conservation authority.

While they each have their good points, I feel **Wildwood** is a bit better. Consider **camping overnight**, as it's inexpensive and the trail is right by the campgrounds. A swim in the lake is a welcome idea after a hot day of riding, too.

Best Mountain Bike Trails in Ontario

Eastern Ontario

Forest Lea - MTB Trail

1864 Forest Lea Rd., Pembroke

Trailhead - 45.80894801, -77.27758506

Length – 30 km

80% MTB singletrack
20% doubletrack access roads

Elevation – Gradual, short climbs; level around the lake and marsh area

Terrain – A mix of random roots and rocks, with smooth soil in between; bridges, berms, flat rock, muddy and sandy patches; some sections are overgrown by late summer

Skill – Intermediate to Advanced

Traffic – Not a busy location; MTB riders, hikers, horseback riders; Nordic skiers, snowshoeing, Fatbikes, snowmobiles.

Maps – Map board at the trailhead, small old signage on trails, bring map, use GPS.

Facilities – Parking lot, outhouse

Highlights – Steady encounter of gnarliness, lake view, bridges, garden gnomes in a wilderness setting,

Trail Fee – Free, but consider the $20 annual membership to support maintenance

Phone – None (signal weak)

Website – Forest Lea Blog

Similar Trails – South March, Hilton Falls, Puslinch

Local Clubs – Ottawa Mountain Bike Association

Access – West of Pembroke at the end of the Forest Lea Rd. at 1846 is a large parking lot. Right side of the Nordic ski cabin is the MTB trailhead.

In the winter, **Fatbikes** can use the snowshoe loops, though they are short. Riding on Nordic ski tracks in the winter is not cool, and damages them. Continue your ride on the side roads or the snowmobile paths, please.

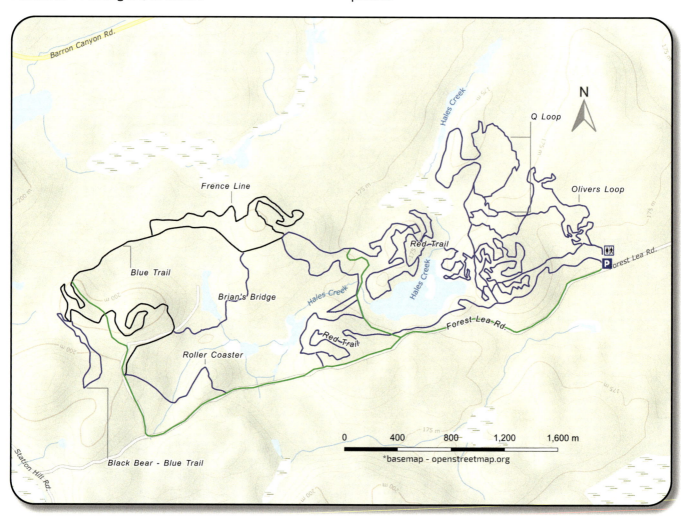

86   *Best Mountain Bike Trails in Ontario*

Review:

Just west of **Pembroke, 30 km** of technical trail await you at **Forest Lea**. All MTB riders keen on a challenging, yet enjoyable, **rocky, rooty singletrack** need to check out this remote location one day.

Tucked away in **northeastern Ontario**, close to the **Ottawa River**, where the **wilds of the north** can be felt, sits this little-known set of tracks.

The terrain undulates with small changes in elevation; a few short climbs are found on the west side.

Mountain bike riders will find little here that is Easy, as much of the trail moves at an **Intermediate pace** with occasional moments that call on your **Advanced skills** to be employed.

Aside from the flat access roads and **overgrown** Nordic ski paths, much of the terrain is a mix of **random rounded rocks** and tree roots on singletrack. Though at times challenging, none of the **gnarly sections** is impossible, insane or endless.

Thankfully the tough stuff is not relentless, and sections of clear trail allow you to relax briefly and set up for the next upcoming series of challenges. A **full-suspension bike** with **large rims** would improve your efforts.

If this sounds like more work than fun, then it's likely not your thing. Mountain bike clubs in the **Ottawa Valley** regularly visit this location. Since it is **not a busy place**, you will need to be equipped not to get lost.

When my son and I were there, we rode the **Red trail** (the most popular), taking in sections of the easier **Green trail** as well. We enjoyed the twisty loop as it took us over **long bridges** to the lake for a scenic view. Then we passed through the playful **Enchanted Forest** section, where **garden gnomes** are scattered between the rows of tall pines.

I have heard others mention that the other trails looping out back are a **tad harder** and have a few **rock drops** you need to be aware of.

I would like to say I rode all the trails, but sadly we eventually got chased out of the woods. By a bear? No (though that is a possibility here). The **deer flies** were just rabid that day!

Seems these pesky, insistent flies are attracted to **moving objects** and **dark blue/black colours.** My poor son, with his dark blue helmet, had a swarm orbiting his head. You can expect the spring bug season here to be bad.

The club-supplied map board is a **simple approximation** of the actual trail. The loops actually twist and turn way more than illustrated. Add **Nordic ski paths** to the mix and the few old (some handmade) signs are barely enough to keep you on course.

A **GPS map app** would be good for reference. We were unsure of the way a few times, but a MTB rider has to be prepared for such situations.

If you need new, **technically challenging**, yet not overly hilly, terrain in your diet, then this place has plenty to keep you at it for the day. It is close enough to **Pembroke** or **Petawawa** to do lunch or stay over when you go.

Best Mountain Bike Trails in Ontario

Eastern Ontario

Harold Town – MTB Trail

2611 Old Norwood Rd., Peterborough

Trailhead – 44.32210447, -78.26119704

Length – 14 km

80% MTB singletrack
10% hiking trail
10% doubletrack access roads

Elevation – Flat, easy trail along hill base, medium-sized hill climbs and descents on switchbacks

Terrain – Smooth loam soil base, some gravel, ramps, berms with optional rock and wooden features

Skill – All levels, but most of it is built for experienced riders

Traffic – MTB riders, hikers, dogs; in winter, Nordic skiers, Fatbikes – no grooming

Maps – Map board at parking lot, signposts on trail

Facilities – Parking lot; outhouse; but no garbage bins, so pack out your garbage

Highlights – Well-cut track, new structures & tracks, lookouts, not busy

Trail Fee – Free

Phone – 705 745 5791

Website – Otonabee Conservation Area

Similar Trails - Ravenshoe, Centennial, Albion Hills

Local Clubs – FB page - MTB Riders of Harold Town, Peterbourough Trailbuilders Assoc.

Access – 5 km east of Peterborough, you'll find a large parking lot just south off 2611 Old Norwood Road.

You are asked to pack out your own garbage.

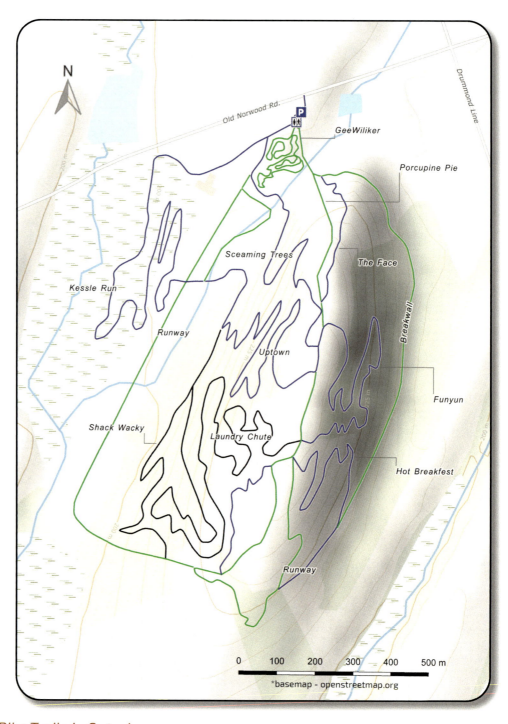

Best Mountain Bike Trails in Ontario

Review:

I was delighted to find, while scouting east of **Peterborough**, some excellent MTB riding to review. At **Harold Town Conservation Area**, local builders have created a winner.

They've used many of **IMBA's** top recommendations in terms of **trail-design techniques**, which means MTB riders will find plenty to explore and **good times riding**. It may not be on your shortlist yet, but here is why it should be.

photo - James Malvern

As you pull into the parking lot, the first thing you see standing in the field is a **large hill**. This is what geologists call an **esker**. There are hundreds of these mounds of **glacial deposits** in Ontario, and this is a tall one at **48 m**. That's what you are going to play on, so **expect some climbing**.

For the beginner, the loops are at the base of the hill and, as you would expect, rather **flat and tame**, except every so often there is a **small ramp** or **rock** as an alternate choice to play on and hone your skills—a nice touch!

There is also an old access path that rings the mound and also runs straight up and over it if you are in a rush.

Regular MTB riders should take the **1.7 km Kessel Run** loop to warm up and connect to the **Uptown**. Since the **ski-hill lift** is long gone, this switchback is the only way you get to the top. It's not too gruelling an effort that you will likely do a few times.

Most of the **trees covering the hill are cedar**. I do not know why, but cedar brings out the mosquitoes, even on a hot, dry day.

Once on top, you have at least **nine choices** to head down. **Hot Breakfast** or **Screaming Trees** are easier routes than the challenging **Laundry Chute** (my favourite) and **Pot Shot** to **Shack Wacky** way.

If you take the **Funyun** or **Honeymoon** loop, enjoy the singletrack down because the trail actually climbs back up to the top at the end.

Beyond the twisty track, there are strategically placed **ramps, boardwalks, rock gardens, boulders, skinnies,** and **log hops** spaced to keep your fun meter in the happy zone.

Harold Town has something for all levels, thanks to great trail design with plenty of variety and challenges for those who want them. As well, there is good erosion management on newly cut trails.

Most of the terrain is smooth, black soil, often with **berms on the turns**. It's sure to be mucky and slick when wet.

There is a map board at the entrance. Each trail is well marked and has signs posting **length** and **amount of climbing**.

The **grand views** from **lookouts on the top** are an added bonus compared to your typical tour featuring acres of trees whizzing by. And, as at many other locations, be nice and **share the trail** with any hikers or dog walkers.

Noted painter **Harold Town** once lived here and now both the area and the local MTB group bear his name; perhaps this is why local riders have so **artfully built** this network: Just **14 km** of trail compressed on a hillside, which works and delivers surprisingly well.

This little-known MTB playground is worth the drive from **Toronto**; it has **all the right ingredients** to make it a hit, and I highly recommend you come on out to try something different and make your list.

Best Mountain Bike Trails in Ontario   89

Eastern Ontario

Larose Forest – MTB Trail

Indian Creek Rd., SE of Ottawa

Trailhead –   45.37585510, -75.24247959

Length – 17+ km

60% MTB singletrack
20% hiking trail
20% doubletrack access roads

Elevation – Near-level terrain with lots of rolling bumps and dips

Terrain – Fine, sandy base; smooth trail; no rocks; few roots; drains well. Flowy, bermed singletrack; some tight turns

Skill – Easy, Beginner level

Traffic – Not busy; two-way trails; typical path users are bikers, hikers, Fatbikes, Nordic skiers and dogsleds

Maps – Well marked, with map boards at the trailhead and junctions with numbered signposts

Facilities – Parking lots, outhouses, shelters; the cell signal is weak here

Highlights – Flowy ride, tall trees, creek valleys, bridges, quiet

Trail Fee – Free

Phone – 613 675 4661

Website – Prescott – Russell County, FB page - Forestlarose

Similar Trails – Limerick Forest, Northumberland, Christie Lake

Local Clubs – Ottawa Mountain Bike Association

Access – South of Ottawa, exit Hwy 417 to Hwy 33 then quickly turn east on Russland Rd and continue for 6.5 km.

Turn north on Saumure Rd. briefly and continue straight onto Indian Creek Rd., which turns north to ride areas.

Best locations to park at are P1 on Indian Creek Rd. and P4 at 4577 Champlain Rd hwy 8, a 11 km drive further east.

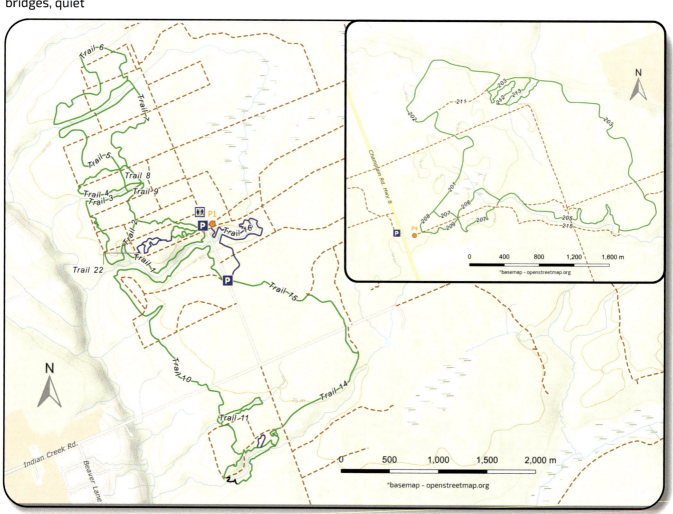

90   Best Mountain Bike Trails in Ontario

Review:

Southeast of **Ottawa** lies the large **Larose Forest,** where mountain bike riders can find **17 km** of fast, flowy loops that offer something to please everyone.

This large forest is typical of many historically clear-cut areas that were either too rocky or sandy for farmers to use. This one, which first began to be replanted in the 1920s, has a **very fine sand base**.

Surprisingly, it's **firm to ride,** with only a few spots loose enough that you could slide out on turns. Even so, there are **berms** at many of these curves so you can keep your speed.

I had the chance to ride the loops near **P1** and none seemed too tough. The track is smooth, with few roots and **NO rocks** at all.

A few log hops set on the route would have been welcome. Maybe they are omitted to keep it as an **Easy, beginner MTB experience.**

At first my group headed into the woods on the **east side**. Here there are a few loops and wider cross-country ski trails that take you way in...but fallen trees and hungry bugs chased us out.

Next, we tried the more established **west side** by the large rain shelter at **P1**. I soon found out this was the better ride, well worn and with good signage.

Several loops run along the ridges above small creek valleys that drain off a rather **flat topography.** Here trail builders have cut a few harder, quick **sidelines** to get a some thrills, and have added drops, a bowl and pump tracks to give it more interest.

The **Ottawa Mountain Bike Association** partnered with the county to build and maintain these trails. Well done!.

(Note – **Clean your chain** after this ride. The fine sand will grind your parts quickly. Use dry lube rather than oil before you start; the sand will stick less.)

In the end it was a hot, humid and dusty fun run. The bugs got fewer and it was time to head to the St. Albert Cheese Factory for ice cream (naturally).

Unlike north of Ottawa, where you'll find plenty of rocky, technical riding, this southern trail was an easy, fast, smooth ride to enjoy. Even my teenage son (for once) loved it.

Further on the east side of this forest, at **P4**, you can find three more MTB loops to ride. There are also Nordic, ATV and equestrian paths, as well as gravel sideroads, to explore in this large forest. In the winter **Fatbikes** would love this spot

photo - Paul McCulloch

Best Mountain Bike Trails in Ontario   91

Eastern Ontario

Limerick Forest – MTB Trail

8773 Forsythe Rd., north of Prescott

Trailhead - 44.83639366, -75.62242645

Length – 180 km

30% MTB singletrack
50% hiking trail
20% doubletrack access roads

Elevation – Rather flat landscape with a few small hills

Terrain – sand, some soil and gravel, rooty sections, large mud holes, wetlands on fringe areas, trails carved out by dirt bikes

Skill – All levels; best for Intermediate riders

Traffic – MTBs, ATVs, dirt bikes, hikers, horses; in winter, Nordic sports and snowmobiles

Maps – At trailhead, signs on posts, a few map boards

Facilities – Large parking lots, outhouses, chalet

Highlights – Plenty of trail / road to explore, drains well, not busy on weekdays

Trail Pass – Free

Phone – 800 770 2170

Website – Limerick Forest

Similar Trails – Ganaraska, Northumberland, Larose

Local Clubs – Ottawa Mountain Bike Club

Access –

- Forsythe South Trails – large parking lot on east side at 8773 Forsythe Rd.
- Forsythe North Trails – parking at 9826 Forsythe Rd. by Shanty trail
- Further north, near 1175 Limerick Rd. by chalet, though not much to ride there

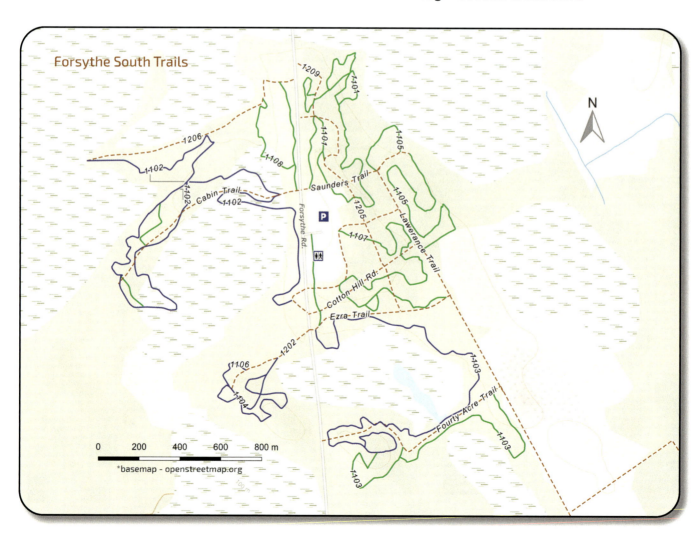

92   *Best Mountain Bike Trails in Ontario*

Review:

Out in **Eastern Ontario**, in the middle of farm country, lies **Limerick Forest** north of **Prescott**. Here you will find a trail system that mountain bike riders can rip through.

This **large forest** claims to have **180 km of trails**, from singletrack to gravel side roads. So there is plenty to ride.

The area is **divided into north** and **south zones**. On the **Forsythe south** loops (which are likely similar to the north), you will find fairly flat **forest terrain**, along with **small, rolling hills**, a few boulders and rutted tree roots.

The **trails drain well, being sandy**, so riding in early spring or right after a rain shower would be cool and gives you a firmer base. There are also **wetlands** that border many of these woodlots. You will know it when you get close and the mosquitoes find you—they are really "friendly!"

There are few wooden structures or jumps to play on, though the trails have **plenty of nice rollers** cut out by the dirt bikes.

Yup, unlike all the other MTB riding locations in this book, this one is mainly a **motocross** and **ATV playground**, and with that, you will find the terrain to be **extremely gouged** and **trashed** compared to the smoother trail base we usually ride. However, mountain bikers are welcome on this turf, and it's interesting to try out a new experience.

G a n a r a s k a Forest is another area where loops on the **west side** are carved out by dirt bikes. **Is this fun stuff?** To some, **yes, it can be**.

Dirt bikes make **wider turns**, so tight switchbacks and gnarly track are just not in here, but you can enjoy a **faster ride**. When you get going, you are almost assured that the next bend will be **well banked**.

Picking your line gets to be important while zooming along, because some runs are literally **troughs and berms**. You need to consistently be deciding to maybe **ride in them or not**.

I did notice how the flow of the trail is carved out for a **motorized bike experience**, for which soft sand, quick climbs and large roots require nothing more than **giv'n it more gas**. Not so with leg power on a MTB. That's how the **trail can fool you** into thinking "Riders before me have made it, here I go..." and you may fail.

That's the challenge: **reading the trail**. As for leg power, there is plenty of soft sand and mud-sucking moments that will tap your batteries, so **have extra power to spare**.

Most routes flow well, though I did find quite a few **spur trails cut** here and there that go nowhere. On the access roads, **ATV** action has created **huge mud puddles/ponds**. Definitely go around them, or they will swallow you up!

I was there on a weekday in the middle of August and only heard one or two motorized play toys far away in the bush. I can't speculate as to how busy it gets on weekends, though.

For the **Fatbike** crowd, all that sand and the short hills make **Limerick** a great summer ride or winter destination. But **eBikes** are currently not allowed. Now, does that seem odd?

With few places to mountain bike in **Eastern Ontario**, Limerick is a welcome destination, though, as mentioned, "different" from the MTB trails you might be used to.

When you look at the size of it on a map, there certainly are more trails here than one can do in a day's outing. The **Ottawa MTB club** makes its way down here at times; perhaps you should, too.

Best Mountain Bike Trails in Ontario

Eastern Ontario

Northumberland – MTB Trail

101 Beagle Club Rd., N. of Cobourg **Trailhead** - 44.09819085, -78.1074739

Length – 40+ km

20% hiking trail
30% singletrack MTB trail
40% doubletrack

Elevation – Lots of gentle rolling hills, some quite large

Terrain – Packed sandy and mixed soil, with a few tree roots and some gravel and rocks; watch for poison ivy

Skill – Easy to Intermediate

Traffic – Quiet and rarely busy; you may see bikes, hikers, horseback riders, ATVs, snowmobiles, x-skiing

Maps – Found at trailhead; the trails have signposts and coloured markers

Facilities – A parking lot and outhouse, but no other amenities for miles; Nordic skiing in winter.

Highlights – Plenty of solitude, provided by a wild pine forest (smells piney fresh!)

Trail Pass – Free

Phone – None

Website – Northumberland County

Similar Trails – Ganaraska, Eldred King, Long Sault

Local Club – Cobourg Cycling Club

Access – From Cobourg, head north on Hwy 45, then left onto Beagle Club Rd.

Within a few hundred metres, there is a large parking lot; the map board at the trailhead will get you started.

The best MTB track is NE across the road a bit.

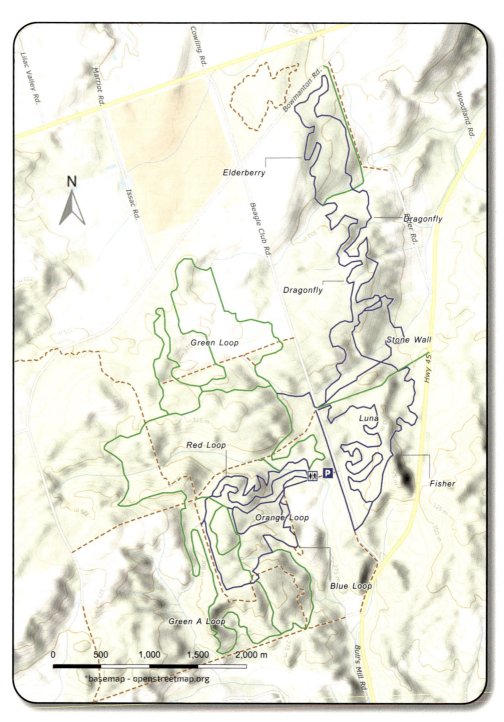

Best Mountain Bike Trails in Ontario

Review:

This little-known **Northumberland County Forest** offers mountain bike riders plenty of choices to let loose and explore.

With over **40 km** of track, riders get a **fast, hilly** set of cross-country-style loops and roads. This area, part of the **Oak Ridges Moraine**, has a smooth, **sandy soil base**, with a few tree roots and the odd rock left from the last glacial melt. I find it feels very similar to riding at **Ganaraska Forest**.

There is plenty here to discover. The forest is large, with a mix of **evergreen pines** and deciduous trees. As a result, it can feel **dry, dusty**, and a tad arid during the hot summer months. You may likely experience that pleasant piney smell.

The best riding is across the road, north of the trailhead parking lot. A local club cut the **4-km Dragonfly** MTB loop that leads further up the path to the **3-km Elderberry** and back on the **2-km Stonewall** trail. This is where any **gnarly, rocky stuff** is found.

South of there, still on the other side of Beagle Club Road, you can continue on **Luna, Flying Squirrel** and the **Fisher** trails to make up a fun additional **6-km** loop to enjoy. These are shared with dirt bikes, but you're unlikely to see one.

Back where you parked are most of the non-motorized trails. These are more mellow and good for a beginner XC - MTB ride experience. Take your pick from among the **Red (2.3 km), Blue (3.2 km)** or **Green (11 km)** loops—or a combination of them—and follow the coloured dots on the trees posted for Nordic skiing in the winter.

While mellow, this part of the trail network provides a fast ride if you want it, on wide track with hills that have gradual inclines for the most part. Take care turning: the mix of sand, leaves and pine needles can wash you out. Need a steeper hill? Find **The Hogs Back** if you dare. It's south of the parking lot on the Green loop.

The curious or driven cyclist can ride the numerous **dirty roads** and **ATV trails** to add more to the day. Look for **raspberries,** too. Yum!

Unfortunately, sand is great for growing **poison ivy**. On less-travelled backwoods trails, watch out: by summer's end, the weed can be **waist high** and encroaching in on the path. Take a ride in the early spring, or in the fall after a frost, and you will see a lot less of it.
Also be aware that **black bears** wander these parts, so making some noise as you ride along could be a good thing.

This **rustic** location is **rarely busy,** so I suggest riding with a buddy. Being prepared and self-sufficient is also wise as there are no services anywhere close by. Print a map or use your GPS phone map app. Your phone signal may be weak.

This is an excellent spot for **Fatbikes!** In the winter, please stay off the Nordic ski trails and ride up the road **3 km** northwest at the **Woodland Trails**, where there is another **9-km** loop that takes you to **Lookout Mountain**. I think you know what's there.

If you seek adventure or solitude, you'll surely find it in this patch of wilderness.

Best Mountain Bike Trails in Ontario

Eastern Ontario

South March – MTB Trail

875 Old Second Line Rd., Kanata

Trailhead - 45.34609903, -75.94661024

Length – 25 km

60% MTB singletrack
40% hiking trail

Elevation – Rolling, small hills with quick ascents, ever-changing grades

Terrain – Smooth soil full of roots; random limestone rocks; flagstone paths; large granite outcrops; land and water bridges

Skill – Intermediate, more fun for Advanced riders

Traffic – MTB riders, hikers, joggers, Fatbikes, snowshoers

Trail Maps – Map board at trailhead, excellent post markings on trail

Facilities – Parking on street or at community centre

Highlights – Well-designed and -maintained MTB playground, pond boardwalks, flat rock, scenic views

Trail Fee – Free

Phone – None

Website – South Marsh Highlands

Similar Trails – Georgian, Laurentian, Buckwallow

Local Clubs – OMBA – Ottawa Mountain Bike Association

Access – Officially you can park at the rec centre SE of the trailhead, but most riders find that awkward and park along the side of the street at 875 Old Second Line Rd. and Klondike Rd., Kanata.

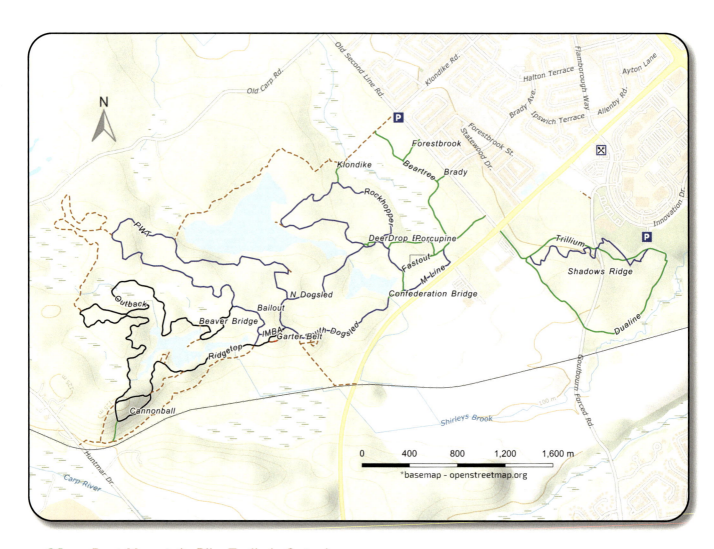

96 Best Mountain Bike Trails in Ontario

Review:

South March Highlands is the best MTB riding for locals on this side of the **Ottawa River**, and **a top pick** in **Ontario**.

At this **conservation area,** you will find around **25 km** of loops, well maintained by the Ottawa MTB club, that will **challenge** and **entertain** any **avid rock enthusiasts.**

Gnarly trails circumnavigate the property, where the exposed, smooth stone of the **Canadian Shield** houses pockets of water and marshland. Narrow bridges, some long, take you over the water (don't lose your nerve) and on a very scenic journey over and among large, rounded, flat rocks.

Don't take your eyes off the track too often; the terrain is ever changing and full of (good) surprises. You have to pick your lines well amid this minefield of stones.

Beyond the large, smooth boulders, there are everywhere loose, jagged and random chunks of rock of the more torturous kind, and roots, too. Parts of this twisty trail are made using these rocks as flagstone, I think to make this an easier ride. At times this is a blessing, and hmmm...sometimes not.

Now, don't get the wrong impression (I'm just scaring away the newbies), this place is serious fun if you own a decent full-suspension bike and have broken it in. The pounding on the **Rockhopper** trail alone will prove your bike's worth.

Loops start out from the trailhead with beginners in mind. A good way to warm up for the real reason you drove this far: the gnarly, foreboding outer zone. Not a super-hilly area, and suitable for skilled **Intermediate cyclists,** this will be a technical journey to practice your agility, timing and grace.

Once you've laid waste to the challenges of the track on the centre loops, take on the **black-diamond** terrain way at the back. This is a bit more technical than the blue loops, and it's **longer**.

Here, the open-rock ride on the **1.3 km Ridgetop** trail is a must for more advanced riders. It needs your attention and wits, as there are moments where you need to decide if today is your lucky day. A few rock drops could easily send you over the bars.

You can always do the by-pass or walk it (no shame in that). It's well signed, so you should have little problem trekking about. Consider wearing padding, and riding with a buddy might be prudent. And the pockets of mud are sure to splatter you.

Watch for hikers, and their dogs, especially on weekends, when it gets busier—this ride is beside an ever-growing local suburb.

Fatbikes come out in the winter, making this is a totally different and smoother ride experience. With sometimes too much snow your guaranteed that. There is no scheduled grooming, but others may have tramped the path before you.

In summer, though, all these scenic marshlands are home to plenty of mosquitoes. Hope it's a windy day, or keep moving and make your own wind.

Just NW of **Kanata** you can find plenty to eat and drink in town as you plan your next rock ride in **Gatineau Park, Quebec**.

What a hoot it is to ride the water bridges and rock humps. Techno rockers must try it. **An excellent spin** with no large climbs and **even more trail** beyond the conservation area to explore. By crossing over Terry Fox Drive there is about **4 km** more of the same fun and games we love.

Best Mountain Bike Trails in Ontario 97

Northern Ontario

Bracebridge RMC - MTB Trail

Hwy 11, N of Bracebridge

Trailhead - 45.11124874, -79.3098965

Length – 17 km

50% singletrack
50% doubletrack

Elevation – Stone ridgeline runs parallel to the highway with the whole area sloping east down to the river

Terrain – Smooth soil base, random rock outcrops, boulders, boardwalks, and a gravel mix on access roads

Skill – Best for Intermediate / Advanced MTB riders

Traffic – Two-way trails; light use by local hikers and cyclists; active Nordic skiing area in winter. Fatbikes permitted only on the snowshoe trails in the winter; no grooming is done

Maps – Map at the trailhead, as well as new signpost maps

Facilities – 2 parking lots with outhouses, a shelter and benches and picnic tables on the trails

Highlights – New MTB track on ridgeline, additional trail being developed, scenic river and rapids

Trail Fee – Donation post – pay what you can

Phone – None

Website – MORCA, BRMC on Facebook

Similar Trails – Buckwallow, Porcupine Ridge, Walden

Local Clubs – _Muskoka Off Road Cycling Assoc._ FB page

Access – Two parking areas now exist. A new south end parking lot was added, with the entrance on the north side, on Holiday Park Dr., 100 metres east of Hwy 11 interchange. This new entrance is best suited **for seasoned MTB riders.**

Note: The main parking area is 2.5 km further up, right off Hwy 117. There is only one highway sign posted mere seconds before the turnoff (!), so start hitting the brakes as soon as you see it—the turnoff comes up suddenly, I find this a tad dangerous.

Do not miss that turn, or you are in for one long loop around with a rather significant U-turn up, around and back down to the interchange. If you need to go south to get back home later, you'll need to drive up the highway to the next crossover a few kilometres up the road.

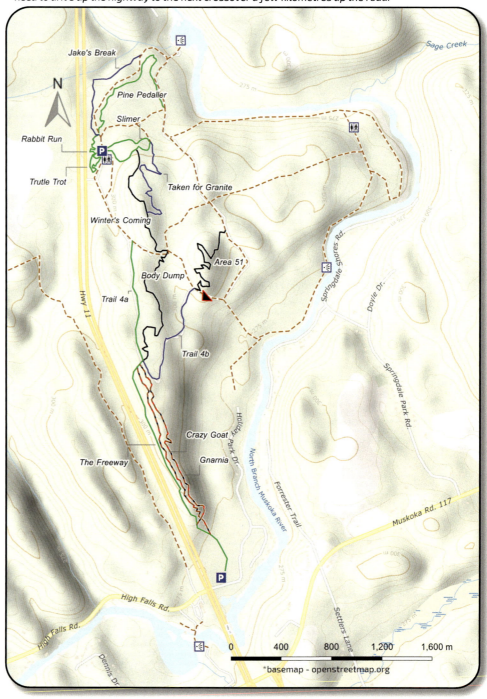

98   Best Mountain Bike Trails in Ontario

Review:

An **exciting transformation** has taken place recently at the **BRMC**. The **addition of MTB trails** has made this area worth the drive to **Bracebridge**. There are **9 km of new singletrack,** this is good news in the mountain bike world.

The highlight is a **hidden long rock ridge** that has been maximized by an avid new MTB club, the Muskoka Off-Road Cycling Association — MORCA. Along this rock feature run five trails that are a blast!

On my recent visit, club riders eagerly took me on a tour of **their fine work**. From the new south parking lot off **Holiday Park Dr.**, we headed uphill to take on the Advanced double-black-diamond **Crazy Goat**. What an introduction and immediate challenge for this old goat! LOL.

Another trail, **Gnarnia**, runs parallel with the same insane difficulty. These trails ride up over large humpback **smooth rock mounds**, around and down fast descents and across **boardwalks** in a somewhat flowy line.

If your skill level is **Advanced** and your mountain bike has **29" wheels** and **shocks** to match this rocky terrain, then you're good to go.

If you're looking for a little less challenge, a third line called **The Freeway** is an easier way up, or a fast, long bomb down to return to your car. There are other, tamer **Intermediate loops** as well (**Jakes Break** and **Taken for Granite**) that do not test your skills constantly, yet are equally well designed and varied to keep it fun.

You will find on the north end a few short **Easy loops** for mountain bike beginners to navigate (e.g. **Rabbit Run, Pine Pedaler**).

For some, just **9 km** of MTB trail may seem rather short. Ah, but it's never about the distance, it's all about the amount and variety of challenges packed in…and they've got them (and more coming…).

Need more **cycling**? Try the **8.5 km** of paths that loop around on gravel/dirt access roads, which are cross-country skiing routes in the winter.

You will encounter a few **wooden bridges** and some **benches** so you can stop and view (or even swim in) the **Muskoka River**.

There is nothing too strenuous on these doubletrack routes until you go up the **gravel hill** at the south end. A **counter-clockwise** route would be the better riding direction.

The trail is well signed and it's impossible to get too lost. As for the bugs, it's cottage country.

Duck Chutes are small rapids that can be seen from afar on the northern loop.

It is worth mentioning that across the highway, there is a picnic spot by **High Falls** at the **Hwy 117** turnoff. Here, you can see **impressive waterfalls** at any time of the year.

Not often do I get to celebrate **new trail construction**. It's labour-intensive and full of bureaucracy, but the new MORCA club has taken it on with **much success**…and your volunteer help is also welcome.

What once was just an outing for cycling in the woods now also has excellent MTB trails to consider, so add the **Bracebridge Resource Management Centre – BRMC** (can we give this a better name?) to your "**must check out" MTB list.**

Although BRMC is right by the highway, it should be noted the main entrance is tricky to find. (See **Access.***)*

Best Mountain Bike Trails in Ontario

Northern Ontario

Buckwallow – MTB Trail

Hwy 11 & Reay Rd., Gravenhurst

Trailhead - 44.95895288, -79.32451078

Length – 27 km

70% MTB singletrack 14 km
30% doubletrack access roads 13 km

Terrain – Somewhat flat woodland sloping down to a marsh, a few short climbs on the back side, wide access roads with twisty, smooth singletrack branching out

Surface – Smooth, sandy/loamy soil, drains well, large rocks, slabs, stone ridges, a few tree roots, wooden bridges

Skill – All levels, from easy family trails to insane fun for experts

Trail Pass – Day pass $12

Hours – May 1 to Oct. 31, 8 am to dusk, night riding by appointment

Facilities – Parking lot, outhouse, bike wash, bike rentals, KOA camping next door

Highlights – Great rock riding, well maintained, challenges for every level, staff are super friendly

Maps – Paper map given with your pass, signs on trails

Phone – 705 687 8858

Website – No official site, FB page – Buckwallow Cycling Center

Similar Trails – Porcupine, Agreement Forest, Laurentian, South March

Local Clubs – Muskoka Off Road Cycing Assoc.- MORCA

No Fatbike riding in the winter.

Access – Heading north on Hwy 11 just past Gravenhurst, take the interchange at 175 to Doe Lake Rd. Drive briefly north again parallel to the highway on Gravenhurst Parkway, then east on Reay Rd. E. for about 200 metres. Park on the north side; riding is on the south side of the road.

(There are few road signs to "Buck," but following the KOA camping ones will get you there.)

Trailhead is across the road and down a bit from the parking lot

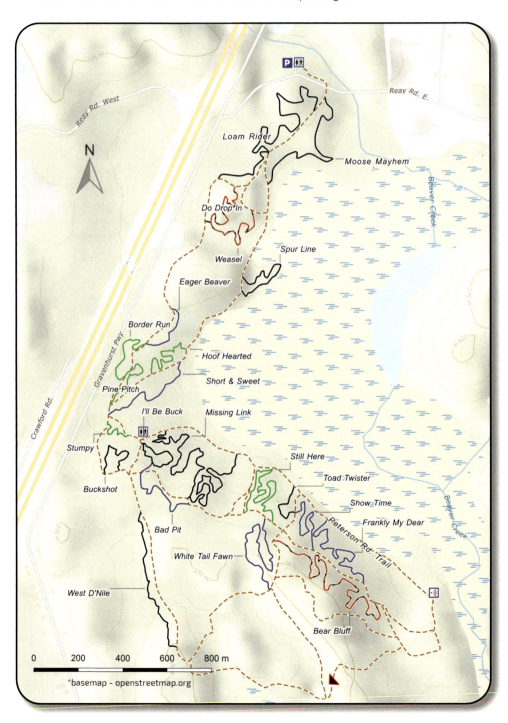

100 *Best Mountain Bike Trails in Ontario*

Review:

Just north of **Gravenhurst** by **Hwy 11**, you will find a bit of everything, from crazy **rock ridges** to friendly, smooth, winding forest trail. **Buckwallow** is one fine mountain bike ride on the **Canadian Shield**.

This location has two key features: **boulders** the size of cars, and trails running over and around rock outcrops and slabs. Yeehaw!

photo - Paulo LaBerge

With plenty of singletrack (14 km) and many undulating rocky challenges to take on, there's **lots of variety**. Yet nothing is too dangerous, though one must **stay vigilant**. Picking your speed and choosing the right lines should always be on your mind.

That said, there is ample riding for a **fun beginner/family outing**, too. Half the tracks in here are twisty, but easy, trail, and there are few hills till you get to the far end.

Mike, the owner, always seems to be there to greet you. If he's not there, you're likely to see his son, and both are chatty, friendly folk. His crew keeps the trails **well maintained** and new routes are added yearly. This trail system just **gets better all the time** (even the outhouse has fresh paint).

You will need the **paper map** given when you pay your fee. I got spun around a few times, even with the yellow signs posted. Trails are not one way, so take heed. The favoured entrances are marked with a nameplate, the exits are not. I wish they were.

Trails are accurately rated with a novel **deer-hoof rating scheme** ranging from one to six hooves. Beyond three hooves, you'd better know what you're doing or walk it. Knee and elbow pads are a good idea in here if you are unsteady or an aggressive rider.

Start by the gate on **Loam Rider** or **Moose Mayhem**—both are favourites for rock enthusiasts. Then make your way up to find fabulous rocky ridges on the **West D'Nile** trail outback.

Bomb down the **Mohawk** access road to start your way back. Now you should be warmed up enough to take on a few surprises on **Bear Bluff** a double-black-diamond trail.

photo - Paulo LaBerge

Other loops in here are more mellow and better suited for mere mortals. Even kids love them. The new **White Tail Fawn** trail has some scenic views as you roll over the **flat slab rocks**, and it flows real nice.

Most loops are under a kilometre in length, except **Missing Link** at 1.7 km—it's not to be missed. There are another **13 km** of wider routes to get you around (these are cross-country ski paths in the winter).

This is cottage country and there is a marsh on the east side, so expect bugs to bite from June onward; so just keep moving...

If you like camping, stay overnight at the **KOA campground** across the road and ride **Porcupine Ridge** or the **BRMC** up the road for even harder rock escapades.

Serious mountain bike riders know **Buckwallow** is **worth the drive** from Toronto. Popular with cottagers, it can get busy on summer weekends around midday. By the **fall, the colours** are out and the bugs and crowds are gone, so it's a great time to ride!

Best Mountain Bike Trails in Ontario

Northern Ontario

Georgian – MTB Trail

4 Nine Mile Lake Rd., Parry Sound

Trailhead - 45.42536116, -80.02818127

Length – 28 km

60% MTB singletrack
40% doubletrack access roads

Elevation – Level area with short hills (some steep); a few small drops

Terrain – Forest with clearings of flat rock and ridges; sandy spots; muddy low sections; boardwalks; some gnarly stone and roots; log hops

Skill – All levels; best for Advanced rock riders

Traffic – MTB riders, hikers, **Fatbikes** and Nordic Skiing in winter

Maps – Map board, signs (perhaps a little confusing)

Facilities – Parking lot, outhouse, shelter

Highlights – Open flat rock, ponds, very scenic, good winter Fatbiking

Trail Fee – Adults $10, under 18 $5, buy online or at bike shops in Parry Sound

Phone – 705 746 5067

Website – Get Outdoors Parry Sound, FB page

Similar Trails – Buckwallow, Walden, South March

Local Clubs – Get Outdoors Parry Sound, Bike Muskoka

Access – Northeast of Parry Sound up Hwy 124; look for Nine Mile Rd. Parking is just on other side of the train tracks.

Trailhead is east up the hill, past the chalet; trails branch off from the central Lynx loop.

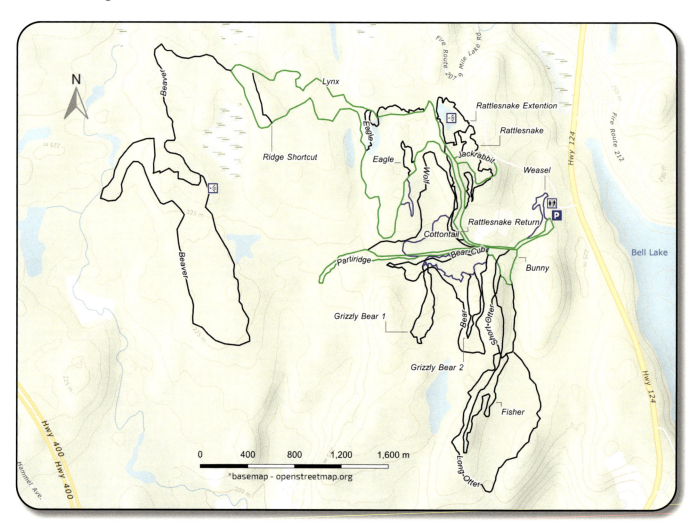

102   *Best Mountain Bike Trails in Ontario*

Review:

Up in cottage country, near **Parry Sound**, resides a MTB location called **Georgian**. If you cross-country ski, you'll know the name: Georgian Nordic. Set on the lowlands of the **Canadian Shield**, it rocks in many ways!

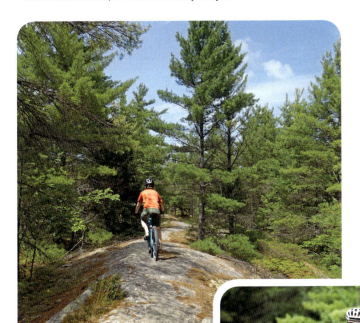

A terrain of open bare flat rock, wetlands and bush, it makes for a unique ride experience not seen in **southern Ontario**.

A relatively new area for mountain bikers to migrate to, it still is developing into an exciting destination for **avid rock riders**. Recently two loops were built on higher ground (yes, that means climbs): they're called **Grizzly Bear 1 & 2**. Rated black diamond and technical, these trails feature some nice open rock ridges. They're on my list this summer.

The easy paths—**Lynx** and **Partridge** loops—use the wider Nordic paths as an avenue to get to the singletrack from the trailhead. Most are difficult, but not impossible to enjoy. The harder **Bear**, **Wolf** and **Otter** loops go into the woods and offer a few tricky, rocky sections. In my opinion, most of it is not too crazy.

But what I really want, after driving 2 ½ hours from Toronto, is a ride I cannot get closer to home. And that's the **open flat-rock experience**.

To get that, you need to head to the **Rattlesnake** and **Extension** loops on the other end, my favourites. You'll get to hit **semi-technical**, really tight, **scenic trails** that open up to ponds, wetlands and slabs of flat rock—thoroughly enjoyable. Follow the boardwalks to a picnic table on a rock outcrop, out in the marsh. It's a perfect stop to refuel.

Right at the parking lot, a quick run on the short **Weasel** loop gives you a feel for what the rest of the harder trails may be like. It's a nice option for the those of you who are still gauging where your mountain bike skills lie (or a tad timid).

Water and **soggy ground** are a problem on the Shield, as the soil is thin and there is poor drainage. If it has rained recently, you would be best to wait a few days, not only for the water to drain but also because wet rocks and roots get too slippery. As for the mosquitoes the moisture produces, that will be your own battle to win.

Depending on your energy and the water level, try going way back into the wilds of the large **Beaver** loop, which is sure to please **rockhounds** who need more of that good stuff.

A recent conversation with management assured me that problems with general signage have improved. Not that we could not find our way back (follow the **Lynx**), it just took longer to sort out.

Good value for the price, the trail fees are an investment in helping to establish the area and cover insurance. You can pay online or at the cash box by the trailhead.

In the winter, **Fatbikes** are welcome here, both on their own trails and sharing with skiers. You can bet they get tons of snow off the bay.

Georgian is a welcomed new riding spot that should not be missed when you head to **Sudbury** or visit **Georgian Bay** this summer. With about **28 km** to ride on **23 trails**, there is plenty here for everyone; just pick your flavour. Now, that's got me thinking of ice cream again... Head to **Parry Sound** after your ride for lunch and a cone.

Best Mountain Bike Trails in Ontario

Northern Ontario

Haliburton Forest – MTB Trail

1095 Redkenn Rd., Haliburton

Trailhead - 45.22425370, -78.59098659

Length – 100 km (400 km)

25% MTB singletrack
15% hiking trail
60% doubletrack access roads

Elevation – Rolling hills among lakes with a few steep sections; access roads are generally level

Terrain – Smooth soil base, can be muddy, wet, mixed with gravel and rocks and boulder outcrops

Skill – All levels, depends how far you want to go

Traffic – MTB riders, hikers, logging trucks, ATVs, hunters (wear bright colours)

Maps – Use paper map given with entry, or download map app files from website

Facilities – Parking, comfort station, showers, picnic area, rental cabins, cookhouse, general store, wilderness campsites, treetop walks, wolf and husky enclosure tours

Highlights – Large, expansive wilderness area to explore; solitude; beautiful fall colours, overnight stays possible

Trail Fee – $16 Adults, under-17s free

Phone – 1 800 631 2198

Website – Haliburton Forest Wildlife Reserve

Similar Trails – Georgian, Minnesing, Kolapore Uplands

Local Clubs – Muskoka Off Road Cycling Association – MORCA

Access – From Hwy 118 at West Guilford, take County Rd. 7 (Kennisis Lake Rd.) north; turn on Redkenn Rd. Drive briefly to compound with red buildings at 1095 Redkenn Rd.

Riding trails fan out north beyond the base camp, office and cabins.

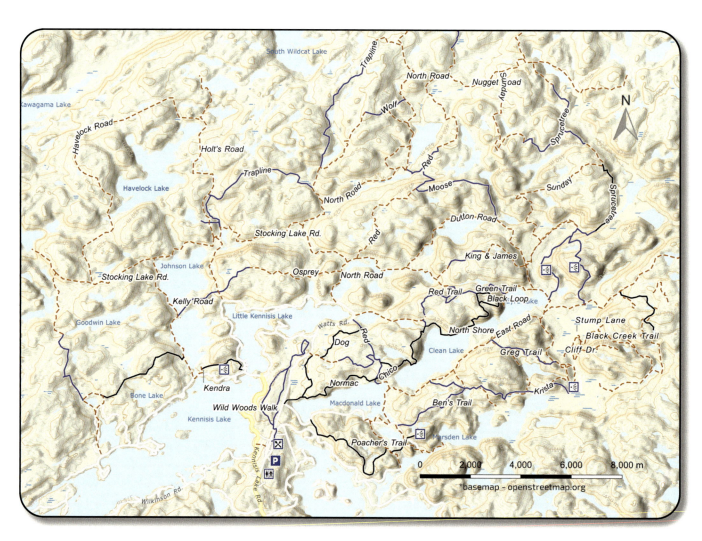

104 *Best Mountain Bike Trails in Ontario*

Review:

Haliburton Forest is Ontario's **ultimate XC** MTB wilderness adventure. With more than **400 km of routes** to explore, you truly can get away from it all. Assorted access roads and singletrack to discover will keep your riding group on the go.

This **huge forest** area (100,000 acres) is below **Algonquin Park** and a 30-minute drive north from the town of **Haliburton**.

Years ago, I would go in the fall, stay for the weekend and ride the trails with my bike group. Good times, no bugs and cool mornings inspired us to ride many kilometres into the bush. With maps in hand, we headed out on dirt and gravel roads in search of **Eldorado**. Would we **find the ultimate trail** today, the one we would all talk about later over a campfire?

Even if we didn't, the journey and adventures with friends were priceless. The scenery here in pure **Northern Ontario,** especially with the fall colours over the many lakes, was beautiful. The **clean air** and **stillness of the forest** were a sharp contrast to the rat race most of us endured during the week.

Since those days, much remains the same at the **Haliburton Forest & Wildlife Reserve.** When I chatted with management in spring 2020, they mentioned a few added services and improvements (you can find more info on their website).

I cannot be specific as to which current MTB trails rock and which suck. This has changed over the years and will continue to do so, as this is a **working forest.** Logging activities will eventually erase today's trails—no matter how wonderful—and create opportunities for new ones.

I was assured that there are **100 km** of **singletrack** to **mountain bike** ride. Wherever those loops lead you these days, the terrain remains the same as it was years ago. It's hilly country with **hundreds of lakes,** ponds, creeks and wetlands. On this journey expect plenty of cardio climbs and with satisfying long descents.

You may ride logging roads that range from a mellow mix of sand and gravel to rock strewn chaos that is all but unrideable. MTB trails consist of smooth black soil, leaf matter, sticks and mud. Be watchful for fallen limbs and trees. Fieldstones and flat rock are also abundant. Down on the lower sections, be prepared to test puddles, some substantial. You are certain to get wet & dirty—what fun!

Generally speaking, the **best riding** is closer to the main gate by **Kennisis Lake.** The further back away from base camp, the less frequented the routes, the rougher, grown in the track. Some bushwhacking and bike hauling may be required.

This **XC MTB adventure** can take you in way back where you may come across hunting camps, logging operations and wildlife (if you know how to find it). Certainly, there are opportunities to find an idyllic lake to call your own. Do lunch, have a swim.

With so much to ride here, and with it being a **3-hour drive from Toronto,** staying over in the area is a good call. Cabins can be rented; there is a general store, cookhouse and other activities like a canopy walkway tour, a visit to the Haliburton Forest Wolf Centre and/or husky kennel, or fishing, paddling a canoe, and more.

So make plans and pack all you need for this **wilderness bike expedition** into the unknown. Experience some freedom and add **a little nature back into your life.**

Best Mountain Bike Trails in Ontario

Northern Ontario

Hiawatha – MTB Trail

Fifth Line E. & Landslide Rd., Sault Ste. Marie   Trailhead - 46.58683194, -84.27954975

Length – 26 km

70% MTB singletrack
20% hiking trail
10% doubletrack access roads

Elevation – Fairly level in the north Pinder area; drops into valleys on the other side of the main road; medium to large hills, some steep and sandy

Terrain – Smooth soil base, sandy spots, some gravel, large boulders, a few mud holes

Skill – All levels

Traffic – MTB riders, hikers, (bugs, bears...)

Maps – Map boards at trailhead, paper map at the Sugar Shack office, numbered posts on trails

Facilities – Parking lot, outhouses, park office, shelter, picnic tables, ice cream shop!

Highlights – Fine quality, well-maintained trail, variety and challenges

Trail Fee – Free

Phone – 705 946 8530

Website – Hiawatha Highlands Conservation Area

Similar Trails – 3 Stage, Buckwallow, Walden

Local Clubs – Sault Cycling Club, FB page

Access – 10 km north of downtown Sault Ste. Marie. Three large parking lots exist close together, with separate trailheads near where the road bends at Fifth Line East when it meets Landslide Road. Look for the blue Soo Finnish Ski Club lodge.

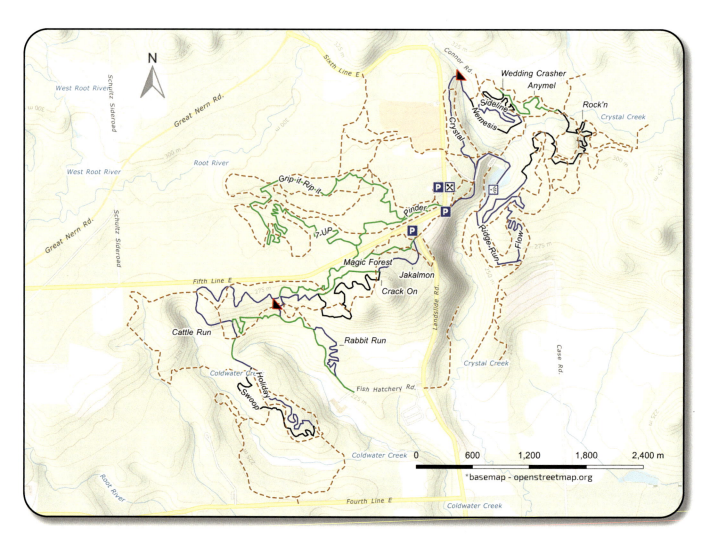

106   *Best Mountain Bike Trails in Ontario*

Review:

North of **Sault Ste. Marie** in the **wooded highlands** not far from town, the Hiawatha trails are the perfect place for any mountain biker in need of a spin session in (or a break from driving through) **Northern Ontario**.

Here you will find about **26 km** of marked trail, pretty evenly split among three different areas. These three zones give every skill level some joy and exercise.

The **5.2 km Pinder** trails are on relatively flat terrain with mellow inclines that are perfect for **Beginners**.

On the other side of the road, the terrain drops into a few valleys. Here are the **11 km Red Pine** trails, **Intermediate** loops composed of old tall pines and long hills. You'll find plenty of twisty track and fast descents with a few more advanced sections.

I rode the **Hiawatha** area on a summer road trip with my son; we only had time to do one section: the **9.4 km** set of loops that make up the **Crystal Creek** trails. We found them **thoroughly satisfying**.

The terrain is a mix of **forest soil, sand and gravel**. Though it's not too hilly, there are **short climbs** and **large rocks** to weave around as you ride (one way) through this mature forest.

Most of the track is **cut for MTB riding**, **flows well** with just enough of a challenge and is well maintained. We found a number of **nice berms** on some fast turns and also a few small mud puddles to zig around.

The more difficult trails are marked **black diamond** on the map, but we found them only briefly harder to do. If you're feeling unsure, you can just walk the tricky bits, as most of the trail is regular fare for any seasoned rider. The long, sandy downhill at the beginning is **steep, so keep that front wheel straight** or you will wash out.

I found the **Wedding Crasher** at post **#21** to be the highlight of the ride, with many **switchbacks around rocky outcrops**—just my kinda buzz. This Advanced section can be bypassed, but give it a try. And **Wave** at post **#17** is fun to crank through. It repeatedly turns back and forth through the trees 'til it straightens out to give you a fast, flowy descent.

At the end of the loops, follow the cross-country ski path down to a **high dam, pond** and a **chance to swim.** As you cross the creek bridge, beautiful **Crystal Falls** are on the right. Follow the ramp to the rushing water.

Finally, you need to do the long climb up out of the valley on the paved road. Yeah, this part kind of sucks, but hey, it leads you to an **ice cream shop** at the top. Timely and rewarding!

Signage is a very simple numbering system on the trails, and one might get spun around when meeting up with the winter Nordic paths. Printing a **paper map** is recommended, or you can obtain one at the **Sugar Shack** office just west down the road from the parking lots.

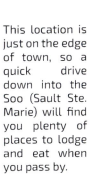

Expect midsummer mosquitoes; keep moving and consider repellent. A **bear bell** might be a good idea if you are on your own. I wouldn't say there is a lot of rock you could crash onto, but padding may be a good choice if you're a risk taker.

Fatbikes are welcomed in summer or winter. They get tons of snow here.

This location is just on the edge of town, so a quick drive down into the Soo (Sault Ste. Marie) will find you plenty of places to lodge and eat when you pass by.

Northern Ontario is a BIG place; I only wish there were more stops like Hiawatha on our tour. It's a worthy destination for any adventure-seeking MTB rider road-trippers (and their kids, too).

Best Mountain Bike Trails in Ontario

Northern Ontario

Laurentian – MTB Trail

Lake Laurentian Conservation Area, Sudbury

Trailhead - 46.46107238, -80.96340150

Length – 50 +km

80% hiking /MTB trail
20% doubletrack access roads

Elevation – Large, smooth rock mounds with a few steep inclines. Level riding by the water.

Terrain – Gravel sand base, with grasses and random rocks and boulders on path; gravel access roads; open rock ridges and rock mounds, big drops, gnarly bits and mud patches

Skill – Intermediate, mostly Advanced – very technical

Traffic – MTB riders, popular hiking area, Nordic skiing in the winter

Maps – Limited map boards and trail swatches on posts

Facilities – Parking lots, washrooms at chalet, food and lodging close by

Highlights – Open, flat-rock riding, challenging, very scenic, hilltop vistas, fall colours

Trail Fee – Free (+ donation box)

Phone – 705 674 5249

Website – Lake Laurentian Conservation Area

Similar Trails – Walden, Porcupine Ridge, Buckwallow, South March

Local Clubs – Walden Mountain Bike Club - WMBC

Access – Three start points:

- **Laurentian University** - Parking lot behind the sports field beside the athletics building (metered parking)
- 2309 South Bay Rd., in the **Lake Laurentian Conservation Area** parking lot
- At the end of South Bay Rd., in the **BioSki Club** lot.

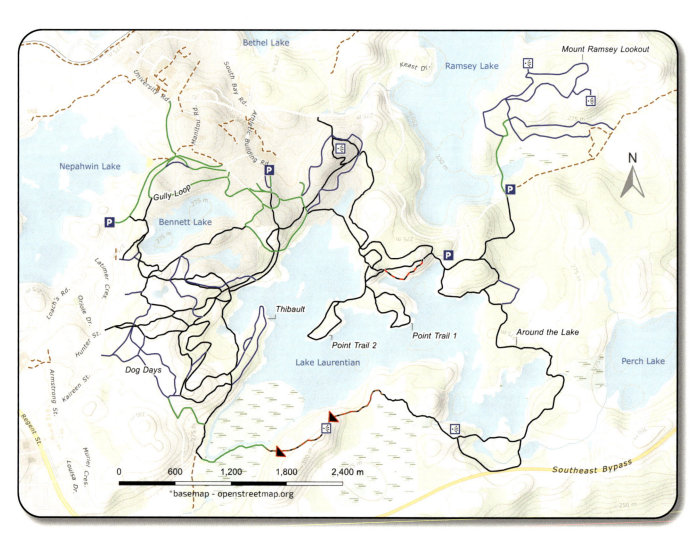

108   *Best Mountain Bike Trails in Ontario*

Review:

If you love to ride **open, flat rock**, you will get more than enough thrills at **Laurentian** in **Sudbury**. You'll find **50+ km** to crank and conquer behind **Laurentian University**, encompassing the **Lake Laurentian Conservation Area**.

This is an **adventurous rock ride** with half of it requiring **Advanced skills** – Attention, you have reached **black-diamond country!**

Beyond the gravel roads used as Nordic ski paths, there is little here for riders who have not mastered the basics. **Big drops, insane climbs** and **precarious lines** are the norms. You need to be in control and brave.

Now that I have scared any wannabes, let's get on to the review, LOL.

Though much of the area is a **technical minefield** of random rocks, there are stretches of smooth soil and beautiful **Precambrian igneous rock** to roll over.

There are **lots of hills**, including some bald ones. Riding to the tops is surreal for this southern Ontario boy. Once you reach the peak on these **treeless rock mounds**, the sights are substantial and there is this buzz of being **"King of the Hill!"**

The **Red trail** by the university and the **Blue marked loops** will keep you busy discovering and climbing numerous **rock peaks** between wooded valleys.

This area has few directional signs or maps, so it is not always certain you are heading where you thought. Packing a map of some form would help, or hey, just wing it.

The **Around the Lake** and **Thibault** singletrack trails run close to the water and when combined make a beautiful ride through the stands of **white birches**.

Another fine set of loops are the two **Point Trail** loops out onto the peninsulas and the adjacent trails to get there.

Head the other way for a **2 km** moderate climb to the lookout on **Mount Ramsey Summit**.

If you want to circle **Lake Laurentian,** have enough stamina for the **5 km** difficult and at times soggy wilderness trek. There is a monster hill (35 m) that will likely be a **hike-a-bike** up and questionable ride down. But the **view from the top**? Wow! (Pack a camera.)

At this point do I even have to mention that a **full-suspension rig**, preferably with **large tires**, is the ticket? Well, it is. **Wearing some armour** is also a consideration, depending on your enthusiasm.

Bugs thin out by the end of July, and millions of **blueberries** are there for the picking. Expect it to be **slippery when wet**, with a few surprise **muddy patches,** and boardwalks built.

This **mecca of rock riding** is on the edge of the city of **Sudbury,** mere minutes from lodging and dining after your **full day of heroics.**

It's a must for those in search of new challenges. You'll improve your skills while taking in a **very scenic day**, and it's great for your cardio, too.

Need more rock'n and roll'n? Head to **Walden**, 30 minutes west. In my opinion, it's different, but just as good.

Best Mountain Bike Trails in Ontario

Northern Ontario

Minnesing – MTB Trail

Hwy 60, Algonquin Park

Trailhead -   45.55572602, -78.60279285

Length – 5, 9, 15 or 23 km loops

70% hiking trail
30% doubletrack access roads

Elevation – A wide path that ascends upwards, with a long run back down and large, rolling hills

Terrain – Mostly smooth soil with rocky inclines, lots of muddy patches, and a few wooden bridges; the back loop sees less use and is overgrown

Skill – Intermediate

Traffic – Remote, with the occasional biker or hikers as well as Nordic skiers, Fatbikes and people snowshoeing in the winter. Wildlife? A bear bell might be a good thought

Maps – Located at trailhead; a few signs at junctions on the trail, use GPS map app, weak cell signal

Facilities – A large parking lot, outhouses, vaulted toilets, ranger cabins, log cabin with a wood stove; bike rentals in the summer on Hwy 60

Highlights – Enjoy as much wilderness, and solitude, as you can handle

Trail Fee – Park day passes, or overnight camping passes, required

Phone – 705 633 5572

Website – Ontario Parks, Algonquin Provincial Park

Similar Trails –
Haliburton Forest,
Wildwood,
Kolapore Uplands

Local Clubs – None

Access – In Algonquin Park, along Hwy 60 near Cache Lake and Canisbay Lake. Take the dirt road north for a few minutes until you reach the large parking lot and cabin.

The trailhead is north of the parking lot, on the east side of the cabin.

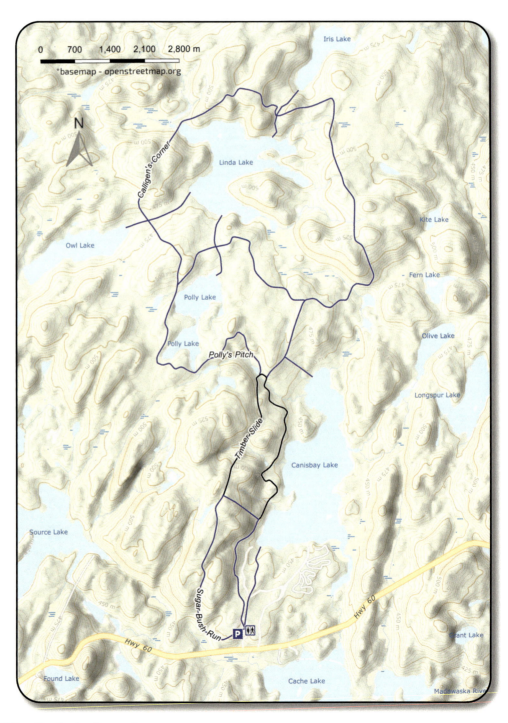

Best Mountain Bike Trails in Ontario

Review:

The **Minnesing** trail in **Algonquin Provincial Park** offers mountain bikers a challenging **cross-country** style ride. It's perfect for those who want wilderness, adventure and mileage.

It has long consisted of **hiking trails** that are now officially also **MTB loops**. Bikers will experience a **long** and **fast forest** ride, mainly along singletrack hiking paths with an old gravel road on the return.

There are four consecutive loops to choose from: **5, 9, 15** and **23 km** approximately.

The flat sections remain a **fast, smooth ride on a black topsoil** with not too many roots. When you can **find a line** between the rocks and roots, **most hills are easy enough to climb**.

As with many hiking trails, **erosion is a problem** and over the years water has washed away the soil from the steeper inclines, revealing round **rocks** and **boulders**. This is a product of blazing a straight trail on a hill. When it rains, water rushes down like a river, washing the soil away. To fix those erosion issues switchbacks and grade reversals are needed.

There are **many large, muddy puddles** at the **bottom** of these hills likely during most of the summer. You have to skirt around or take your chances and bolt through. A few boardwalks help to cross some of this mucky mess, but more would be helpful. According to a park ranger I spoke with,* new ones have recently been constructed.

There are a few small, old signs marking the trails, although I doubt you will come across any other side trails to get lost on.

I found the **shortcut** on the second loop to be so overgrown and steep that a **hike-a-bike was required** to get up it. While it did bring us back, we took plenty of pounding down a gravel road peppered with **large, round stones** and **rocks**. This is an **old coach road** that, many years ago, took **tourists** to a **lodge** from the **train depot**; there is no sign of that lodge now or the station.

Although it is a fast descent on the way back, this is definitely no fun to climb, so I recommend starting the trail in on the **east side** of the log cabin.

I've only completed the first two loops, but have heard the outer **12 km** loop at **Callighen's Corners** is harder to manage, as it is less frequented and likely you will be doing a bit of bushwhack'n. Certainly, it's a ride to **prove yourself** if you are motivated enough!

The last few years, this large back loop has been closed, so call the gatehouse and check beforehand if you are planning to include this on your ride.

Being here sooner than **mid-July** is bound to be **bug warfare**. Later on, if the summer is dry, the mosquitoes are tolerable—if you keep moving.

This can be a fast ride, yet a long journey. It could rain, you could break a chain, need extra water, see a bear... So **be prepared, pack well** and tell someone where you're heading. It's frequented by few, **you may not see anyone on your trek**.

A "rustic ride" it is, but not a dangerous one if you are an experienced rider and adventurous. Make it a day trip or an overnight **Bikepacking** outing with friends. You can also connect from **Canisbay Lake Campground** next door and stay awhile.

This is a great ride for your **Fatbike**, even in the winter, though that does depend on how many others have packed down the snow base before you: Algonquin can easily get a metre of snow by February. There is a cabin at the trailhead that has wood if you need to warm up.

Unfortunately, the Nordic trails in the park do not welcome **Fatbikes**; try the **Rail Trail**. I wonder if in the summer months you could ride those ski tracks?

* I also discussed with the ranger how such a large park like **Algonquin** *has so little to offer to mountain bikers. He agreed there was great potential for new MTB loops.*

As to when and how this may come about, I think we need to voice our interest as MTB riders to get things started. That squeaky-chain-gets-the-oil syndrome.

Best Mountain Bike Trails in Ontario

Northern Ontario

Porcupine Ridge – MTB Trail

Hwy 15, Bracebridge

Trailhead - 45.02633567, -79.36111200

Length – 12 km

60% MTB singletrack
20% hiking trail
20% dirt road

Elevation – Slopes up to the ridge with a steep climb; levels off in the back, with rock mounds and small slopes

Terrain – A mix of smooth soil track and flat rock. Plenty of rocks and boulders to navigate around and over, plus wood structures

Traffic – Light MTB use, with hikers near the entrance

Skill – Intermediate to (very) Advanced

Trail Fee – Donation post; be nice and pay something

Facilities – Parking lot, outhouse, camping at Whispering Pines next door

Highlights – Great rock riding, challenging, lookout, possible swim in the river

Maps – Map board at the trailhead, new signposts for each loop

Website – Porcupine Ridge on Facebook Muskoka

Similar Trails – Buckwallow, Agreement Forest, Laurentian, South March

Local Club – Muskoka Off Road Cycling Assoc , MORCA on Facebook

Access – Park across the street from Santa's Village theme park. Parking is in the new location (the second lot).

The trailhead is at the back, past the sign and pay station.

Open May 1st to October 31st

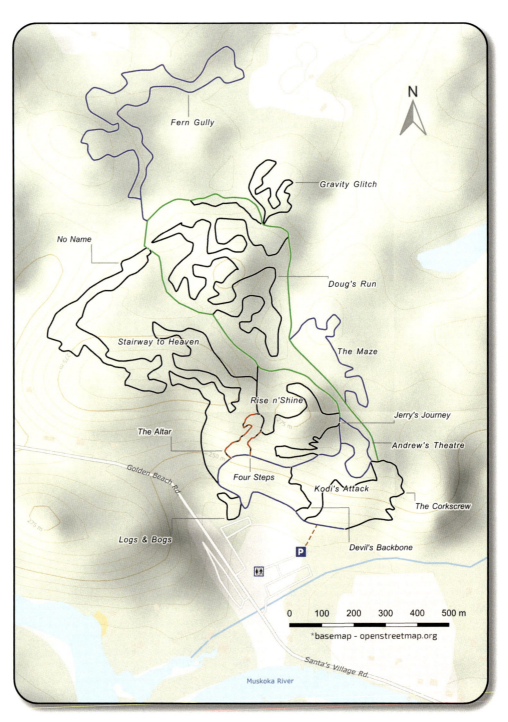

112   Best Mountain Bike Trails in Ontario

Review:

Porcupine Ridge is one of the most **advanced mountain bike** trail areas to ride in Ontario.

It's truly a **technical playground** of loops with plenty of rock to ride, steep, slow gnarly sections and tempting structures to take on. You'll find massive granite **flat rock** with **steep inclines, rock gardens** and **high bridges** on this awesome trail network.

And if you need to test your skills and give the legs a good workout, well, here it is.

Recently reopened, the trailhead and car lot have shifted to the right (south) 100 metres. Almost all of the **12 km** of trail has been cut for MTB riding by locals, and they did a great job! Signs have been updated and you should not be losing your way.

From the trailhead, the ride starts with a **climb to the ridge.** On the right is the easier (but not that easy) **Corkscrew** to work your way up. Or go at it on the shorter **Devil's Backbone,** where a minefield of rock awaits.

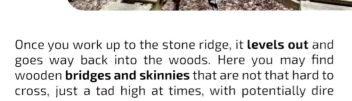

Once you work up to the stone ridge, it **levels out** and goes way back into the woods. Here you may find wooden **bridges and skinnies** that are not that hard to cross, just a tad high at times, with potentially dire consequences if you fall off. For those who live dangerously.

Trails marked **double black diamond** here are exactly that: **difficult X2!!** So much fun if you are game. The variety of gnarly trail plus scenic views makes this place a **gem.** (Which we almost lost.)

If I have scared away half of you, that's good, because this place is **for experienced riders** on solid MTBs with **big rims** and **dual shocks.** You want easy, then ride the road. This will wake you up and spank you if you daydream!

Before you ride some of the nasty structures and technical bits, I would suggest first scouting them out for surprises.

On weekdays, few riders are in there, so be sure you have a **rescue plan.** Your cell signal can be weak out there. **Ride with a buddy** if you can, and carry a spare of everything in case you get trashed. Wearing some padding is a thought...Oh, and expect hungry bugs in the spring.

Enough warning for the inexperienced. If you are a **fearless, hardcore,** full-on MTB rider, then you have to go and give it a try. **You will love it!**

MORCA, the new local MTB club, has done a wonderful job maintaining these loops. **Drop a donation** at the trailhead post on the way out (or online later) if you got your thrills in.

Need more crank'n? ...then drop in at the **Bracebridge Resource Management Centre, BRMC** where they are building new wicked track.

Best Mountain Bike Trails in Ontario   113

Northern Ontario

Seguin – Rail / MTB Trail

Parry Sound to Kearney

Length – 80+ km (one way)
95% rail trail
5% roads, crossings, detours

Elevation – This route is not as flat as most rail lines, and it dips down to cross smaller bridges

Terrain – A crushed-stone base with larger rail bedding rocks; rather sandy in areas; large puddles after a rain; rock cuts for the MTB rider

Skill – Easy

Traffic – Busy on summer weekends with bicyclists, hikers, horseback riders, and ATVs (main users); snowmobiles in winter

Maps – Adequate signage at gates; post markers along the trail have been improved

Facilities – Parking, food and washrooms can be found in the towns of Parry Sound, Sprucedale, and Kearney, as well as at Hwy 400 and Oastler Park

Trailhead - 45.30813313, -79.89506969

Highlights – A scenic, hillier ride with rock cuts and wooden bridges. Enjoy the falls and the ghost town of Seguin Falls, as well as wetlands, many creeks, and farmland

Trail Fee – Free for non-motorized use

Phone – 888 587 3762

Website – Park to Park

Similar Trail – Algonquin, North Simcoe, Two Lakes

Local Clubs – MORCA, Bike Muskoka

Access – A few good access points may be found at:

- Parry Sound Harbour at Glen Burney Rd.
- Hwy 400, approximately 10 km south of Parry Sound at Horseshoe Lake Rd.
- Orville Community Centre; the trail starts 400 m east
- Seguin Falls at Hwy 518 N and Nipissing Rd. E; roadside parking as trail crosses Nipissing Rd.
- Sprucedale at Hwy 518 N and Stisted Rd. S; street parking

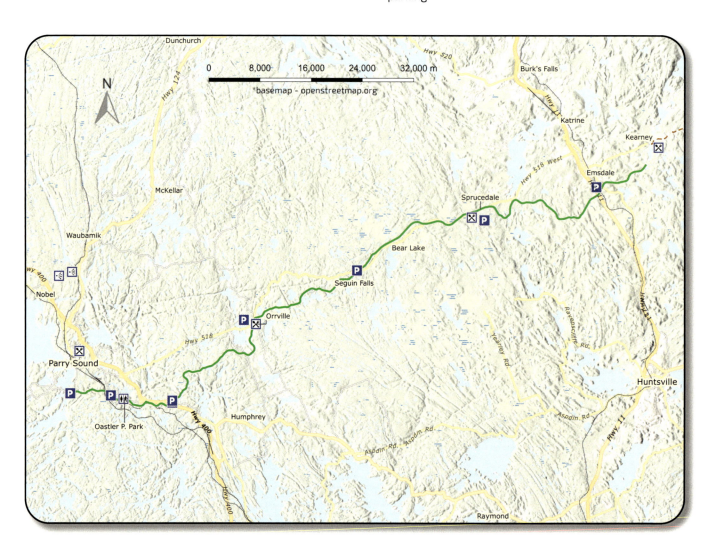

114   *Best Mountain Bike Trails in Ontario*

Review:

I have recommended this **Rail Trail** in this guide because not only do you need a MTB bike to ride it, it's also is a **XC adventure** different kind from the usual twisty trails we do.

Starting at the **Parry Sound** harbour on **Georgian Bay**, this old rail bed passes over **Hwy 400** and crosses **Hwy 518** many times, leading to **Hwy 11** and eventually fading into the bush somewhere past **Kearney**.

This is not your average **Rail Trail**, although it is well-maintained and gets plenty of use by **ATVs** and **snowmobiles.** This causes the terrain to get chewed up and dusty, with large rocks, loose gravel, and sand everywhere.

Different sections have **large puddles** (more like ponds) that are wide and deep, and you may have no choice but to ride through. Expect flooding in the spring.

So this terrain is best suited for mountain bikes, **Fatbikes** and perfect for a **Bikepacking** trek.

Although it doesn't deliver lots of thrills, it still travels through serene cottage country around lakes, through forest, farm fields, wetlands and rock cuts. And unlike most Rail Trails, which are rather flat, this one delivers some small hills where the original bridges (sold for scrap when the track was lifted) were replaced with small wooden ones at a lower grade.

This gives riders a **short hill** down in order to cross and head back up the other side. That said, the full length actually slopes gradually up **150 metres** from **Georgian Bay**.

At **80+ km one way**, this is a long trail, and you need to choose just a section of it for a day's ride.

I suggest a **43-km** loop I have done a few times. Head out from **Hwy 400** to **Orville**, then back on **Hwy 518**. At **Oastler Park Dr.**, ride south to meet up with the trail before again crossing the **400**. I found the road traffic not busy on the return, and the paved shoulders on **Oastler** were surprisingly spacious.

Another good starting point is at the south end of **Parry Sound**, with an option to make a loop using **Oastler Park Dr.**, but this time head the other way through town for a short but hilly loop.

On the east side is an excellent place to pick up the trail, in the town of **Sprucedale**. Unfortunately, I am not so sure about **Kearney;** it could be overgrown and swampy.

For the more **adventurous MTB rider**, this can be a great **Bikepacking** trip. Take your tent, pack some food, and make it a three- to four-day trek from end to end. I saw signs of scenic, rustic campsites along the route, and Oastler Lake Provincial Park, which provides a few more comforts, is on the trail and makes a good base for completing the loops mentioned.

Consider going in the autumn when there is less traffic and fewer bugs, and the fall colours are out. Either way, enjoy this wild, rugged part of northern Ontario—start planning!

History – The railway was built by the former **Ottawa, Arnprior and Parry Sound Railway** in **1891**, funded by lumber baron **J.R. Booth**.

Trains carried timber from **Ottawa** to **Georgian Bay** for shipbuilding and grain was sent eastward until 1933, when the **Cache Two-Rivers** bridge needed repair.

The bridge was deemed too expensive to fix, so rails west of it were abandoned and by the **1950s** they had been removed and sold as scrap. Now it's a wonderful place to ride.

Best Mountain Bike Trails in Ontario

Northern Ontario

Sir Sam's – MTB DH Trail

1054 Liswood Road, Haliburton Area

Trailhead – 45.12996980, -78.48180813

Length – 23 km

70% MTB singletrack 14 km
30% Downhill runs 9 km

Elevation – Picture a ski hill: you ride up, bomb down, most trails are on flat, lumpy top

Terrain – Smooth soil base, sandy spots, some gravel and roots, can be muddy

Skill – All levels, but best for Advanced riders

Traffic – MTB and downhill bikes, hikers

Maps – Map board at trailhead, lots of signage on trail

Hours – Opens mid-May till mid-October. Chairlift, services, lodge open weekends during summer and fall, honour system during the week

Facilities – Large parking lot, lodge, washrooms, food, pro shop, rentals, lessons, racing

Highlights – A chairlift makes it easy to go up; great views from the top

Trail Fee – $15 for 2 hrs., $20 all day (includes one chairlift ride)

Unlimited chairlift/trail access $35 for 2 hrs., $45 all day

Trail-only access during off-hours (place $10 in honour box, sign waiver)

Phone – 705 754 2298

Website – Sir Sam's

Similar Trails – Blue Mountain, Horseshoe, Kelso

Local Clubs – None

Access – From Hwy 118, taking Hwy 6 or 14 will get you to Eagle Lake. Follow Sir Sam's Rd. to 1054 Liswood Rd. Park by the lodge at the bottom of the ski hill.

The easy way to the top is riding the chairlift, or you can pedal up the switchback, which starts close to the lift on the centre of the ski hill.

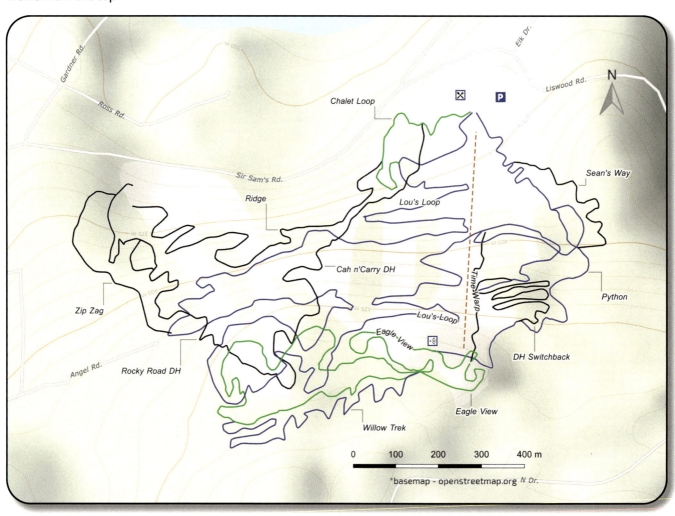

116   *Best Mountain Bike Trails in Ontario*

Review:

Unknown to many, **Sir Sam's** is a downhill ski resort north of the town of **Haliburton**. In the summer it transforms into a great little **DH** (downhill) and XC ride park.

This **90-metre** ski hill has **23 km** of runs heading down the slope and circling the top. The terrain is a smooth clay/loam base with gravel and sandy spots and not as rocky as I expected.

In the forest trails on top, which are not that hilly, you will find some stone, roots and mud patches. These twist around nicely and are a great place for a beginner to hang out. There is also a **BMX pump track** and a few **structures** to play on out in the open area.

Time spent in this wooded area on top will take longer to cruise as the bombs down the hill can be over comparatively quickly.

Most trails here can be managed by any seasoned MTB rider on a sound bike. The black-diamond runs going downhill are a blast—you do need to know what you're doing. Thankfully the resort has plenty of signage to warn you of any perils.

If you are just getting into the crazy world of **DH riding**, this is a good starter hill before taking on Blue Mountain or heading to Quebec. There are some sweet bombers and a few small jumps to go aerial.

Riding the lift up is an unusual treat. And the vista from the top is **gorgeous** looking out over Eagle Lake.

The basic two-hour fee gets you one **ride up the lift**, then you are on your own next time. The 1-km pedal-power climb is a gradual **switchback** up the open face of the ski hill. **Not too hard** the first time...by the fourth, I was getting a good workout.

Learn your way around so you do not accidentally take a trail going down too soon. When you are ready, if you're not that experienced, take the **Intermediate** long cruiser criss-crossing the hill on **Lou's Loop** to find your way to the bottom. The next time, you can do the faster way down on the **2-km Python**: Hold onto your brakes, kids.

Now you are ready to try the **expert black** runs (or maybe not). More vertical, tighter turns and rock outcrops are served up as you fly down. These are sure to please most DH riders. The **Zig Zag** DH trail is tons of fun, but remember at the bottom there is no working chairlift on that end of the hill. You will have to grind it up partway on the **Ridge** trail, then cut across for the express chair to the top.

The ski hill is a mix of smooth soil and aggregate that can get dusty in the hot summer months and too slippery after a good rain. In the spring, it takes a while for the snow to melt and the trails to dry out. Add the June bug season and you might want to wait till at least July to show up. **Sir Sam's** is a beautiful experience into the fall season, with the colours out.

The lodge is open on weekends when the place gets busy. It's one of the few places you can rent a set of wheels and get bike repairs.

The mountain bike riding here is different, enjoyable and a thrill. I just wish it were twice the size. You will likely ride everything many times.

For riders coming in from their cottages, this is a great day trip. The town of **Haliburton** is 15 minutes south of here for eats and a bed. From **Toronto** and elsewhere, you might wish to stay over, as the drive is considerable and the riding will certainly tire you out...in a good way.

Best Mountain Bike Trails in Ontario

Northern Ontario

Torrance Barrens – MTB Trail

Hwy 13 Southwood Rd., Gravenhurst

Trailhead - 44.94151396, -79.51361098

Length – 10 km

100% hiking trail

Elevation – Rather level ground with undulating rock mounds and rocky crevices.

Terrain – Flat stone, smooth soil, grasses, muddy sections, puddles, stairs, boardwalk, large ponds

Skill – Easy to Advanced

Traffic – MTB riders, hikers (and bugs, LOL)

Maps – A few signposts; stone or paint swatches as markers on the trails

Facilities – Parking lot, outhouse

Highlights – Open spaces, flat-rock riding, photogenic, solitude, blueberries!

Trail Pass – Free

Phone – 705 765 3156

Website – Muskoka Trails

Similar Trails – Bracebridge RMC, Buckwallow, Georgian

Local Clubs – Muskoka Off Road Cycling Assoc.- MORCA

Access – One entry point at parking lot; there is a sign for the Barrens; loops can be taken in either direction

Directions – From Hwy 169, turn south onto Southwood Rd. (Muskoka County Rd. 13) and travel 7 km to the Torrance Barrens sign on the north side. Park on the flat rock.

From the south, take the large exit off Hwy 11 just past the Severn River Bridge onto County Rd. 13 (Southwood Rd.) and drive about 25 km until you reach the parking lot.

This drive is gorgeous when the fall colours come out.

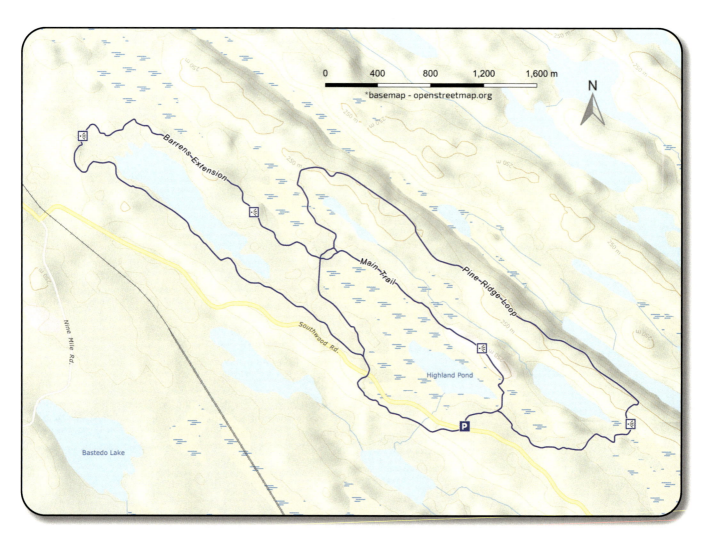

118   Best Mountain Bike Trails in Ontario

Review:

Torrance Barrens Conservation Reserve is a **unique 10-km trail ride** with large, **open flat-rock** areas along most of the three loops.

This **very scenic**, remote location has few trees, numerous ponds and great vistas.

The ride over tabletop rock mounds is **easy for most MTB riders**, with the more tricky parts between them.

As you descend between the mounds, the trail typically gets vegetated with a few trees (and their roots) and loose rocks.

When you get to the bottom, **some crossings have mud and puddles to manage**. The level of recent rain will determine how much of this you get (and the bug population).

This pattern of smooth, open rock followed by bush and loose rock, then mud patches, repeats itself throughout the ride.

There are a few stairs to haul your bike up and **boardwalks** to cross, as this is a somewhat straight hiking trail, not a twisty track cut specifically for MTB bikes.

Regardless, it's **a joy to ride for any level.** Beginners will likely need to walk the drops, quick climbs and mud. The rest of us will love it.

This hiking trail has **three main loops**, which may have a few hikers on them. That said, even on busy weekends when the car lot fills up, you can still find your own space.

This is a very secluded, quiet place, so take care to not go out too late or on your own. Help is far away. **Bala,** 12 km to the north, would be the closest town.

The trail is marked with **stone cairns, white paint marks on rocks** and a few metal signs which are not always easy to find. There are a few maps on posts, too, but none at the parking lot.

Pay attention to where you're going, because you could get totally lost in the open spaces if you wander too far.

The area is called an **oak savannah** for its lack of vegetation and types of plants. Look for **blueberries** in July if it's been a wet spring.

We need to talk about the bugs. They will be there ripping you to bits in June and early July on a hot day. **Deer flies** are attracted to movement, dark hair, shades of black and dark blue. Using

photo - Paulo LaBerge

DEET bug spray and wearing beige, white or green colours can help… or outride the critters, LOL! Another idea is to ride this trail from late August into the fall season, to avoid bugs and enjoy the amazing fall colours.

This seems like a great spot for a **Fatbike** ride, though winter snows may be too deep.

Enjoy the drive there on **Southwood Rd. – County Rd. 13**; from either direction, it is wonderful. Winding through the savannah, so remote, it's likely my **favourite highway** in all Ontario.

Best Mountain Bike Trails in Ontario   119

Northern Ontario

Walden – MTB Trail

1 Denis Ave., Naughton

Trailhead -   46.40387658, -81.19238974

Length – 22 km

60% MTB singletrack
40% doubletrack ski trail

Elevation – Easy section is flat, the rest is on the large hill; a few tough climbs and big drops

Terrain – Open, flat rock; smooth soil; wood chips; roots; boulders; main x-country ski paths, tall grass and boardwalks bridge soggy sections

Skill – Beginners will appreciate the few flat, easy loops and the x-c ski trails; the rest is best for the Advanced rider

Traffic – Light use from mountain bike riders and hikers. In winter, Nordic skiing, **Fatbikes** and snowshoeing

Trail Maps – Map board at trailhead; well-signed markers on trails, painted dots on rocks; six routes mapped; paper map at trailhead with a donation

Facilities – Parking lot, outhouse, Fatbike rentals in the winter

Highlights – Advanced skills required, open bare rock riding, lookouts

Trail Pass – Free

Phone – None

Website – Walden Mountain Bike Club

Similar Trail – Laurentian, South March, Porcupine Ridge

Local Clubs – Walden Mountain Bike Club, Sudbury Women's MTB Group

Access – Drive approximately 20 km west of Sudbury on Hwy 55 to the town of Naughton. Turn north at St. Louis St., then head west to 1 Denis Ave., the Walden Nordic Centre.

Trails are open June to middle of October.

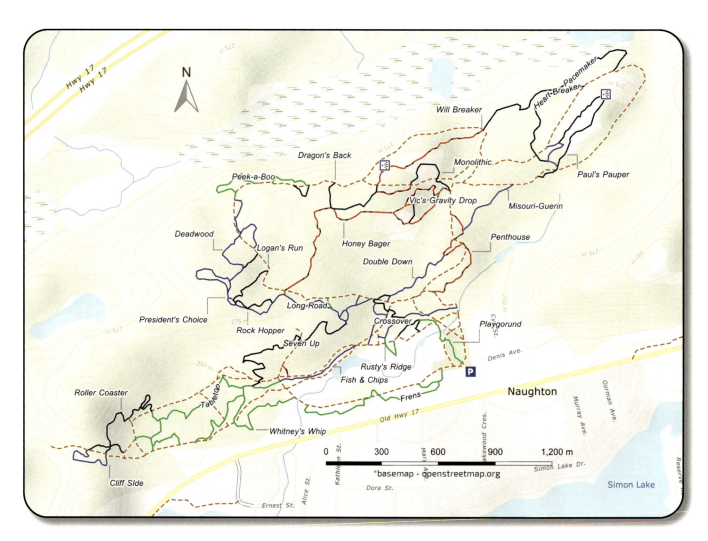

120   *Best Mountain Bike Trails in Ontario*

Review:

Visit **Walden** (formaly **Naughton**) for your fill of classic **Northern Ontario** mountain biking at its best. An even mix of difficulty and terrain keeps everyone happy. Wonderful, flat, **open slabs of rock** are the draw!

This spot in **Naughton,** 20 km west of **Sudbury,** is your typical dual-purpose sports area, home to Nordic skiers in the winter, MTB riders in the summer. As such, you have the usual interplay between the two sets/types of paths that's seen at many MTB locations.

Wide Nordic winter routes circling the property, with singletrack loops cutting in and out from them, give you about **22 km** to ride here. The narrow, sought-after MTB tracks make up **13 km** of that, and they are a blast to take on.

Down at the base, west of the car lot, run all the **easy beginner loops** to warm you up for the climbs. Some of this lowland area can be soggy.

If you have had enough of level terrain, commence your ascent to the main large rocky hill by turning off onto the difficult **Seven Up** trail. Or continue on for a more moderate climb at any of the other forks going north a few minutes later.

Next, find the **Long Road** trail and you'll be well on your way to all the good stuff. Depending on your skill and bike, there are many options to take. The club website has even listed **six tours** as route suggestions. Bonus!

Up by the top of this hill, the trees thin out and reveal bare, flat rock, which I find a joy to ride over. This gets interrupted by steep lines and rock drops. There is some **serious technical riding** here that will test your skills and fear factor. In these parts when they say it's a double-black-diamond run, they mean it! **Honey Badger** is one of these.

The last time I rode here, my favourite loops were **Dragon's Back**, **Will Breaker** and **Pacemaker,** which make a great combo ride higher on the northeast side. Stop for a moment and **take in the views from the top**. Few rides in Ontario get such open vistas.

Since then, new trails have been cut, so now I need to check these out—best reason to go back!

The wide main ski paths at times have the aid of boardwalks to get over the muck and filth, or you can just gun it, if that's your thing.

Originally a Nordic ski area, Walden is also the home of the **Walden MTB Club,** a large, active club that has started hosting major races and a women's bike group.

They keep the trails **well maintained** and the signs keep you moving in the right direction. (This seems to be clockwise, though most loops are technically two way.)

In the winter, **Fatbikes** can play on separate loops away from the skiers.

Wet weather will make this a **slippery, muddy place,** so please avoid after a rainy spell. The bugs are not too bad by the end of July, but **bears** have been seen, so a bear bell is a good idea. You would certainly benefit from travelling on a full-suspension MTB and perhaps use some padding if unsure (or kamikaze).

For all you southern MTB riders in need of adventure, fewer trees, and more rock to crank on, this is the place. If you are driving through the **Sudbury** area it's worth a visit...and be sure to try **Laurentian,** too.

Best Mountain Bike Trails in Ontario

What Is Mountain Biking
& Would I Like It?

Every spring, there are **new cyclists** who consider buying a mountain bike to get into the sport. If you are curious and want to try MTB trails, here is an **overview** of what to expect.

If you are fit and have a decent mountain bike, that's a good start. There is **a certain mindset** to MTB riding that you need to be in tune with or else it can be a frustrating experience.

Let me elaborate on the personality, the zen of the ride and the gear you should have.

Who is Suited for Mountain Biking?

Anyone—kids, men and women—can do mountain biking, at any age, and enter at any skill level. There are **easy rides** in this book for beginners to learn and safely progress on. You manage how much risk you wish to take on. This not usually a dangerous sport unless you take risks, and certainly has fewer deadly consequences than riding in road traffic!

Though 70% of the riders I see on the trail are guys, **women who ride enjoy it** just as much,. Riders' ages go from kids with their dads to old veterans who can't quit (like me). I've noted the **average age** of MTB visitors to the Ontario Bike Trails website to be somewhere between 40 and 50.

Some young riders who have done **BMX** and **Skateboarding** take on MTB trails as a similar added activity (once they have bucks to buy a MTB and car, LOL).

What you do need is a **reliable mountain bike** and **good health**. This is an enjoyable sport, but also a **full-on exercise**. You sweat and work hard for your thrills—the **cardio benefits** are a bonus.

You can be a **casual rider**, take it easy or be aggressive, even push yourself to train to **race** some day.

If you are already a **road rider** and you have strong legs, that will help with the climbs. From there, you will need to hone your skills in **turning, shifting, braking, balance** and **perspective** as you weave between the trees. It's **a different kind of cycling** and can humble the most experienced of road Sportifs.

If you love going long distances really fast, MTB may not work for you. Mountain biking is all about **technique,** riding slower and taking on the ever-changing challenges of the terrain. It can be a grind at times, but it also offers fast descents and moments of nervous uncertainty. The constantly shifting trail is an enjoyable **problem-solving journey** through the woods that keeps you engaged and **is never monotonous.**

As I said, it's not about speed or distance; it's all about taking on a challenging landscape and overcoming it (and of course, staying on the bike, too, LOL).

Sure, we all go over the bars at some point, but **we rarely do** (unless a stupid idea pops into our heads). The trick is to **be aware of your surroundings** and **have a plan** at any given moment if you do crash. That way you can manage the impact, brush off the dust and be smarter for it.

The key to MTB riding is to challenge yourself, grow your skills and not have a **bad crash** that takes you out. There is no shame in passing on a tricky structure or walking a steep hill so you can **ride another day.** Nothing is worse than sitting out the summer because **you overdid it** in the spring. Perhaps defer any questionable rocky verticals, skinny boardwalks and risky jumps to later in the season, when you feel more comfortable and steady on your steed.

What you see on **YouTube videos** of guys flying down insane hills, leaping over canyons and performing aerial flips is not what 99% of the rest of us average MTB riders do. And don't kid yourself, those riders have practiced those moves and failed hundreds of times.

Entertaining as they are, these **sensational videos** continue to perpetuate in the public's mind the notion that mountain bikers are a reckless lot to be feared. Well, we are not. We lead normal lives, work, pay taxes, and on the weekends **need more excitement** than pedalling along a paved road, and I bet you do too.

When you've gotten in a few years of solid riding, you may eventually graduate to jumps and tricks. It's a **long, gradual progression** in skill and confidence that leads you to try and eventually succeed. Like learning to play the piano, but with more bruises.

photo - Paulo LaBerge

What Is It Like to Ride a MTB Trail?

Ontario, unfortunately, has **no mountains**. But that's no problem, because we do have plenty of hilly, varied terrain (some very steep), to make your legs **feel the burn** after a few hours. You would be surprised how enjoyable a well-cut MTB trail can be, even if it's built into what seems like uninspiring terrain.

Most mountain bike trail areas consist of a few fairly straight, **wide, dirt "access roads"** (I never see vehicles on them). These are often **Nordic ski tracks** in the winter. Then there are usually assorted random **hiking trails** that are narrower, though still rather straight and simple.

Finally, the blessed third type are the trails cut specifically for MTB riding. Amen!

Called **singletrack**, this kind of trail twists and turns, going nowhere in a hurry. Add some mean hills, roots, rocks, logs, mud…yeah, it gets to be a technical, slow grind sometimes, but **that's the draw.** Then, minutes later, the payoff of a fast, winding descent. Hold on to your bars, it's more thrilling than a roller coaster.

Some trails are smooth and easy, with hardpacked soil, while others can feature **loose sand** and **gravel** or **slippery mud** and **water crossings**. Up in cottage country, you have large **flat rock** (slickrock) and **giant boulders** to ride over—Oh, what fun!

Often, locations have added **man-made structures** to entertain and dare you. **Dirt jumps, wooden ramps, skinnies, bridges, teeter-totters**… but if you're a newbie, for now, keep the rubber on the ground until you earn some experience.

At times you may want to **challenge yourself**. How far can you go without putting your foot down? Or how fast you can you take a turn before the bike starts to slide out? Or you might want to try your skills at cleaning a log pile or rock garden without getting stuck.

You are **one with the machine,** taking on the challenges, **winning every metre** as you go.

Your **focus is the terrain three metres in front.** There's no time for daydreaming here: assessing the oncoming consequences is top of mind. This sport **demands your attention** and if you're not focused, you may go down.

A typical MTB ride can take **2 to 3 hours** and yet only cover **15 to 20 kilometres**, but you earn them!

Best Mountain Bike Trails in Ontario

Most **trails run both directions,** so heads up on blind corners, call out that you're coming or passing. In addition to the odd other cyclist about, you may see **hikers** for a walk, maybe with their **dogs** and **kids**, but not often.

Be **polite, slow down** and announce yourself, especially if **passing horses**. You now represent the MTB fraternity and we want to stay friends with all trail users. As for noisy **ATV** or **dirt-bike traffic,** there is next to none on the loops I have reviewed on in this book.

Half of the MTB trail loops in Ontario have only a few signs to guide you, so a **GPS mapping app** on your phone or a **paper map** & **compass** can keep you on track. The other locations do have good signage; some are a tad confusing, but they will eventually get you home. Remember it's a **recreational outing,** not a race.

Being out in nature, in a never-crowded, **peaceful forest** environment is a welcome change from our hectic city life. And there are **no cars** to be seen! If you like hiking and Nordic skiing, mountain biking is sort of similar.

Most rides are in a **treed forest setting**, shaded from the **burning sun,** which **blocks the wind** and any **light rain. Expect bugs** in the spring (and all summer when close to wetlands). Keep moving to keep them from finding you. And check for **ticks**, a new problem in the province.

Almost all MTB locations are in rural country areas, so look at putting in **an hour or more of driving** to get there...and then the same back (factor in **traffic**), plus likely a **lunch break**. So heading out for a ride can easily take up **half your day.**

You will be sweaty, a little dusty and dirty, and really tired after the ride—a **good, happy tired.**

What Kind of Bicycle Do I Need?

You just **can't take a road bike** on a singletrack trail. It's not built for that terrain, and you will lose control or get a flat soon enough. To enjoy mountain biking, you need to rely on the right equipment to **perform well, give some comfort** and **keep you safe**. Using the wrong bike (or a cheap one) puts you at risk of ending your MTB days sooner.

Wheel rims that have grown from 26" to 27.5" and now to **29"** tires (the larger circumference gives **better traction** and ease in rolling over obstacles). All mountain bikes have wide, **knobby tires;** many are now **tubeless**.

Gearing has evolved from **three chainrings** to one at the front (called a one-by), and the gears of the **rear cassette** have increased proportionately to still give us low gearing to mount those cursed hills. This has eliminated the **front derailleur** and the associated shifting/breakage problems.

Brakes have evolved from **rim to disc brakes**, from wire cables to hydraulic oil lines that are so effective, you can now lock your wheels with two fingers.

Shocks also continue to change and get refined. Front, back, coil-sprung, air, locked, adjustable, and all varied in design. They keep the pounding to a minimum and add more control to your ride. Locking them reduces energy loss when pedalling uphill or on the road.

Four Main Types of Mountain Bikes

There are a myriad of variations in weight, tire size, geometry, rigidity, suspension, gear ratios... it has gotten super-specialized if you've got the money, but here are the basic four kinds for those new to the sport.

Rigid: As the name implies, having no shocks at all makes for a bumpy, hard ride, but it also makes for a

124   *Best Mountain Bike Trails in Ontario*

lighter bike to haul. **Hybrid and gravel bikes** could work for a first outing on MTB trails, but, to varying degrees, these all limit the terrain you can manage and are not a good choice for newbies.

Hardtail: A mountain bike with suspension shocks on the front forks. The rear end is still stiff. This is a good choice for a regular trail ride, XC loops, racing and **beginner bikers**. Lightweight, firm handling and half the price of the next category.

Full-suspension: Shocks on both wheels give riders more **comfort, control** and **speed** over rough terrain. Mountain bikes with dual shocks are **heavier, durable** and expensive.

Fatbike: These have large, wide, low-pressure tires to **spread your weight** over sand, snow and swampy ground along with a stiff frame with regular components. Shocks are not needed. Can be customized for Bikepacking.

If in doubt, don't buy right away. A few places in Ontario **rent mountain bikes** for you to check things out, or see if you can borrow one from a friend. Buying a lightly **used MTB** (make sure it was not stolen) might be OK, but any well-worn rig may have a worn drivetrain or too much out of alignmentto be worth it.

There are many **subcategories** of **mountain biking** that you may gravitate to:

- ✦ **Trail Riding** – General recreational riding on marked, unpaved MTB trails (this is you as a beginner).
- ✦ **Cross-Country (XC)** – Long distances, faster rides over varied terrain in the woods, open fields, gravel paths or over flat rock.
- ✦ **Bikepacking** – Similar to bike touring on the road, but XC-style on dirt and gravel paths, for more than one day, using a MTB or Fatbike. A rider is loaded with bags to carry clothes, food, tent, etc.

- ✦ **All-Mountain/Enduro** – Racing either mostly downhill or a mix of climbs and descents on singletrack, lasting a few hours or spread out over a number of days.
- ✦ **Downhill (DH)** – Fast gravity runs take riders on bermed turns and over large jumps. A shuttle or ski lift takes them to the top of the hill.
- ✦ **Freeride** – A broad discipline that includes big jumps, BMX tricks and stunts on natural and built ramps, bridges, and large drops on descending trails.
- ✦ **Dirt Jumping** – Mounds of dirt shaped to send riders into the air to perform aerial tricks, usually placed close together in a loop.
- ✦ **Trials** – Requiring good balance, this consists of hopping and jumping over obstacles without putting your foot down.

What Do I Need to Bring?

A few words, especially for **Beginners**. I'm not going say much here, as I get into preparing for a mountain bike ride at the end of the book.

What you **don't need** is a kickstand, bike lock, fenders, bike rack, basket or saddlebags. These are all **dead weight** and useless on the trail.

Wearing a helmet is cool on the trail, so don't be a fool, everyone wears one.

Where Can I Learn to MTB Ride?

Getting into MTB riding is a gradual progression of testing and honing your skills.

Ideally, you should **ride with others** to learn from them and as support, if something breaks or you get lost or hurt.

Best Mountain Bike Trails in Ontario

Joining a local MTB club or a ride group organized out of a bike shop is a good idea. Be sure other seasoned riders don't mind a slow learner and are willing to teach and wait for you. (Some advanced ride groups are hyper and never stop or wait for anyone.)

A few MTB locations rent bikes and have lessons. This can help you decide if it's your thing, because actually MTB riding vs. watching YouTube videos will be **harder than you thought.**

Riding techniques are all about **balance** and knowing what **speed** and **gear** to be in to get up over the next hill or log or across rock gardens, skinnies, down drops and rooty switchbacks. It's about **picking the right path** to navigate your way through, **assessing the next three to five metres**, making adjustments, and repeating on and on… Once you **get into the flow of it**, you will learn to **save your energy** and find the best riding lines—and **you will love it!**

MTB Trails for Beginners

If you're just starting in on mountain biking, **start small; don't overdo it**. Ride conservatively and don't rush it. You stand a better chance of doing it again if your MTB experience remains pleasant rather then painful.

This list has locations where many trails are **rated for beginners** (not all, some trails may be too difficult for you to try).

Please review maps, note posted trail signs and **ride within your skill level** so as not to not get injured. Mountain biking is a thrill, and sometimes a spill. It has its dangers which you need to be aware of…and avoid. Ride at your own risk, but have fun, too.

Toronto - GTA

Don Valley – easier trails run along the river's edge

Centennial – all MTB track, hilly, flows well, a great place to learn

Eldred King – forest dirt paths with some hidden singletrack

Jefferson – some good riding, avoid the big hills

Albion Hills – easy, wide Nordic track with some singletrack for beginners

----

Christie Lake – north of Hamilton, perfect for beginners, almost all MTB trail and easy

Midhurst – Barrie – half of the trails are easy

Short Hills – a few hills, varied terrain, wide hiking paths

Turkey Point – Many trails are easy, flat and twisty

Coulson's Hill – Brantford – hilly, many trails, twisty but not too tough

Guelph Lake – most trails are easy, a few roots

Torrance Barrens – flat rock, little climbing though muddy

Hardwood – bike rentals, lessons, enough easy track

Northumberland – Port Hope, most trails are easy

Dufferin Forest – not too hilly, smooth track, but don't get lost

Larose Forest – flat, curvy and with no rocks

Brant Tract – flat and smooth track on much of the route

Wildwood or **Fanshawe** – varied, long cross-country ride

Horseshoe Valley – a good place to try downhill riding, rentals and lessons

ALSO: These locations have wider dirt access roads beginners can try and a few MTB tracks (but not many at easier skill levels). Look them up on the OBT site.

Bendor – north of Toronto, mellow, no singletrack

Whitchurch – easy, flat, no MTB trail

Heber Down – a few hills, a variety of terrain to try

Long Sault – smooth, sandy base; a few sizable hills

Awenda – long and easy forest paths

Bracebridge RMC – one hill, access roads and a few beginner MTB trails

Buckwallow – access paths, some easy MTB loops, not too hilly

Georgian – a few beginner loops, not too hilly

MTB Groups & Clubs

Not only is mountain biking in a group plenty of **laughs and good times**, mates can **push you to ride farther** and **faster when if you're feeling lazy**. You can learn and teach each other new techniques and spot riders trying risky ones. It's also much **safer to travel** in packs and there is always someone with extra homemade munchies or the ability to fix anything.

My old TBN MTB crew

Having led many group rides, I have seen some basic **group dynamics** you should be aware of. Here are a few thoughts to **keep it a good vibe**.

Whoever calls the ride leads it. Do not overthrow the leader; make your own ride group if you must.

As the leader, invite like-minded riders who all have the same skill and endurance. Plan a route and **meet their expectations** or you will lose rank. At some point there will be **bad weather**; what's the protocol for cancelling a ride?

Email or post on a website where and when to meet, how hard the ride will be. Give **detailed directions** to the trailhead. A 15-minute grace period is your call; after that, head out.

A group ride of more than **10 to 15 cyclists** gets to be a bit of **wagon train** and should be **split by speed** and **ability** level into at least two groups that can meet up later.

Riders need to be sure the person behind them knows which way to turn at the next trail fork. When there is a mechanical problem or injury, **stick together**. What's the rush?

Every rider has a different outlook on what their ride should be. Some like to hammer it non-stop, with hardly a snack or pee break to be seen. Others may only want to see singletrack, and the moment you lead them down a dirt access path, the complaining starts. There are the tech-heads who stop to often to check the latest stats and map apps, and to compare notes. Some ride mountain bikes that need serious tuning and always break down, delaying things—or have no pump, patch or tools for the inevitable. **Be ready for these characters.**

And then there is **liability**. Legally, if you lead a rider down a sketchy path and they get hurt it could be your fault. You may think, "My friend knows what he getting into, he would never sue me," and this is likely true, but if he's in a coma, his partner or parents (or their lawyers) may not be so understanding. A grim thought.

Tell everyone they are **riding at their own risk**, but is that worth much? I am not a lawyer, so to lessen that predicament, let me move on to the next topic.

Join a MTB Club

One of the side benefits of joining a bicycle club is that they have **liability insurance** to cover group rides. This is actually a large chunk of your club membership fees.

Now, the main reason most cyclists join a club is to **meet other riders, improve their skill**s and **be social**. Some MTB clubs have group rides, kids' camps, race events, social parties, weekend trips. It depends on the club's size and dynamics…and your willingness to **give back and chip in**.

Yes, **putting in your time** is important in some form, to help maintain and build trails, to lead rides, organize trips or volunteer for a board position.

Wild Bettys MTB Club

Form a MTB Club

If no MTB clubs exist in your area, it might be time to form one with your ride group. Why? Well, beyond all the great reasons in the last few paragraphs, it gives you **strength in numbers.**

Any and all **rogue trail builders** need to take notice of this. Your beautiful handiwork is in jeopardy of being repeatedly removed until you **make it legal**. Or do you dream of cutting tracks in a woodlot you have been eyeing, but don't know how to make it happen?

Well, showing **landowners, politicians** and the **public** you are organized, serious and **have a vision** will make things a reality. It may take a few years, but when your trail work is approved, it will become **permanent.**

Post a **club website** and you are on your way to building your ranks, because **good volunteers only work for good organizations.** And please keep that website current.

Be certain to **talk with other bike clubs** on how they got set up. We are all a friendly MTB family, just a little busy; but do ask around, because other clubs have **solved may problems** you will encounter. They will know how to **talk to landowners**, who are the **best local officials** to contact, and how to **deal with red tape.**

Best Mountain Bike Trails in Ontario

Ontario Geography

If you take a moment to understand the lay of the land you ride on, it will reveal why so many MTB locations are where they are. It's all about **terrain, availability** and what merriment can be constructed on a location.

Way back in time, billions of years ago, what's now the province of **Ontario** was forming. What you see is a combination of volcanic activity, movement of the earth's crust, centuries of erosion and a few enormous lakes, rivers and glaciers passing through.

What was left eventually filled in with trees until **settlers arrived** and began to clear and farm the land. Many current MTB locations are **failed farming ventures,** abandoned due to poor soil conditions. Too sandy, full of stones, cursed with poor drainage or too steep to farm? It all suits us nicely to ride on.

In **western Ontario,** out by **London**, agriculture is doing well. The terrain has little stone and is rather level, with only a few valley woodlots to consider. Thus there are few opportunities to carve out some tasty track.

More and better MTB trails exist eastward, toward **Hamilton**. Here the **Niagara Escarpment** curves up to the **Bruce Peninsula** and beyond. A significant limestone ridge pushed up by the earth, it offers many locations for rocky, gnarly trail building.

As we move further east above **Toronto,** the 160-km wide **Oak Ridge Moraine** plays a key factor in other MTB trail locations. We now have glacial melt and ancient lake runoffs depositing sandy soil that cannot sustain farming. Here come the bikes...

The terrain north of **Lake Ontario** slopes up and starts to get hilly from glacial deposits until we meet the **Canadian Shield**. This stone bedrock has been exposed by the movement of many **Ice Age glaciers** grinding the stone and scraping away the soil, leaving bare rock and a thin layer of topsoil.

The Shield extends north of the **Trent-Severn Waterway** and across to the **Brockville** area, then cuts across back up by **Ottawa**.

This terrain is the best MTB riding to build on, with flat, bare rock, boulders, valleys, hills and lots of forests. So much potential, yet not that close to the largest population of keen riders to the south. There are a few great places in cottage country and beyond as far as **Sudbury.**

Give it a few more decades and we should see more up there, it's just so untapped. And I am wishing one day **more involvement by our Ontario Parks services** to offer MTB riders more to ride then the meagre amount that exists.

GPS Accuracy

In collecting GPS data to make my maps, it became evident that achieving a high state of accuracy was an **elusive target**. There are just too many factors playing into the quality of the data.

Here is why. First, your GPS device has to receive a faint signal from **satellites orbiting the earth**. Then your unit needs to calculate some **quick math** on the fly to record your position as **time, longitude, latitude** and **altitude** in a data file for each point.

After the ride, these track points are typically saved as a **GPX file** to export to a mapping program or be uploaded to an online **fitness tracking service**.

A **vector line** joins each **track point** to create a long, winding line of the route you just did. Altitude and time data are used to **plot elevation** and **speed graphs**, and reams of other stats some of us bike nerds love.

Sounds like a good setup, but here is where trail line inaccuracy, deviations and errors are inherently prone

Best Mountain Bike Trails in Ontario

to happen. A good GPS signal is achieved when at least **three (four is better) satellites** can give a fixed position at any given moment. Any less, and the data will deviate, or it might not even register as a track point. This is evident when your GPS tracks have **long, straight lines**, a sign that your device was unable to record data points during that stretch of the ride.

Adding to the complexity of this task, **we are erratic, fast-moving objects** on our bikes.

The most accurate GPS units receive on **two frequency bands.** Your phone does not. Your best accuracy may be **offset by three metres** or more from your actual position.

The weak GPS signal transmitted by satellites will **get even dimmer** when atmospheric clouds and/or the forest canopy absorb some of the signal, or deep valleys and high cliffs **block and bounce** them. (Stuffing your phone way into your backpack will weaken that signal, too.)

Truly amazing technology but, as I mentioned **not as accurate as you might think**. Recently I did a test you could try. I rode my bike back and forth down the same forest trail. What I got are not identical trail lines. The deviations from the main trail were at times major and none of them matched.

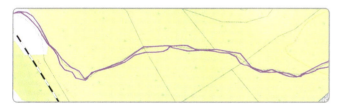

Did you know a GPS signal is free? You neither need data on or even a phone plan to get a reading. And you can preload the app and base maps at home using wi-fi even for an old phone with no sim card.

It is best to set your GPS apps to **log every few seconds.** The shorter the interval, the more data points—but also the more your **battery drains.** This high stream of data may overwhelm a cheap unit or poorly designed software.

Map Making

As I was making the MTB trail maps for this book, I tapped into many resources, including government map data, openstreetmap.org, satellite images, paper maps, and my own GPS tracks and that of friends and clubs. The variations in data were sometimes huge. Considering the issues in achieving accuracy as mentioned above, **who had the most accurate tracks?**

With no way of knowing, I eyeballed it, and **averaged it out.** Rest assured, none of my maps will have you swimming in the lake or riding through walls. But despite my determination to **create the ultimate MTB maps,** I had to admit it's just not possible.

Well, OK, it is if I pay a **surveyor** to walk every trail, with a fancy GPS gizmo to plot every hill, rock and shrub. Not happening on my budget, nor is it necessary.

You see, I had to stop myself in the midst of my mapping anguish and realized the **spirit of mountain biking does not need it**. Riders have always sought out MTB trails on a whim and a rumour. Who needs maps? When the trail calls you, you take it. OK, we don't want to get totally lost, so maps can help us save time and find places.

Actually, if you're good at map reading and interpretation, **a well-made map has a ton of information.** Mine do, and they sure are nice-looking, too.

Early on in MTB history, a **paper map** was what you would pull out of your pocket at a trail intersection to discuss options with other riding mates. Light, portable, made of paper and **needing no batteries**, it worked.

Well sort of. It just couldn't tell us **where we were**. When fancy cycling odometers and GPS wristwatches arrived, we now had our current position fixed in relation to the map. Very cool, then the advent of smartphones just busted everything open with colour screens, GPS and altitude sensors, and countless free mapping apps.

Whatever you use on the trail as a guide—**your intuition, a paper map or a GPS device**—enjoy the journey.

Best Mountain Bike Trails in Ontario

Trail Building Concepts

When **designing a trail system** or even a single loop, here are some key points to consider.

From the trailhead, bike trails should **start off easy**. This delivers a good **warmup** for seasoned riders and an opportunity for **beginners to get comfortable** on their mountain bikes and sort out the local terrain.

As the trail loops fan out farther into the woods, **Intermediate** and then **Advanced** singletrack is introduced. These offer **more and greater challenges** for those who make it that far in.

In a perfect world, **at the start of any new loop**, a sign would indicate the name, **skill required,** and perhaps length and elevation gain. A map board at large intersections with a trail marker reference numbers and a **"you are here"** arrow would be ideal.

At the entrance, or very soon into any trail, there should be a challenge at the trail's highest skill level. This **warns riders what lies ahead**, hopefully filtering out overconfident riders to reduce accidents farther in.

Durham MTB Assoc.

The trail lines that builders map out must not only produce a safe and enjoyable ride, but also **control trail wear**.

A well-designed MTB trail does not run straight up hills as old hiking paths do; it will be stretched out, running along at **less than a 10% grade** across the hillside, or be some form of a **switchback**. If done well, the **elevation gain is subtle** and is hardly noticed by users. It also reduces future erosion.

Incorporated into the path should also be small **trail reversals in elevation**. Also, a slight **pitch to the outside edge** allows the trail to drain and prevent or lessen mud puddles. When it does rain and the water channels down the path, it hardly has a chance to pick up speed and volume before **draining off it at each dip** on the route. (And you thought all that terrain undulating was for your amusement.)

Other aspects in good trail design help **reinforce trail paths** or **retaining walls** with gravel, stones and logs.

Boardwalks and **bridges** can be constructed to pass over water, soggy or sensitive areas. **Factor in a little bit of overkill** with sound building practices, using screws and timber to make your project last. Also be aware of the **fall zone** on the sides of your structure. Keep it friendly if someone veers off for a spill.

And why not **add some fun** into it? There is no reason that practical trail building can't also make a new trail more enjoyable by adding challenging elements to the ride.

Stony rock gardens, boulders, log paths, boardwalks and bridges all can be made enjoyable while keeping us dry and off sensitive environments.

Ottawa MTB Assoc.

Everyone loves flowy, effortless cruising through the woods with **fewer climbs** and **more bliss**. See what you can do the next time you pick up a shovel or saw.

To learn more about trail-building techniques, contact the **International Mountain Bike Assoc. (IMBA)** in **Canada** and your local bike club. It has become a real science.

And a word of advice from someone who's made a lot of MTB trail maps: **don't give short trails, long names.** The text will not fit on the trail line—or might collide with other trail names on the map—and is likely to be omitted.

Trail Hazards

Beyond the obvious obstacles that we enjoy riding over or around, there are several other hazards to be aware of. And I don't mean to be alarming, Canada does not have tigers or alligators. It's a pretty safe country to cycle in; just keep your head up.

If you are visiting Ontario, we do not have too many nasty plants to avoid or animals to escape from. Please look into any of these if you are in doubt about how to identify or avoid them. I am keeping this brief as the focus of this book is on finding good trails.

Bugs that Bite

Rushing water breeds **black flies** in the spring, and standing water gets the **mosquitoes** multiplying. If you have a flat tire deep in the woods, you will learn exactly how many there are. They start to thin out by mid-July. Carry or apply some **DEET** insecticide before you head out. (I hate the stuff and just ride faster then they can fly, LOL.)

Deer flies are active in hot weather and can make your ride a misery. DEET is not as effective on them. I've heard of riders using double-sided tape on their helmets to trap the little darlings.

Black, dark blues and **reds,** those colours and **movement** attract bugs; even **your breath** and **hair** can attract them (if you have **dark hair**). You just can't win! Try wearing lighter shades of beige, yellow, orange, and green, and ride known buggy areas on windy days, when it's cool, or later in the fall.

Tick sizes on a finger

Be on the lookout for **ticks**. These may carry **Lyme disease**, which can be a debilitating illness if not treated. They hang around tall grasses and are ready to hitch a ride as you brush by. Know how to check for these tiny critters after the ride. It can take up to a day to get infected, so when you get home, be sure to shower and wash your clothes.

Plants that Sting

Ontario has a few **unpleasant plants** you may encounter that could give you an itch or a bad rash if you chance to brush against (or fall into) a clump of them.

Starting with just the **annoyances**: **raspberry** and especially **blackberry** bushes – large thorns on the thicker canes will scratch you up if you zip by too close. They do have an obvious up-side: delicious berries. Yum!

Poison Ivy – common in sandy soil. Oils from the plant affect different people in different ways. It has not bothered me, but could give you a serious rash.

Giant Hogweed

Stinging Nettles –This leafy plant grows waist high and stings like a mosquito bite. The sensation lasts briefly and is mild.

More uncommon, but still out there, are **poison oak, spotted water hemlock, wild parsnip, pokeweed** and **giant hogweed**. All have nasty sap to avoid getting on your skin or in your eyes.

If you think you've come into contact with or rolled over any of these plants, avoid spreading the sap around and shower and wash the bike and your clothes asap. At the very least, wash your hands.

We have one poisonous snake, the **Mississauga rattlesnake,** and **black bears** in Northern Ontario. Neither likes to get surprised. A **bear bell** or talking a lot will alert the bears to head the other way. As for the snakes, they could be out on the rocks taking in the sun before you arrive, but are rarely seen.

So now you know what's out there. Rarely do I hear of anyone having an issue, but it's worth adding these potential hazards, along with trees, rocks and gravity, to your MTB **trail gauntlet**.

Best Mountain Bike Trails in Ontario   *131*

Loose Bike Parts

- Health, eMTB, Theft, Etiquette

Rider Health

After many years of plying the trails, I'm here to tell you that the sport of mountain biking has a lot of **wonderful benefits**, and a few not-so-good side effects.

Mentally, it **relieves all your stress.** All that **cardio**, solitude and attacking the trail is going to mellow out everyone in time. If you have work, house chores or relationship **issues on your mind, forget 'em!** There's no room to think about them; your focus is down that trail. Your life depends on it, literally.

Hills are part of the MTB experience and so are steep old hiking trails with routes that suck, but we still climb them like goats. When you're young, nothing is impossible, but eventually the **stress on your knees and back** cranking up a wall will tell you it's time to walk it or find another route.

Lower back pain can also come about from too much **pounding on the trail**. Riding a **hardtail** is fun, but a **dual-suspension bike** is the way to go for many of us, especially as we get older. God, the ride is like floating on a river! Your back will thank you for it (and you can go harder on the downhills—it's a win-win).

Riding down crazy white-knuckle runs likely has you **gripping the handlebars** for dear life, which is not so good in the long term. This tight grip and the jarring terrain can produce **numbness in the hands**, which may lead eventually to **carpal-tunnel** issues. Padded gloves and wider handlebar grips help, and so does remembering to loosen that stranglehold a tad.

Having a sore butt the first ride in the season might happen. If you still are getting pain in the posterior, you're sitting down too much. **Get off the seat** and ride the bumps standing on the pedals, using your legs as shocks.

Dropping your saddle on a steep descent is good form. But often I see beginner riders with seats far to low for most of the ride. **Bring them up!**

I hate to say this to the veteran riders out there, but as we age, **our balance** starts to go on us, and dodging trees is part of the sport. Oh and you **break easier** and it takes longer to mend... By your sixties, you might find **Road Riding, Park** or **Rail Trails** looking better every year.

eMTB – Electric Mountain Bikes

I am talking about **power-assisted mountain bikes**, not electric scooters and motorcycles. On these bikes, you still crank the pedals most of the time, but there's a little electric motor to help you go up a hill or farther into the woods. These can **extend a senior MTB rider's years** on the trail, or give access to a person with a disability.

As a new means of transport, electric mountain bikes are still evolving every year. I asked around in early 2020 what the stance was on these new fan-dangled contraptions. Most bike clubs and land managers have a **"wait and see" policy**, and so do I.

A few locations officially allow power-assisted MTB bikes, while many look the other way. It's an insurance liability issue that will have to be sorted out after there's data from a few years of usage.

If you're in doubt about whether you can bring your new e-steed, **check first.** I think if eMTB riders behave and do not **tear up the trail** or ride at **top speed,** we will sort this one out for the better.

As regular MTB riders, we now have to factor in that an **oncoming bike could be faster** than we think, coming up a hill or when passing at an intersection.

132   Best Mountain Bike Trails in Ontario

Bike Theft

Theft is a real thing, as you know, and I think we have all had a bicycle stolen or know someone who has experienced this. A **MTB is expensive**, making it a high-value item for thieves, and it's so convenient to steal—it turns into the **perfect getaway vehicle** after the crime.

Take a few good pictures of your bike as reference, including a photo of the **serial #** stamped underneath the frame where the crankshaft is. Have your store receipt filed away at the ready. And **register your bike** with the **police** online so if found or there is an attempt to sell it, you are **listed as the owner**. (Before you buy used, check the police database.)

Don't make it easy for those who wish to prey on you. Saving money is smart, but buying a cheap lock is a false economy—get the best you can afford. **Don't advertise** that you have the latest and greatest MTB on Facebook, Strava or bike forums, and don't ever share your **bike's storage location** online. Some thieves are just opportunists, but others are more clever and will do research to find **soft targets**. But they will move on if your bike is a hassle to steal.

I have always taken the front wheel off and put my beloved bike in the car or van while in transit. Better **security, less wind drag** on the highway. I cover it with a car blanket overnight or take it in when I stay at a motel. Sure, the vehicle has an alarm, but that won't stop a smash and grab from happening.

After a ride, if you're going for a meal or a beverage, look for a restaurant where you can **sit on the patio** or inside by the windows so you can keep an eye on your expensive toys, especially if your bike is hanging on your rear rack or standing on top of your car's roof (btw, great advertising).

It breaks my heart every time I hear a bike has been taken. It will break yours, too. So don't make it easy for thieves.

Trail Etiquette - part II

The irony here is that the riders who need to read this are the ones least likely. So I am going to skip all the usual etiquette blah-blah, 'cause you already know it. Thanks for not being a jerk.

A few extra annotations, ladies and gentlemen:

Be Seen – How can other riders avoid you when you are apparently **trying to be invisible**, dressed all in black or forest green?

Be Aware – If you've got music blasting in your **earbuds, you're oblivious** to your surroundings. You won't know that other riders are headed your way or trying to pass.

Call Out Your Intent to Pass – Don't be a stealth rider or stalker. If you are behind me and wish to pass, no problem, just **let me know,** ("on your left") and this way we both feel good about it. Do not blast by me unannounced. That's rude and dangerous.

Pick Your Stops – I get it, you're tired or your bike is making some weird noise, but don't stop in the **middle of the trail.** Pull over to one side—you might be there for a while. And do not stop on the **crest of a hill**; go beyond to where it levels out. Otherwise any riders right behind you will have no place to stop.

Sliding Out – You might think it's cool to drift out on a curve, sending dirt flying everywhere, but if everyone did this, the **erosion** would get so bad the trail might have to be closed.

Skidding Down – Locking your brakes in fear as you slide down a trail is a sign that **you are not ready** for such steep endeavours. It's dangerous for you and not good for the trail. When you can handle the pitch without skidding down, we welcome you back.

Avoid Muddy Trails – It's a hoot to ride in the rain and you're impatient and can't wait, but landowners and trail builders are going to be pissed. So hold on to your horses, cowboys and cowgirls, give it a day or two to dry out.

Shortcuts – Whether you're tired or just lazy, do not redesign the singletrack with your custom shortcuts. Not only does this add confusion for new riders, but slapdash ridearounds are in no way fun to ride.

Removing Obstacles – Hey, if we wanted the going to be easy, we would have paved it. If you can't ride it, you are not ready. Others can and they love it this way, so **let it be**—the stones, boulders, logs, the whole mess. It's all good, ya hear?

Best Mountain Bike Trails in Ontario

Prep for the Trail

As you get to the end of this book, here are a few parting words to send you off down that lonesome trail into the bush... and back again, **smiling!** The smiling, happy part is important for **YOU**.

Bad experiences will dampen your spirits so that next time, **you may hesitate** to go out. Even worse, a bad experience may end up with your breaking something, so that you need to stay home to mend. Do not end up on the couch, watching extreme MTB videos all day!

A little preparation for the trail makes a **big difference**. You can then relax and **ride with confidence**, knowing that you have a sound bike and provisions for the duration, you know where you're going, and you've got a backup plan.

Even when the worst besieges you, this advice will **lessen the grief.** (It also reduces **the chances** of it happening at all.) **Risk management, dude!**

photo - Paulo LaBerge

If you're not inclined, then take your trusty steed to the bike shop for a tune-up. Compared to car maintenance costs, bike repairs are so cheap. **There is no excuse.**

So your clean bike(s) is (are) ready in the garage, sleeping. Nice job! How are you doing on the apparel front? You've got a few sets of clean jerseys, bottoms, a jacket and socks at the ready, I would hope.

Pack a bag and leave it by the door with almost everything you need: **helmet, bike gloves, glasses, cycling shoes, spare shirt and socks, thin jacket, tool kit, bug spray, energy bars, camera** and anything else you always bring to a ride.

When you leave, in a rush or sleepy-eyed in the early morning, you'll only have a few things to remember to do. That would be to **fill up your water containers,** grab **your phone** and **wallet,** and off you go. You could also take some **fresh fruit/veggies as a snack** for the drive or **bring a lunch** to eat when you return to the car if you are not heading to an eatery.

2 – Sports Apparel

Wearing the proper clothing on a ride will regulate the sweat and heat you generate...and there will be lots of it. It is best to **wear polyester blends** as a first layer to wick sweat. These **dry fast**, unlike cotton, which gets heavy and can give you a **chill when wet.** Your choice: tight fit or loose. Same with riding shorts with a chamois (padded inner layer).

If you need another layer, a light, breathable shell jacket is a good idea. Add a fleece jacket inbetween for those cooler spring and autumn rides. If it's really chilly, jogging tights under your shorts could be needed then, too.

Whatever your wardrobe, dress in layers and **start the ride slightly chilled**. You want to eventually warm up to compensate and hit a **comfortable balance**. Work the zippers and vents to regulate. Leave some space in your backpack to ditch a layer if the day warms up even more—and you do too. Otherwise, overheating will send you back to the car early.

Packed & Ready

You never know when the mood will arise or a friend/partner will call on you to go for a spin. Having your **bike ready to roll** and your **gear clean** and **packed** will make it so much easier for you to join them.

1 – Bike Prep

If your beloved bike is not shifting well, has slow leaks, creaks and groans for lube, or is still covered in mud from the last ride, **get on it and fix and clean it!** ("Bike"—who am I kidding? Bikes! This applies to **all your bikes.**)

134 *Best Mountain Bike Trails in Ontario*

If you're out for just a short spin, you can keep it **light and simple:** all you may need is a water bottle on the frame and a tool kit under the seat, and maybe an energy bar.

A **sport-specific backpack** has become the norm. It's not always comfortable, but it's indispensable for self-reliant riders out in the bush. It carries your **water, repair kit, food, phone**...and has storage to carry all your junk on the trail. Find one that works for you.

Bring ID in case you crash and can't remember who you are (it happens) and some emergency money (not that you can buy anything in the woods). Have **bug repellent** at the ready in the car. You will know soon after arriving if you're going to need it; you can also ask returning riders how bad the bugs are. That said, a little emergency container for the trail might prevent a hungry invasion if you are stuck fixing a mechanical problem or hurt. It's poison, so I refrain from using much and I tend to put it on my clothes rather than my skin.

Riding with fingerless **gloves** (or full length in cold temps) keeps the calluses away as you grip the bars. The padding helps and it spares me any "road rash" when I fall and inevitably put my hands down to break the fall (so the theory goes).

Dark sunglasses in the woods? Not my first choice. Instead, consider wearing clear **sport** or **safety glasses** to protect your eyes from those pointy branches. Try **yellow-tinted** glasses on a cloudy day. Just like you're ski goggles, it brings out the relief in the terrain.

The Black Look

As much as black is in fashion, it's a poor choice for bike riding. Especially for road cyclists, and bike club jerseys!

Too many of you are dressed in black, on a black bike, with a black helmet and backpack. Commandos, police and robbers wear black so as not be seen. It works. But YOU need to be noticed.

As a cyclist on a tiny, thin, metal frame, wouldn't you **feel safer** knowing you could easily be seen by oncoming traffic? **Why make it any harder** for the distracted and the poor sighted? It's in your interest to avoid potentially nasty accidents that could end your cycling days.

And on the trail, wearing bright colours reduces collisions on blind turns, hills and trail intersections. (Also, hunters will not mistake you for a deer.)

There are **two other reasons** why **black** is not the best choice.

1 - Biting bugs are attracted to dark colours. **Black** and **dark blues** are great advertising: "Dinner over here, everyone!"

2 - Sun radiation is absorbed by black more than any other colour, **making you feel warmer**.

Please consider a little **colour in your life** to be seen and to better the odds that you can continue to enjoy riding.

(So this has got to be my biggest pet peeve and now I've said my piece. I'm just trying to think of your well-being, kids.)

---

3 – Shoes

Whatever you wear, your shoes need to give you **traction**. Wear **polyester socks** so you can avoid blisters and let your feet breathe. Perhaps high socks in poison-ivy country.

I sometimes use bike shoes that clip in but prefer a good pair of **hiking shoes** on flat pedals. There is an ongoing discussion of what works. You will find your own conclusion. Here is how I see it.

Sure, you get **more power** out of a pedal stroke when you're clipped in. It really helps on the hills after two hours of riding to keep up with the other stallions.

Best Mountain Bike Trails in Ontario

But when a crash is imminent, I believe there is a microsecond **delay** to twist and unclip before you can bail. That could be all you need to end up a tangled wreck still attached to the bike. You didn't quite have enough time for evasive action.

My solution is to unclip one foot (or both) any time I think there's a possibility of having a spill. My pedal clips have an outer rim so I can ride either way. So far, I've had no serious accidents, just dumb ones, LOL.

4 – Food & Drink

Water is the most important item to carry. Without any (or enough), your ride may end too soon. **Bring more than you need** and leave an **extra bottle in the car** for your return. You can hang water bottles in cages on your frame and/or carry a small backpack that has a water bladder with a tube that you can drink from while riding.

Gauge how much you are sweating and **drink before you are thirsty.** Wait too long and cramps will set in. Another way to offset this is to add an **electrolyte-replacement tablet** to your water for those long, epic rides.

Mountain biking can be intense. **Your body needs energy** to keep those legs pumping. Pack enough **quick carbohydrates** to eat on the trail so you do not bonk out. Pick lightweight, easy to eat, nutritious food.

photo - Wild Bettys MTB Club

The typical choice that fits this bill are **energy/protein bars** of some sort. Grocery-store **granola bars** are fine if you're on a budget. **Bring a few extra** for those on the ride who forgot or are still hungry—or for if you get lost and need this to be your dinner.

Other **backup energy** supplements that weigh nothing are **gel** and **chewable** products. These may one day come to the rescue when you find you've underestimated the ride and the tank is low, and you still have hours of riding to get back.

Generally speaking, the cooler the weather, the less you sweat, and the less you drink, BUT the more you may eat to stay warm.

5 – Repair Kit

You must pack a repair kit to help yourself and others on the ride. Repairs may not be pretty, and only temporary, but should be good enough to get you back to the trailhead. What you bring is based on the odds of certain things breaking and tools/parts you can easily carry. Here's what I suggest.

Bring a **spare tube** and **a pump** (or compressed air) that fits your **Presta** or **Schrader** valve ends. And protect that rubber tube from getting a hole while in transit. As plan B, throw in a tiny **tube patch kit**.

Buy a large, quality **multitool** with a chain-link remover and all the driver heads, spoke wrenches and Allen key sizes you need to tighten down your bike. Pack a few "**quick chain links**" and a plastic tire lever (one is usually enough for MTB tires). Add a few plastic **cable ties** to secure things, and perhaps a **derailleur hanger**.

Wrap all this in a grease rag and put in a small bag. This goes with you every time you ride, either under your seat or in your backpack. Promise. Otherwise, lessons will be learned the hard way.

Now you are packed and ready to "Take off, eh!" ...on any given day into the **wilds of Ontario.**

Best Mountain Bike Trails in Ontario

Get Your Motor Running

So today might be **a great day for a MTB ride**. Plans are in the making and you're pumped. Just a few suggestions before you bolt out the door.

1 – Good Directions

Know where you are going and **how to get there.** Check **traffic conditions** and look up **road closures,** too. Some MTB locations host lots of races—is there one on today?

If you are going solo, then it's simple: everyone's in agreement. If you are planning to ride with a group, be sure you **know what to expect** out of the ride. I mention **MTB group dynamics** elsewhere in the book.

Print a paper map, pack a **small compass** (it's a good backup and they need no batteries) or save the base map of that MTB location on your phone for your **GPS mapping app.** There is no guarantee you will get much data in the middle of a forest.

2 – Check the Weather

Not the weather out your window, silly! The **weather at the location** where you are headed. It may be completely different, even better than you thought. If it's going to be a hot day, start early. Not warm enough? Wait til the afternoon.

Every weather service seems to predict what's coming a little differently. (Really, who knows for sure? I have seen it hail on a sunny day.) Once you size up the forecast and you are still keen to go, that's great.

As they say, **dress for the weather** and you can ride any time. Leave extra clothes in the car just in case it does rain on you, or the temps drop big-time, or you fall in the creek.

Notice how I have not suggested packing a **raincoat**. Seems pointless somehow. Ever ride in a plastic raincoat? It a is a sauna. You're sweating anyway; what's a little more water? In the forest you're sheltered. It has to pour before you really need to bail and if so, just beeline it to the car, which usually is close enough.

That said, I would not suggest purposely riding in rain or just after. Things get **mighty slippery** out on the rocks and leaves, and any clay soil turns greasy. When the injury-probability meter is heading to 11, stay home.

photo - Peter Istvan

Now, in some areas I mention in this book, the soil is loaded with **sand** and **gravel**. Many of the trails in these locations will **drain fast** and handle erosion well, even firm up, so I would guess they'd be better choices than others that really need a **few days to dry out**. You be the judge. Not all trails may be suitable, so **ride with caution and respect**.

Ride Here After It Rains:

Sandy soil base – Ganaraska Forest, Northumberland, Eldred King, Dufferin Forest, Limerick, Larose, Durham Forest

Gravebase – Puslinch, Carrick Tract

Flatrock and stony – Buckwallow, Torrance Barrens, South March, Laurentian

Indoors - Joyride 150

If you must ride just after it rains, you could always consider a gravel **Rail Trail** or a paved **Park Path,** and a road ride is always an option. No, it's not MTB riding, but you are on a bike and it could be good for your sanity or training.

Best Mountain Bike Trails in Ontario

3 – Leaving Home

Grab your **bike, helmet,** the **backpack** you prepped with all those items I mentioned, any extra **food/clothes,** your **wallet** and **phone,** and fill up your **water containers.** I have seen riders show up with no front wheel—game over. Others with no seat, no helmet, no food, not enough water …yup, the list goes on. Don't be that guy or gal, LOL.

Have you told someone **where you are going** and **when to expect you back?**

Double check…… all good, gas in the car?….Hit the road!

Ridin' the Trail, Yee Haw!

1 – Parking Lot Prep

When you get to the parking lot, find some shade (if you can) and unload. If this is your first time, asking riders who have just finished can give you some valuable insight. They may **recommend routes**, tell you what to avoid, or alert you to recent fallen trees blocking the path, logging activity, swampy sections or bug-infested parts.

At this point, apply bug juice or sunscreen if you need to. There is little sunshine to be seen on most MTB rides, but maybe out on the **Torrance Barrens,** down the **Seguin Rail Trail,** or at a **Downhill ride park** you might need protection.

Now is a good time to **add lube to your chain**. Less friction, bike lasts longer: a good thought. You have two choices: dry lube or wet.

Dry lube has Teflon, silicone, and other slippery waxy additives that keep your chain in motion. Dry lube does not attract dust and sand that grind your gears and wear down your drivetrain. It also has to be applied almost every ride, so stay on it.

Wet lube is oil based, long lasting and great for preventing the formation of rust. Water and wet mud will not stick too badly, but sand and dust do, and then grind away. I prefer dry lube; you decide.

Is your **tire pressure** still OK? Tighten the quick releases on your wheels. I bend mine back, tucked in into the frame, so no branches can catch them and flip them loose.

Almost ready… Put your **reserve water** in the car, ideally out of the sun, with your return snack (a banana, apple, sandwich, ice cream?!) and cover it with a blanket to help insulate. Now **lock up** and put those car keys in a pocket you can zip up. Actually, any pocket that does not zip is at great risk of emptying out on the trail. Yard sale!

As you pass the map board (if there is one), you could **take a photo of the map**. It might come in handy.

You're on your way! Have a fantastic time. With a little prep and planning, you've earned it—and **you reduced the chances** of telling sad stories at the next BBQ.

2 – Emergency Recovery

Do you have a good plan in case bad things happen?

Riding in semi-remote locations means when something breaks and/or you get hurt, there are few able hands to help you and no easy way to get a lift back to your car.

138   *Best Mountain Bike Trails in Ontario*

The first thing is to **tell someone** where you are going and when you should be back. The next nugget of advice is to **ride with a buddy or larger group**. If you **go solo**, it's better to pick a familiar area that has some traffic.

Certainly, cell phones have made staying connected with others much easier and lowered the potential risks. A call or text for help is usually possible. Yet there are rides where your **cell signal may be too weak** in the middle of the forest to be reliable. Finding a high point or a clearing may help.

If you **get lost or hurt**, stay on the trail. It may take a while, but someone will come by to aid you. Do not take a shortcut through the bush; no one will find you there. If you can manage, **head back the same way** you came. At least you may recognize the way back and how long that will take.

If you are badly hurt, which actually **rarely happens**, I have little medical knowledge to pass on—sorry. If your bike gets hurt, though, here are a few helpful comments.

3 – Bike Repairs on the Trail

Unlike other leisure and road cyclists, MTB enthusiasts are pretty rough on bikes. We use them and abuse them. Mountain bikes sure do take some punishment, so you can expect **more things to break and to wear out faster.**

You've got mud and sand grinding down your parts, plus the strain on chains from cranking up hills and all that shifting we do. Add the stress on the frame and rims as you pound your way down a pile of rock or land a two-metre jump, and yikes, it's cruel!

Here are some things you may need to address, in the order I've most commonly seen them occur:

Flat tire – The #1 bummer on the trail. It can be caused by many things, and low pressure in your tire can make it happen sooner. Check the inside of your tire to see what villainous object has pierced it. It may still be stuck in there, ready to give the next tube a leak.

You have three options: 1) Replace the tube with a new one. 2) Patch the tube; this takes longer. 3) Walk back 10 km to your car if you did not carry a tube or patch kit.

Don't forget you also need to bring a pump for option 1 or 2 to work out.

If you are riding on **tubeless tires** they tend to fix small leaks themselves with the internal sealant. When it's worse it's time for plugs, a patch or a tube. Ask the bike shop what to bring for your wheel setup.

Broken chain – The more you ride hard, the more wear and stress you put on your drivetrain, and the more your chain stretches and gears misalign. Stomping on your pedals up a steep hill while desperately shifting gears is asking for your chain to go PING.

Without a **multitool** that comes with a chainlink remover, you're going to start walking... again. The best remedy is a **"quick link"** to get going. Pack a few of these. Otherwise, you can usually pop out any bent links and connect them back together. Perform this surgery on clear ground. If you're working over a pile of leaf matter and you drop the links, you're done.

Bent rim/ broken spokes – By not planting a good landing, hitting a log or rock hard, or crashing, you can cook your rims or snap a spoke.

Depending on the severity, a few broken spokes can be easily removed so you can still ride out carefully. A slightly twisted rim will have a wobble—you can try to straighten it out or live with it. A spoke wrench or brute force may either improve it or make it worse, you be the judge. If you taco your wheel (bend it like a taco), start walking...

Derailleur – The rear derailleur is your steed's **softest target**, the easiest part to wound. I wish they could invent something better! The culprit that inflicts this grief is often **a stick** the thickness of your handlebar,

Best Mountain Bike Trails in Ontario

lying across the path. Snapping one of these in half with your wheels can flip the pieces into your spokes or chain assembly, stopping you in a blink.

Sliding off a log, dropping off a boardwalk, or taking a minor tumble with the bike may **bend or twist** this precarious hanging chain arm, and suddenly your shifting is not quite right.

What really will end your day is when your derailleur gets twisted right around or snaps off. Now you're walking again, and this time it's 15 km and the bugs are hungry.

But you may be able to check the ailment and give it a tweak. And actually, there is hope: **carry a replacement derailleur hanger**. This part connects between the frame and the main derailleur arm and is supposed to bend/break first. If it's your lucky day, you can just replace it. If it's not, then shorten your chain so you can at least ride out on one gear. Pick one in the middle.

Loose crank arms – This is seldom an issue, but if you are pedalling and you notice that your pedal is getting loose or wobbling a little, stop immediately and tighten it. Otherwise, going up the next hill will strip the threading and you'll have to pedal back to the car with one foot. Not a circus trick you want to perform.

Broken seat – This is not very common, but my seat post snapped once, so it can happen. Standing up on my pedals for the 40-minute ride back was, ummm... interesting.

Sure, though the odds are low, there are other things that can break or bend. But how many tools and parts do you want to haul "just in case?" Well, that depends on **how hard your ride** and **how far you venture**. Being self-reliant is important. This also means you should **learn how to do these repairs (**or start walking, LOL).

Stay Longer

In Canada, we drive everywhere and longer distances than in most countries. Sure, it's a **big country,** but **reducing your pollution footprint** is a responsibility we all have. Don't shrug it off or think it does not matter. As I am writing this, the **heatwave outside** is warning us all to be nice to our planet.

Mountain biking almost any trail in this book requires driving—lots of it—to get there and back. This book is going to put more cars on the highways. Consider carpooling or staying overnight to reduce pollution and cut your gas costs.

I find the **hardest part of my MTB outing** is not the grind up any brutal hills, but **the drive home**. I'm totally spent and tired, and now I have to fight my way home in hot, stinky traffic. (If you know Toronto traffic, no need to explain.)

Make it a weekend or a longer **road trip.** This saves you time and gas, and you can check out a few more ride locations while you're in the area. After the ride, your tent or motel will be closer, so you can shower and relax with a pint sooner. And in the morning, the next riding spot is just down the way, with no marathon needed to get there.

A word about **carpooling**: cyclists are by nature an independent lot. When everyone shows up in their own vehicles and rides together you would think they don't mind each other's company. Yet I never see much carpooling going on, even when I know riders live close to each other or on the way.

I'm a fan of carpooling for environmental reasons. But be aware that **good carpooling etiquette** is required or things fall apart. Everyone should make an effort to be friendly... and try not to smell too ripe.

Passengers: Be ready on time. Pay your way. Appreciate that you are not doing the driving. Chatting and being a little social is good, but refrain from talking constantly for hours just to fill the nervous silence. Read a book, play with your phone, snooze, chill, look out the window.

Drivers: Yes, it's your car, but don't be a dictator. Find a happy medium so everyone is comfortable with the type and volume of music (or none at all), and seek consensus on the cabin temperature, when to stop and where to eat.

Winter Riding

Using a **Fatbike** or a regular MTB in the colder months can extend your riding **year round.** A few changes in how you prep and ride can make this a very enjoyable outing. Apply what I mentioned for summer riding and customize it with these added remarks.

Check the weather and pick the right day. There can be dire consequences if you get lost in a snowstorm, and even on a sunny day, the temperature may range from **+5C to -30C or worse.** Try some **short excursions** first and test your gear setup before launching into a full-day outing or race.

photo - Paulo LaBerge

Start early, knowing that there is **less daylight** in the winter. Bring bike lights, you never know... Check how deep the snow base is and if others have perhaps been there before you to pack down the trail. If the location is **groomed**, well, how luxurious! Enjoy.

Ice is to be feared. Avoid! Unless your treads have studs, it's just too easy to have your bike slide out from under you and BOOM, you've broken your wrist.

Dress in layers—more of them. But don't overdress, as you'll sweat and then get a chill when you stop. You will **need more food energy** to keep you warm when you ride in the snow. **Keeping water from freezing** is a challenge you need to solve. Your hands and feet also need solutions to stay warm and dry. **Wool socks** are great and electric heated gloves and boots may be called for. **Do some research** on gear and clothing that will help you be comfortable.

Nordic skiing or snowshoeing can be a great cross-training option for cyclists in the winter. It adds variety to your outdoor activities, is a great cardio workout, and works other muscles, and you can do it at many of the same locations we ride. And now a little plug for my other site: **ontarioskitrails.com**.

MTB the World

You could be in **Alberta** or **Arkansas** with your MTB bike, ready to go. But where is the sweet stuff you want to ride in the little time you have?

What has worked for me is to contact local clubs and MTB groups for advice. You can be sure their riders know where the best trails lie. What would really rock is if they invite you on a group ride, if the timing works out.

Search the internet for MTB club websites or Facebook group pages. It can be a lot of fun riding with locals and ensures you don't get lost or waste time looking for that best track. Keep in mind this is their home turf and they can probably outride you because they know the trails very well.

Travelling and have the urge to ride, but don't have a bike? **Rent a rig** from a bike shop in town. You can bet they know a few choice spots to let loose, maybe even give you a lift to get there. And make sure they give you a repair kit too.

There are so many **incredible places** in this world to ride, seek them out, they will be such memorable experiences. Start that wish list today!

Best Mountain Bike Trails in Ontario

Glossary & Lingo

Some common MTB terms and a little local bike jargon/slang I have heard.

ARMOUR: 1) Padding you wear for your knees, shins, elbows, etc. to limit bruises and breakage. 2) Trail-building techniques to repair erosion and/or prevent future erosion using stone, bricks, rocks for reinforcement.

BABY HEADS: Round glacial rocks or river stones the size of baby heads. Random or piled on the path, they make a rock garden.

BAIL: To disengage from your bike when crashing. You don't want to land on the bike, or have it land on you. Lose the bike and save yourself: you can repair the bike.

BENCHED: A trail running along the side of a steep slope has been dug out and benched into the hill.

BERM: This is a banked corner to enable riders to turn faster. Built out of dirt, it may be armoured with stone or shored up with timber.

BEARTRAP: To slip off the pedal and have it come around and smack your shins, leaving a scar shaped like a trap.

BOARDWALK: A wooden structure, usually a metre wide or less, built to bridge across water, wetlands, crevices and other impassable terrain. When they are built just for MTB fun, they're often referred to as ladder bridges.

BOMB: To zoom down a hill with great speed and zeal.

BONK: To bonk is to run out of energy. The tank is empty; you can't go on.

BOTTOM OUT: When your shocks reach their maximum compression.

BUNNY HOP: A quick, short jump to clear logs and rocks.

CHAIN SUCK: When your bike chain comes off and gets jammed between the wheels and the frame. Also mentioned when a chain is slow to separate from the gearing teeth due to a worn-out drivetrain.

CHAIN TATTOO: A greasy stain or worse left from your chainring hitting your leg.

CLEAN: To clean a trail loop is to ride it perfectly without losing control, crashing or putting your foot down.

CLIPLESS: A confusing term, dating back to the days when pedals had toe cages and riders using those were said to be "clipped in." Today, when your shoes are *actually* clipped into the pedals, this is not like the old toe cages, so you're said to be "clipless." (Yeah, dumb, now you know. I try to use another word.)

DAB: When your foot touches the ground, you have dabbed it to keep your balance.

DH: Downhill! Trails ridden on sturdier bikes, often accessed via a chairlift or shuttle.

DIALED IN: You are in that happy place when all is working well and your riding is awesome. See ZONE

DROP: When the trail drops suddenly and there is gap and air under at least one of your tires, so you can't roll down. Usually the best way to handle a drop is to jump down.

ENDO: A crash that sends you over the handlebars. If you mess up your DROP, the likely result is an endo.

FACEPLANT: When you do an ENDO and you kiss the ground with your face.

FLOWY: for a MTB trail with FLOW: that is, it's well designed and carries you along quickly with the least amount of effort, climbing or braking.

GAP: A jump with an opening in the middle. This adds more risk/thrill—be sure you have the speed to clear it and land safely on the downside of the second part of the jump.

GNARLY: Adjective for anything related to challenging, difficult trail terrain with rocks, roots, tight turns, tricky structures, etc. to overcome.

GRAB SOME AIR: Getting your wheels off the ground on a dirt jump or wooden ramp.

GRANNY GEAR: You're in granny gear when you're using the largest gears on the rear cassette and the smallest on the front chainring. This gear ratio gives you more and easier pedal strokes to help you climb mean hills.

GRINDER: A long, slow climb up a hill that takes forever.

GRUNT: A tough, steep climb that makes you work hard.

142 *Best Mountain Bike Trails in Ontario*

HARDTAIL: A MTB with shocks on the front forks and no suspension in the rear.

LADDER BRIDGE: A boardwalk section that changes in elevation. Wood slats look like a ladder. These can be thinner than a metre wide, often feature angles with tricky turns, and can be elevated up to several metres off the ground.

LID (AKA BRAIN BUCKET): Your helmet is your friend.

LINE: The route a rider picks on the trail through a rocky or rooty area, or to climb or descend a gnarly hill. Picking the best line is the objective.

LOG ROLL/LOG PILE: One or many logs piled up to ride over. With enough speed, you are able to roll over or jump off it.

NORTHSHORE: Referring to the type of riding made famous in the North Vancouver area, where riding on raise boardwalks became popular.

OFF-CAMBER: The width across the trail is not level but angles down with the slope of the hill. Off-camber trails are greasy when wet, so you need more traction. These trail sections are good candidates for being BENCHED in the future.

PINCH FLAT (SNAKEBITE): This happens when your inner tube gets compressed between the wheel rim and something hard like a rock or log. The tube gets pinched and a hole or two holes are made that resemble a snakebite. It tends to happen when your tire pressure is too low.

PUMP TRACK: A looped track designed with banked turns and small, rollercoaster hills. Rather than pedalling, you use the motion of your body to maintain momentum.

QUICK RELEASE: Levers for each wheel that when moved loosen the wheel axles. You also have one on the seatpost.

RATCHET: A riding technique in which you pedal in partial strokes in order to clear obstacles (usually large random rocks, roots or logs) where a full, circular pedal stroke would hit the obstacle and cause you to get stuck.

RIGID: A MTB with no shocks/suspension. One bumpy ride.

ROCK GARDEN: a trail section littered with big rocks, maybe the sizes of BABYHEADS

SIDEWINDER – A gravity switchback that descends the two banks of a valley. Momentum carries you from one side down and up the other side of the valley and back again.

SHRED: To ride a trail fast, with skill and control, and have fun doing so.

SKINNY: A narrow structure not much wider than your tires that you ride on top of to challenge your balance and nerve. Skinnies can be made from fallen logs, rock ridges, or built with lumber. The higher up they are, the better a rider you must be to clear them.

SWITCHBACK: A trail-building technique that allows riders to gradually climb a steep hill by zig-zagging across the slope. This reduces the angle of the climb and erosion issues. Some switchbacks can have difficult tight 180 degree turns.

TABLETOP: Like a GAP jump, but with the gap filled in so the jump is flat across the top. The goal is to land on the downside of the jump, but if your takeoff lacks speed, you land safely on the flat part and can still recover and roll out. These are good for beginners because they offer less risk than gaps.

TRACKSTAND: The ability to balance on your bike while stationary and not pedalling.

TRAVEL: The distance your shock can compress, from no load down to fully compressed.

TREE GATE: Two closely spaced trees with the trail snaking between them. This can be a challenging trail feature to manoeuvre through.

WASHOUT: When your tires start to lose control in deep sand, mud or gravel, usually on turns.

WASHBOARD: Regular undulations of the terrain, seen mainly on gravel roads where it's usually made by cars. On trails washboarding may also be caused by horse hooves or water erosion problems.

XC: Cross-country style MTB riding, usually a fast pace on smoother, straighter trails.

YARD SALE: When you crash and everything you own gets scattered about. Or when you leave a pocket or bag open while riding and lose stuff as you ride.

ZONE: When you are in the ZONE, the bike is operating as it should, and you are too. You are having a great ride. See DIALED IN
(this is a MTB loop)

*Other terms are defined in the **Using This Guide** section.*

Best Mountain Bike Trails in Ontario

My MTB Top 5 List

(in no particular order)

Epic Runs

All-around great big serving of MTB junk food, yum! Trails may not be that tough, but there is a lot to consume if you're a glutton.

Ganaraska Forest
Dufferin Forest
Kolapore Uplands
Haliburton Forest
Oro Trail Network

Beginner Country

You're a newbie (or your kids are). Keen to learn, brave and full of energy. Enjoy a good time… without the crashing part.

Centennial Park
Guelph Lake
Christie Lake
Larose Forest
Fanshawe

Rock & Rollers

The need for gnarly, rocky, techno insanity is in your blood. Get your dose of pounding and pain here. Plant a few jumps and track those skinnies.

Walden
Porcupine Ridge
Bracebridge RMC
Agreement Forest
South March

Scenic Sights

Sure, the riding is good, but you want something more than endless greenery to look at. Cliffs, lookouts, lake and streams… Take in the natural beauty of it all.

Torrance Barrens
Kelso
Short Hills
Georgian
Laurentian

XC – Trek'n

Serenity and harmony matter to you. Move those legs, put in some mileage, wander and explore freely on two wheels. Become one with your machine and lose yourself in the wilderness side of life.

Minnesing
Kolapore Uplands
Northumberland Forest
Haliburton Forest
Seguin Rail Trail

Need for Speed

Direction > Downhill - DH is the way to go. The faster you go, the better the buzz. Defiant of danger, gravity is your friend, until…you bounce.

Blue Mountain
Sir Sam's
Copeland Forest
Horseshoe Valley
Kelso

Pure Fun in the Saddle

A buffet of different flavours makes for a full meal. A delightful experience with your bike and friends leaves everyone fulfilled.

Buckwallow
Turkey Point
Puslinch
Oro Trail Network
Joyride 150

Optimized Trail Design

Take a chunk of Ontario turf and sculpt it into hours of non-stop MTB bliss. Well-crafted, twisty runs full of surprises, challenges and rewards.

Dagmar
Ravenshoe
Harold Town
Hydro Cut
Hardwood

Gnarly Insanity

What's the hurry? You do not seek the easiest or straightest path. Twisting and turning, up and over, then repeat. For those who love the technical ballet and victory of MTB strategy.

Agreement Forest
Ravenshoe
South March
Puslinch
Three Stage

Surprisingly Good

Loved by few, little known but worth the drive. You likely have never been here, yet you should go. Never crowded, always welcoming, and ready to entertain.

Hiawatha
Forest Lea
Carrick Tract
Waterdown
The Pines

You Want Hills, We Got 'Em

Working on the cardio for the next race? Or just keen on vertical climbs & fast descents? These have the pain for the gain, baby.

Durham Forest
Copeland Forest
Albion Hills
Jefferson Forest
Don Valley

Named with Creativity

What in a name? When it's a MTB trail name, it could be just silly or a warning of impending carnage.

Johnny's Swamp Of Doom
Dragon's Back
Moose Mayhem
Laundry Chute
Superfly Alley

Bonus 5 more
Big Meany
Redneck Express
Minion's Rush
Gravity Cavity
Wedding Crasher
+ Jen liked
Dave's Not Here! Man!

Best Mountain Bike Trails in Ontario

About the Author

Dan Roitner has been riding on two wheels since a he was a kid with a banana-seat bike. In 1985, he headed to Northern Ontario for a camping road trip. Hanging off the back of the car was a new red **Norco Bushpilot** mountain bike.

He drove around the North, eager to find those elusive tracks spoken of in MTB lore. With no guidebooks in existence nor the internet (yet to be born), where to go? Inquiring at **Ontario Parks**, he got cautionary advice from the park rangers. This new MTB sport seemed dangerous, reckless, there was no such place here for such behaviour, they told him. Stick to the gravel roads, son, be gone.

Alas, fifteen years passed, and he was road riding with the **Toronto Bicycling Network (TBN).** Heading down yet another straight, paved country road, bored. He got to thinking there must be others who wished for more out of cycling.

With a dozen other similarly minded wannabe mountain bikers, he commenced taking weekend trips to local trails. Soon a MTB group was formed within **TBN**, and Dan ran it for over 10 years. It seemed natural to share the knowledge he'd gained from riding many trails over a decade on a website when the opportunity arose.

In 2013 **ontariobiketrails.com** was launched, featuring about 30 trail locations; now the site lists close to 130. Dan has always loved cycling, photography, looking over maps, and exploring the Canadian wilderness, so this was a good fit.

A year later a sister site, **ontarioskitrails.com,** was launched for his winter pastime, Nordic skiing. Same format, different flavour.

Living on the east side of **Toronto,** north of the Beaches area, he still MTB rides with friends and his son Trevor while his wife Teresa stays home and worries (ha! not true at all, LOL).

This is his second bicycle trail guidebook. The first is called **Best Bicycle Park & Rail Trails in Ontario.**

You can contact Dan at staff@ontariobiketrails.com

Acknowledgements

I guess it all began when my parents gave me my first bicycle. In doing so, they gave me freedom on two wheels and some foolishness… but I thank them for setting me in motion. That was the beginning of the long road—correction, _trail_—to get this book published.

Leading MTB rides has provided many memorable social experiences and adventures. Thanks to all the **good company** friends gave me over the years on bike club rides. You pushed me further and gave me courage in all sorts of fine and foul weather.

I am grateful to the **Ontario MTB community** for developing and maintaining so many wonderful trails to ride. Your volunteer efforts have expanded and improved the sport immensely in the last few decades.

I appreciate all the helpful insight and updates from bike club executives—you know who you are.

I also wish to acknowledge the **open-source community** that has enabled me to publish this book in house on a thin budget. Free (but not always bug-free, alas) software—WordPress, QGIS, XnView, LibreOffice—helped create this book. I am grateful as well to openstreetmap.org, the Ontario Government (MNR), cycling friends and clubs for sharing tons of raw map data I could have never amassed myself.

I'm thankful to **my sister,** for years of patiently proofreading my work, and **Jen Groundwater,** my book editor, for keeping the tone of my writing intact and wanting to ride everything she proofed (she lives in BC).

Cheers to **Paulo LaBerge**, Peter Istvan and a few other shooters; your added pix have spiced up the book nicely.

And finally, at home, I appreciate the endless support and patience that my wife **Teresa** and son **Trevor** have given me, which have made a long and complicated project that much easier.

I have watched with pride Trevor grow and improve as a mountain biker. Thanks, son, for trusting me enough to follow me down some dubious runs. You stayed on your bike and ended up a better rider for it. I look forward to do many more.

BONUS eBOOK OFFER

As an extra bonus supplement to the printed book, I am offering you a free copy of the eBook version.

To download it, go to this private page on the OBT site: **https://ontariobiketrails.com/mtb_eb**

Once there, to get the password, you will be asked a question that refers to this book. Enter the secret password to download the PDF file. Also visit the website to stay current and to subscribe to my **Newsletter**.

Please do not share the eBook file.
Just because you can, does not mean you should.
Don't be a MTB pirate!

Manufactured by Amazon.ca
Bolton, ON